T·O·W·A·R·D·S T·O·M·O·R·R·O·W

Canada in a Changing World
History

DESMOND MORTON

Contributing Author
Rosemary Neering

Harcourt Brace Jovanovich, Canada

TORONTO • ORLANDO • SAN DIEGO • LONDON • SYDNEY

Canadian Cataloguing in Publication Data

Morton, Desmond, 1937 -
Towards tomorrow: Canada in a changing world: history

For use in high schools.
Includes index.
ISBN 0-7747-1281-3

1. Canada—History—20th century.* I. Title.

FC170.M67 1988 971.06 C88-095004-8
F1034.2.M67 1988

Cover photograph : © Chris Speedie/Image Finders

Printed and bound in Canada
93 94 95 MMT 6 5 4 3

TABLE OF CONTENTS

STUDYING HISTORY **1**

How Can We Study History? **2**
Checking Some Facts **4**

CHAPTER 1 *Into The Twentieth Century* **6**

Macdonald's Heritage **7**
The Laurier Boom **10**
What Kind of Canada? **15**
Living in Laurier's Canada **20**
A Nation, an Empire—or Both? **24**
The End of the Laurier Era **30**
Chapter Summary **34**

CHAPTER 2 *A Nation Steeled in War* **36**

The International Background **37**
Canada's Response **38**
How the War Changed Canada **42**
Canadians at War **47**
A Crisis of Commitment **54**
Canada's Role in the Postwar World **60**
Chapter Summary **66**

CHAPTER 3 *A North American Nation* **68**

Growth and Discontent **69**
Americanization and Canadianism **74**
The Great Depression **79**
A New Deal? **89**
Isolationism or Involvement? **97**
Chapter Summary **104**

CHAPTER 4 *Canada's World War* **106**

"This Is Not Our War" **106**
Total War **112**
Canada's War: At Sea and in the Air **116**
Winning the War **121**
Setting a New Course **127**
Chapter Summary **132**

CHAPTER 5 *First of the Middle Powers* **134**

Canada's World Role **134**
Canada and the Cold War **139**
At Home After the Wars **147**
The Limits of Affluence **152**
National and Nuclear Choices **158**
Chapter Summary **164**

CHAPTER 6 *A Nation in Conflict* **166**

Prosperity and Problems **167**
The Matter of Québec **170**
Bilingualism—Cure, Compromise, or Calamity? **174**
The Liberation Decade **176**
Canada and the World **180**
Chapter Summary **183**

CHAPTER 7 *The End of "Liberation"* **184**

The FLQ Crisis **185**
Québec: Moving Towards Independence **189**
Inflation and Unemployment: Battling the Two-Headed Monster **190**
A Community of Communities **195**
Chapter Summary **200**

CHAPTER 8 *A Canadian Society* **202**

Unfinished Business **202**
Our Home and Native Land **206**
Who Should Come to Canada? **212**
Citizenship—Joining Canada **217**
A Multicultural Nation **219**
Into the Future **222**
Chapter Summary **225**

Glossary **228**
Index **229**

AUTHOR'S FOREWORD

Towards Tomorrow may seem an odd title for a book about the past, but it has certain logic. While history may be the study of the past, it is written in the present for the future. Historians are fascinated by what happened years ago but they understand those happenings with minds shaped in their own time and they address future readers. History, like experience, is knowledge you may need to apply in tomorrow's world.

Like experience, collecting and understanding history is a very personal matter. However, scholarly and objective an historian may claim to be, all knowledge and its interpretation is filtered through an author's experience and prejudices. Recognizing that fact may be the beginning of disillusionment; it should be the beginning of wisdom.

ACKNOWLEDGEMENTS

Text

Every reasonable effort has been made to trace the owners of copyrighted material and to make due acknowledgement. Any errors or omissions drawn to our attention will be gladly rectified in future editions.

p. 5, Estimates of unemployment in Canada, 1921-1940: Figures compiled by Dominion Bureau of Statistics, 1940. Reprinted with permission of the Minister of Supply and Services, Canada. p. 11, Sir Wilfrid Laurier quotation: by Réal Belanger from THE CANADIAN ENCYCLOPEDIA, 1985; Vol. II, p. 983. Reprinted by permission of New Canadian Encyclopedia Publishing. p. 17, quotation by Armand Lavergne: from CANADA 1896-1921: A NATION TRANSFORMED by R.C. Brown and R. Cook. Reprinted by permission of the Canadian publishers, McClelland and Stewart, Toronto. p. 20, excerpt from SUNSHINE SKETCHES OF A LITTLE TOWN by Stephen Leacock. Copyright © 1948. Reprinted by permission of the Canadian publishers, McClelland and Stewart, Toronto. p. 23, excerpt from MY NEIGHBOURS by J.S. Woodsworth. Copyright © 1972. University of Toronto Press. Reprinted by permission. p. 29, excerpt from LIFE AND LETTERS OF SIR WILFRID LAURIER by Dr. O.D. Skelton. Copyright © 1921 by The Century Company and Carleton University Press, 1965. Reprinted by kind permission of Mrs Sheila Skelton Menzies. p. 41, excerpt from THE DUTY OF CANADA AT THE PRESENT HOUR by Henri Bourassa. Printed at *Le Devoir*, Montréal, Québec. p. 46, excerpt from THE UNSOLVED RIDDLE OF SOCIAL JUSTICE AND OTHER ESSAYS by Stephen Leacock from THE SOCIAL CRITICISM OF STEPHEN LEACOCK edited by Alan Borden. Copyright © 1973 University of Toronto Press. Reprinted by permission. p. 50, excerpt from THE GREAT WAR AND CANADIAN SOCIETY edited by Daphne Read. Copyright © 1978 New Hogtown Press, Toronto. pp. 50-51, excerpt from WITH THE FIRST CANADIAN CONTINGENT, edited by Mary Plummer. Hodder and Stoughton and The Musson Book Company, Toronto, 1915. p. 61, quotation from CANADA AND THE AGE OF CONFLICT: A HISTORY OF CANADIAN EXTERNAL POLICIES, Vol. I: 1867-1921 by C.P. Storey. Copyright © 1974. Used by permission of Macmillan of Canada, A Division of Canada Publishing Corporation. pp. 90-91, The Regina Manifesto from CANADIAN PARTY PLATFORM by Edward Corrigan. Copyright © 1968 Copp Clark Pitman Ltd. pp. 92-93, excerpt from THE BENNETT NEW DEAL: FRAUD OR PORTENT? edited by J.R.H. Wilbur. First published in 1968 by Copp Clark Publishing Company. Reprinted by kind permission of the author. pp. 93-94, Letters to R.B. Bennett: as quoted from THE WRETCHED OF CANADA edited by L.M. Grayson and Michael Bliss. Copyright © 1971 The University of Toronto Press. p. 100, excerpt from DECISIVE DECADES by A.B. Hodget and J.D. Burns. Copyright © 1973. Used with permission of NELSON CANADA, A Division of International Thomson Limited. pp. 128-129, excerpt from SO YOU WANT A WAR JOB! by Charles Clay. Copyright © 1942. Reprinted with permission from Oxford University Press, Toronto. pp. 153-155, How Would You Have Voted?: Reprinted by permission of MACLEAN'S MAGAZINE. p. 172, excerpt from AN OPTION FOR QUEBEC by René Levesque. Copyright © 1968. Used by permission of the Canadian Publishers, McClelland and Stewart, Toronto. p. 173, excerpts from FEDERALISM AND THE FRENCH CANADIANS by Pierre E. Trudeau. Copyright © 1968. Used by permission of Macmillan of Canada, A Division of Canada Publishing Corporation. pp. 186-187, excerpts from THE OCTOBER CRISIS by Gérard Pelletier. First published in 1971 by McClelland and Stewart, Toronto. Reprinted by kind permission of the author. pp. 187-188, excerpt from TOMMY DOUGLAS SPEAKS: Till Power is Brought to Pooling edited by L.D. Lovick. Copyright © 1979 by L.D. Lovick and Oolichan Books. Reprinted with permission of the publisher, Oolichan Books. p. 215, excerpts from MACLEAN'S MAGAZINE, March 2, 1987: Reprinted by permission of Maclean's. pp. 220-221, excerpts from BLACK LIKE ME by Fil Fraser. Published in Saturday Night, January 1987. Reprinted by permission of Fil Fraser.

Cartoons

25: Julien, Montreal Star. 32: McConnell, Toronto Daily News. 59: Batsford, Manitoba Free Press (PAC/C 9040). 89: Dale, Winnipeg Free Press. 95: Chambers, Halifax Chronicle. 143: Wright, Hamilton Spectator. 167: Macpherson, Toronto Star. 173: Roschkov, Toronto Star. 178: Roschkov, Toronto Star. 181: Donato, Toronto Telegram. 191: Roschkov, Toronto Star. 194: Macpherson, Toronto Star.

Photographs

Key to abbreviations: t-Top; b-Bottom; l-Left; r-Right.
CP-Canapress Photo Service.
PAC-Public Archives of Canada.
DND-Department of National Defence.

Chapter 1: Intro: CP. 9: (t) PAC/C 3693; (b) PAC/C 6536. 11: PAC/C 932. 12: (l) PAC/C 30620; (r) PAC/C 30621. 15: PAC/C 6196. 16: PAC/C 5610. 18: PAC/PA 67271. 19: PAC/Vancouver Public Library/C 38611. 21: PAC/C 891. 22: City of Toronto Archives, James Collection #138. 23: (t) United Church of Canada (Toronto) Archives; (b) PAC/PA 30820. 24: PAC/C 15300. 29: (l) PA; (r) Erindale College Archives. 30: PAC/Topley/PA 11664.

Chapter 2: 39: PAC/PA 717. 41: PAC/C 116599. 42: PAC/C 19945. 43: PAC/C 95282. 44: (l) PAC/C 119446; (r) PAC/C 57358. 45: PAC/PA 72521. 46: CP. 48: (l) CP; (r) PAC/PA 1291. 49: PAC/PA 1326. 51: Canadian War Museum. 53: CP. 54: (t) PAC/C 42420; (b) PAC/C 95732. 55: PAC/DND/PA 880. 56: PAC/C 6859. 59: Dalhousie University Archives. 61: Fenelon Falls Museum 64: CP. 65: CP.

Chapter 3: 69: CP. 70: PAC/PA 48397. 72: PAC/PA 269877. 73: PAC/C 104535. 75: PAC/PA 89595. 77: PAC/PA 139063. 78: National Gallery of Canada, Ottawa. 80: CP. 81: PAC/Turofsky/PA 52600. 83: (t) PAC/CBC/C 20594; (b) PAC/C 13236. 84: PAC/C 20012. 85: PAC/C 29399. 86: Vancouver Public Library #1276. 87: Glenbow Museum # ND-3-6343. 89: CP. 90: PAC/C 121613. 92: PAC/C 623. 96: (t) PAC/C 9338; (b) PAC/Montreal Gazette/PA 129184. 100: CP. 101: CP. 103: PAC/NFB/PA 112663.

Chapter 4: 107: Manitoba Public Archives. 108: PAC/Montreal Gazette/PA 107909. 109: PAC/C 49742. 111: World Wide Photos/948273. 112: PAC/C 19380. 113: CP. 115: PAC/C 47394. 117: PAC/DND/PA 115005. 118: PAC/DND/MILNE/PA 116969. 120: PAC/Montreal Gazette/PA 108268. 121: PAC/C 25. 122: (l) PAC/DND/PA 132648; (r) PAC/DND/Rowe/PA 107935. 123: PAC/DND/Stirton/PA 115032. 125: (t) PAC/DND/Stirton/PA 115195; (b) PAC/DND/Milne/PA 122765. 126: PAC/Milne/C 29452. 127: PAC/NFB/C 29457. 128: (l) PAC/C 33441; (r) PAC/Montreal Gazette/PA 108300. 129: PAC/C 49455. 130: (l) PAC/C87517; (r) PAC/C 90883.

Chapter 5: 135: CP. 137: CP. 140: PAC/Montreal Star/PA 129625. 142: PAC/DND/Brown/PA 142437. 143: PAC/PA 93736. 145: PAC/DND/PA 122737. 146: CP. 147: Financial Post Archives/NFB. 148: PAC/NFB/Harrington/PA 111390. 149: PAC/Legget/PA 136704. 150: PAC/CBC/C 66501. 151: PAC/NFB/LUND/PA 11358. 153: PAC/PA 936524. 154: CP. 156: unknown. 159: CP. 160: PAC/Catherwood/C 39893. 161: CP. 162(l) CP; (r) CP.

Chapter 6: 168: CP. 169: CP. 170: PAC/PA 11350. 171: CP. 175: PAC/PA 133222. 176: CP. 179: CP. 180: CP. 182: PAC/PA 93759.

Chapter 7: 185: CP. 187: PAC/Montreal Star/Bird/PA 129911. 193: CP. 197: SSC-Photocentre/Pearce # 68-14947. 198: CP. 199: CP.

Chapter 8: 204: CP. 205: Miller Services Ltd. 207: CP. 208: CP. 209: CP. 211: CP. 213: CP. 214: CP. 216: CP. 218: unknown. 221: (t) Fil Fraser; (b) Fil Fraser. 223: CP.

75

STUDYING HISTORY

Has the twentieth century belonged to Canada? Sir Wilfrid Laurier, Prime Minister at the start of the century, predicted that it would. As the end of the century draws nearer, Canadians can begin to evaluate his prediction. What happened in and to Canada during the twentieth century? How were we affected by world wars, economic depression, mass immigration, new social movements, and technological change? What kind of a people have Canadians become? What is Canada's role in today's world? Some answers to these questions form the foundations of this volume of the *Towards Tomorrow* series.

Before you examine the people and events that formed Canada's twentieth century history, however, it will be useful to look at history itself. Consider this idea: If you were to describe Canada as it is at this very instant—its people, government, laws, industry, resources—could you do so without mentioning history even once? Think about it. You will probably conclude that the task would be almost impossible. There are two good reasons for this. The first is that we can only truly know that which has already happened. The second is that almost everything people do today or will do tomorrow arises from prior experience. Simply put, history is just another word for experience.

Now try another experiment. Pick something that happened about a week ago—a game, a party, even a class. Then try to recall every last detail: what people wore, what they said, the exact time, how the furnishings were arranged. Hard, isn't it? Better yet, ask some friends or family members to write down individual versions of some experience you all shared. Who got the details right? (No arguing, please!)

To some extent, this is the way in which history is written. Every individual has a personal view of events. Government representatives collect statistics, but, as you will soon see, they don't always ask the right questions, or interpret the answers consistently. Some people keep very careful notes, but their own perceptions and opinions creep in despite any amount of care. Others write exciting, witty accounts of events which may or may not be true. Still others, who may have much better information, lack the time, ability, or inclination to keep a record. Who is more likely to know how it really feels to work in a company, an assembly-line worker or the chief executive officer? Whose description is more likely to get written and published?

Because history can rarely be recorded with complete accuracy, some people want to ignore it. "History is bunk," said Henry Ford. Yet surely we must all agree that, without the past, without experience, we are like small children.

Until quite recently, most history has been written as if the only people who matter are "captains and kings". Yet everyone has a share in history. The exciting current research in history looks at women, children, working people, Native people, and all the others who were most often overlooked in earlier books. Each of these groups has a different experience, a different viewpoint of the past. Your family was probably touched in some way by war, the Great Depression, and other events of this century, whether your parents or grandparents were living in Canada or another country. One good reason to study history, then, is to get a better understanding of your own past.

Nevertheless, it is possible to have too much of a good thing. We all know people who are so weighed down by their experiences that they will never try anything new. We also know of people who use history to nurse a grudge. Always remember: The past is a great place to visit, but no place to live.

How Can We Study History?

All historians are like detectives, collecting evidence and trying to make sense of it. Sometimes there is very little material to serve as a guide—a few ancient scrolls in an unknown tongue, some tomb inscriptions, half-remembered traditions. For more recent times, the evidence multiplies; historians have access to mountains of books, newspapers, letters, photographs, films, recordings, and videotapes. Yet even now there is much historians would like to know but never will. What was said behind the closed door or on the telephone? What was so-and-so really thinking? How is it possible to make sense of the vast array of fact, opinion, fiction, and contradiction that the past provides?

The best approach to the past is to start with a question or a series of questions. What happened, and why? Who settled the region? Did they succeed or fail? Chances are that someone has already written about the topic. Books and articles written after the event are known as **secondary sources**. Some secondary sources are better than others. Sometimes authors have relied on a quick glance or on hearsay; others have dug out all the evidence they could find.

Some writers tell you how they did their research, in the form of footnotes or endnotes. These direct you to other books or articles, or to **primary sources**, the records, letters, diaries, interviews, and other material produced by people who saw or participated in historical events. This is the real stuff of history. But keep in mind that you are acting as a detective, and that some of the most obvious clues may be misleading. Not all the witnesses tell the truth, whether intentionally or unintentionally. For example, King George IV convinced himself that he led a cavalry charge at the Battle of Waterloo. His courtiers never contradicted him, but they knew the king never even visited Waterloo until 1817, two years after the battle.

Like careful detectives, therefore, historians keep checking. They root out generalizations and track down fresh evidence. More and more, they recognize that the "big names" in history are not the only ones that matter. And they know that truth in history is complex and never complete. That is the big difference between history and a detective story. If you read a history book with every detail tied up neatly at the end, including the villain, you are, in fact, reading fiction.

It is only recently that historians have reached these conclusions about the study of history. Some historians still do not agree with them. Well into this century, there was a strong conviction among historians that their work could be scientific in its accuracy. History could be used to prove the validity of "laws" of human behaviour. The best-known historian who held this view was Karl Marx. Marx and his followers certainly made a great contribution to the study of history. They made others recognize the importance of economic forces and the problems of ordinary people in history. Yet few of Marx's readers now believe that he was right in saying that history evolves according to a **dialectic**, a logical process of development which always progresses through certain defined stages. It is very often the case that anyone, whether a historian or a scientist, who sets out deliberately to prove a theory will overlook contradictory evidence.

Thus, it is very often true that historians—like most people—do not settle down to the enormous labour of writing a book unless they have ideas that they want to put across. If you recognize this fact in your own reading and research, you will not be misled into thinking that one particular view is the only valid one. The truth is not finite and static; it is infinite and dynamic, and everyone can share in it.

Checking Some Facts

If what you have just read sounds like a lot of theorizing, consider some "facts" and what they really tell us.

1. How many Canadian soldiers died in the First World War? Many textbooks say that about 60 000 were killed. But does anyone know for certain? The *Official History of the Canadian Army in the First World War* reports that 51 749 members of the Canadian Expeditionary Force were killed, died of wounds, drowned at sea, or were missing and presumed dead. Another 7795 died of disease, injuries, or accidents, for a total of 59 544.[1]

However, there were also about 35 000 Canadians serving with the British Army and the British flying services. The *Official History of the Royal Canadian Air Force*, Volume I, claims that 1388 fatalities represents "an almost complete record for Canadians in the British flying services".[2] Sadly, no one has any idea of how many Canadians serving with the British, French, Belgian, or Italian armies died. Even so simple a question as how many Canadians died in World War I can never be answered accurately.

2. During the Great Depression of the 1930's, many Canadians looked in vain for work. How many? Today, unemployment statistics are published monthly. Surely historians know how many people were hunting for jobs when unemployment was a national crisis?

The answer is "no". Before unemployment insurance was made law in 1940, neither the federal nor the provincial governments kept official estimates of the numbers of the unemployed. The only regular information was collected monthly by asking trade unions how many of their members were looking for work. However, at that time, perhaps one worker in twenty belonged to a union. The only other source of information was the census, taken every ten years, in which Canadians were sometimes asked whether they were working or looking for a job. The information took many months to process; it was obsolete before it was published.

In the absence of clear evidence, historians do the best they can. Here are two sets of results, one compiled by the Dominion Bureau of Statistics (now Statistics Canada) in 1940, the other from *Historical Statistics of Canada*, a highly respected reference first published in 1965. Both are based on census results and estimates. You can find out

[1] G.W.L. Nicholson, *Canadian Expeditionary Force, 1914-1919: The Official History of the Canadian Army in the First World War* (Ottawa, 1962), Appendix "C", p. 546.

[2] S.F. Wise, *Canadian Airmen and the First World War: The Official History of the Royal Canadian Air Force*, Vol. 1 (Toronto, 1980), p. 645.

how these conflicting figures were obtained by reading the article by Udo Sautter.[3]

TABLE A *Estimates of Unemployment in Canada, 1921–1940 (%)*

Year	*Dominion Bureau of Statistics (%)*	*Historical Statistics of Canada (%)*	*Year*	*Dominion Bureau of Statistics (%)*	*Historical Statistics of Canada (%)*
1921	8.9	5.8	1931	17.4	11.6
1922	6.9	4.4	1932	26.0	17.6
1923	4.9	3.2	1933	26.6	19.3
1924	7.0	4.5	1934	20.5	14.5
1925	6.9	4.4	1935	19.0	14.2
1926	4.6	3.0	1936	17.3*	12.8
1927	2.7	1.8	1937	13.8*	9.1
1928	2.5	1.7	1938	—	11.4
1929	4.2	2.9	1939	—	11.4
1930	12.8	9.1	1940	—	9.2

*Calculated from figures in *The Labour Gazette*, February 1938, p. 181.

[3] Udo Sautter, "Measuring Unemployment in Canada: Federal Efforts in Canada Before World War II", *Histoire Sociale/Social History*, XV, 30, 1982, p. 485.

CHAPTER 1

Into the Twentieth Century

At midnight on June 30, 1867 the British North America Act *became law and Canada legally became a nation. Some people doubted that the new nation could survive into the twentieth century. After all, its people were divided by language, custom, and regional loyalty. Its economy would have to compete with that of the rapidly expanding United States of America.*

The job of holding Canada together fell to Sir John A. Macdonald. As Prime Minister for almost 20 years between 1867 and 1891, Macdonald led Canada through its first crises in nationhood. During these years, three new provinces, Prince Edward Island, Manitoba, and British Columbia, became part of Confederation, extending Canada from sea to sea. A transcontinental railway was built, linking east and west. The country withstood the divisions created by two rebellions, both led by Louis Riel. Despite these accomplishments, the task of building Canada into a nation was incomplete when Sir Wilfrid Laurier became Prime Minister in 1896. It was Laurier who would lead Canadians into the twentieth century, a century he said would belong to Canada.

In Chapter 1, you will look at the transition from the nineteenth to the twentieth century, to discover why a nation-building system that did not work in the late 1800's began to work as Canada entered the 1900's. While reading this chapter, keep the following questions in mind.

- *What was Macdonald's nation-building strategy?*
- *How was Canada's economy influenced by outside forces during the 1890's?*
- *How did Laurier's immigration policy change Canadian society?*
- *How did life in Canada during the Laurier years differ from life today?*
- *What issues divided English Canadians and* Canadiens *during the Laurier years?*
- *Was Laurier a nationalist or an imperialist?*
- *Did Laurier build a stronger Canada?*

Macdonald's Heritage

The roots of the twentieth century lead back into the nineteenth. In 1867, Canadians had cheered the Governor General's proclamation of their new nation. Scores of new national organizations, from a National Lacrosse Association to a Canadian Labour Union, reflected a new sense of identity. Canadians hoped that their country of fewer than one million square kilometres would soon spread west and north to fulfil the national motto, *a mari usque ad mare*. In 1871, when delegates from British Columbia set their price for joining Confederation as a wagon road across the Rockies, they were promised something much better—a railway, and within ten years!

There was much to do. By 1873, Prime Minister Sir John A. Macdonald could boast that he had completed Canada by adding British

FIGURE 1.1 *Growth of Canada 1867-1891*

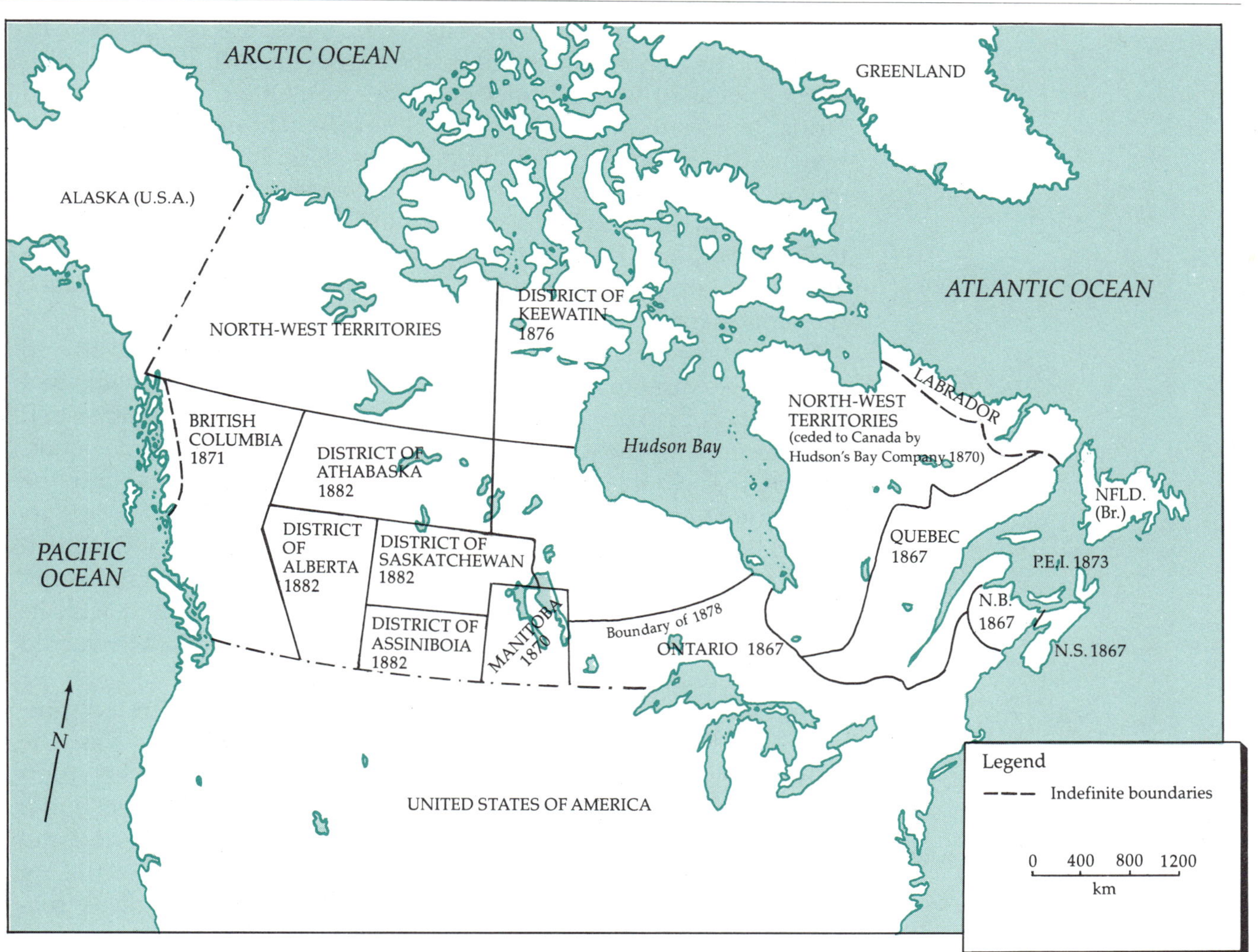

Columbia and Prince Edward Island as provinces and by buying the vast North-West Territories from the Hudson's Bay Company. A rebellion led by Louis Riel, a Métis, had forced Ottawa to admit a small corner of the Territories as the tiny province of Manitoba. In the Treaty of Washington in 1871, Macdonald had worked with the British to settle many bitter quarrels with the United States. A syndicate was organized to build a railway to the Pacific. However, many Canadians criticised Macdonald's handling of Riel's rebellion and his concessions to the Americans. Even more were shocked to learn that the Pacific Railway syndicate had paid much of the cost of Macdonald's 1872 election. In 1873, his Conservative government was defeated in Parliament. Alexander Mackenzie's Liberals won an easy victory in 1874 by promising honest government and strict economy.

Mackenzie and the Liberals were unlucky. A world-wide economic depression began to hurt Canada in 1874. The collapse of European and American banks made money scarce. Investors became cautious about big projects such as a transcontinental railway. It was very difficult for Mackenzie to complete the Intercolonial Railway to the Maritimes and impossible to make much progress on the Pacific Railway. The depression meant fewer buyers for such Canadian products as timber, wheat, and fish. Prices fell. Other countries raised tariffs, taxes on imports. The federal government earned most of its revenue from Canada's own tariffs. Less trade therefore meant less money in the federal treasury. Yet the Liberals, who believed in **reciprocity**, kept tariffs as low as they could. Their critics complained that their policies hurt Canadian business, cost jobs, and favoured British and American interests. In 1878, the Liberals were defeated by much the same margin as that by which they had won in 1874.

Back in power, Sir John A. Macdonald and the Conservatives offered Canadians a three-part nation-building strategy. First, there would be a "National Policy" of high tariffs to make imported goods expensive. It was intended to encourage Canadians to buy Canadian-made goods. In turn, that would create industries and jobs in Canada. Second, the government would fill the vast prairie region with settlers. The settlers would link eastern Canada and British Columbia, stake the Canadian claim to the region, and provide a growing market for the industries protected by the National Policy. Third, to connect the East with its prairie market and to fulfil the promise to British Columbia, Macdonald was determined to build the transcontinental railway.

No part of the strategy was easy to achieve. The depression continued, distorting and defeating Macdonald's nation-building plans. The railway was not finished until late in 1885, four years after the promised date. Macdonald's harsh measures to suppress Louis Riel and a second Métis rebellion in 1885 were designed to reassure investors and potential settlers that Canada's West would be safe and peaceful. Yet few people came. Prospective settlers, including many Canadians from

Lord Strathcona drives in the last spike on the Canadian Pacific Railway on November 7, 1885. Could Confederation have survived without the CPR?

Ontario, went instead to the United States, where the *Homestead Acts* promised them free land. During the 1880's many people gave up on Canada. Only a high birth rate kept the Canadian population from falling.

Ottawa's harshness towards the Métis and the execution of Louis Riel cost Macdonald many *Canadien* supporters. Elected in the aftermath, Québec's new premier, Honoré Mercier, pledged to fight for greater provincial powers. Ontario's Liberal premier fought Ottawa's attempts to limit his powers. In 1886, Nova Scotia's Liberal government was angry enough that it voted to withdraw the province from Confederation.

The continuing depression persuaded the Liberals to campaign in 1891 for "unrestricted reciprocity" with the United States. The idea seemed popular, but an ailing, exhausted Sir John A. Macdonald fought back. Dropping the National Policy, he insisted, would be the end of Canada. Crowds cheered when the old Prime Minister denounced the Liberals' "veiled treason". Business supported his campaign. Voters rejected the Liberals and their young leader, Wilfrid Laurier. The next five years were harsh for many Canadians. The 1890's saw renewed depression, high unemployment, and bitter quarrels in Canada over religious and language rights. In 1896, when Canadians again had a chance to vote, Macdonald was dead, four more Conservatives had followed each other as Prime Minister, and many people wanted a change.

An 1891 election poster, showing Sir John A. Macdonald carrying the flag while being supported by a farmer and an industrial worker. What is the "Old Policy" referred to in the slogan?

QUESTIONS

1. (a) Describe Macdonald's three-part strategy for building a Canadian nation.
   (b) How did the depression that began in 1874 affect this strategy?
2. (a) What is a tariff?
   (b) Why would a country impose high tariffs during an economic depression?
3. Give two reasons why few settlers arrived on the Canadian prairies during the 1870's.

The Laurier Boom

For Canada, the twentieth century actually began in 1896. The year opened with the last of many threats of war between Britain and the United States. The reason was a quarrel about the border between Venezuela and British Guiana, but the battleground would have been Canada. Fortunately, the two antagonists settled their disagreement peaceably. From 1896 on, Canada could enjoy peaceful relations with its southern neighbour.

There were other developments in 1896 that would soon transform Canada, though Canadians might not have realized it at the time. That year, the United States had no more free land of good quality for homesteaders. Thus, one of the magnets which had attracted settlers away from Canada no longer existed. In August of the same year, gold was discovered near the Klondike River, bringing a flood of prospectors to the Yukon. New technology, too, played its part in changing Canada: The first Canadian hydroelectric plant was built on the Niagara River.

The year brought political change as well. On June 23, Wilfrid Laurier's Liberals got fewer votes than the Conservatives, but they won 30 more seats. After 18 years of Conservative leadership, the Liberals would bring Canadians into the twentieth century.

The new Liberal Prime Minister had been the leader of his party since 1887. At first, Laurier's ill health made some believe that he would go no further, that a new party leader would be found. Yet Laurier led the Liberals until his death in 1919. Those who tried to take advantage of him soon found out how tough and resourceful he could be. He was also cautious, resisting change and hard choices. Laurier and his government continued many of the Conservatives' policies. One concession was to remove the import tariffs from the twine which farmers used to bind their wheat sheaves. Another was to lower tariffs on British goods in 1897 as an "imperial preference" timed to coincide with Queen Victoria's sixtieth year on the throne.

It was to the Liberals' advantage that, as they came to power, the

CLOSE-UP

Who Was Sir Wilfrid Laurier?

They called him the "plumed knight", this man who led Canada into the twentieth century. Born in 1841 at St-Lin, Québec, Wilfrid Laurier became a Member of Parliament in 1871, a Cabinet Minister in 1877, and leader of the federal Liberal Party in 1887. After winning the election of 1896, he served as Prime Minister until 1911.

Laurier was knighted in 1897. He was an eloquent and charming man who won his followers' hearts even when they disagreed with him. Historians have rendered different verdicts on him. Some call him eloquent but lazy, tough but resistant to change and unwilling to make a decision. Others call him skilful, pragmatic, and charismatic, a forger of the compromises that held Canada together. One historian describes him as follows:

> A clever and eloquent politician, a true legend in his own time, Laurier has been judged in a variety of ways. For some, he was the spiritual successor to Macdonald, who pursued and consolidated Confederation. For others, Laurier, in the name of national unity and necessary compromise, too often sacrificed the interest of French Canadian Catholics to those of a majority little inclined to support the ideals of Confederation. Finally, some think he too often governed his country with only Quebec's interest in mind. Support for each of these opinions can be found in Laurier's actions in Ottawa, but the last view is most open to argument.
>
> –Réal Bélanger, in *The Canadian Encyclopedia*, Vol. II, Edmonton: Hurtig Publishers, 1985, p. 983.

QUESTION

1. Give reasons why different historians hold such disparate views of Laurier and his achievements.

Sir Wilfrid Laurier meets some of his admirers. These women could not vote for him. Why, then, would Laurier have listened to their views?

world's economy began to improve. The change began with the discovery of huge gold deposits in South Africa. At the time, the money supply was linked directly to the amount of gold in the world, so the amount of money suddenly increased. The Klondike discovery also contributed to the availability of funds for investment in factories, buildings, and ships. The cities of Europe and America boomed as people flooded in to work. Shipping was cheap; Canadian products could be exported to feed and house the new city dwellers. High American tariffs still restricted Canadian exporting, but Europe presented fewer obstructions to trade.

All points of Macdonald's ill-fated nation-building strategy now made sense, especially western development and the railway. The grain markets clamoured for wheat; the pioneering farmers had their market. New hardy varieties of wheat were developed for prairie growing conditions to help satisfy the demand. But there were not enough farmers to grow enough wheat.

Clifford Sifton, Laurier's Minister of the Interior, set out to find the settlers Canada needed. He simplified immigration regulations and hired agents, arming them with posters advertising "The Last Best West". Many people in Europe believed that Canada's Prairie was a sub-arctic desert. Sifton knew he had to change that image. The scarcity of good land in the United States helped to bring farmers' sons north to settle in Canada. They were joined by thousands and then hundreds of thousands from Europe. For the first time, many immigrants were Central and Eastern Europeans. The land, Sifton said, would make them Canadian. Sifton wanted people who were willing to settle the West; what he did not want were immigrants who would crowd into the cities.

The Canadian Pacific Railway had started life in the 1880's as an expensive symbol of Confederation, unable to obtain enough business to pay for itself. By 1901, ever-increasing freight and passenger traffic created bottlenecks on its single line, and prairie farmers complained about its high rates. The federal government considered another transcontinental line. At the time, the Grand Trunk Railway already had

Why was Laurier's government more successful in attracting settlers to Canada than Macdonald's had been?

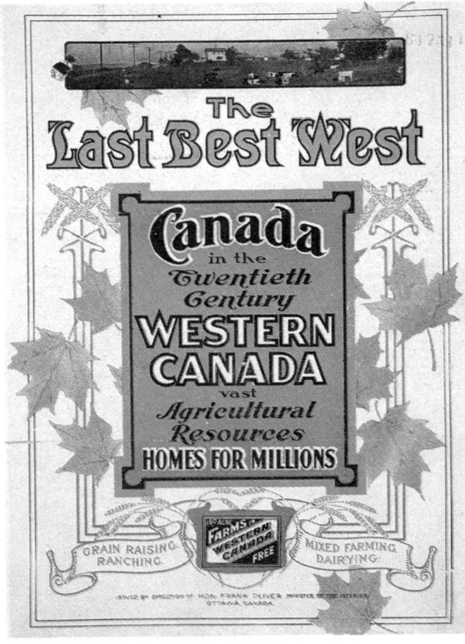

FIGURE 1.2 *The railways of Canada, as of 1914*

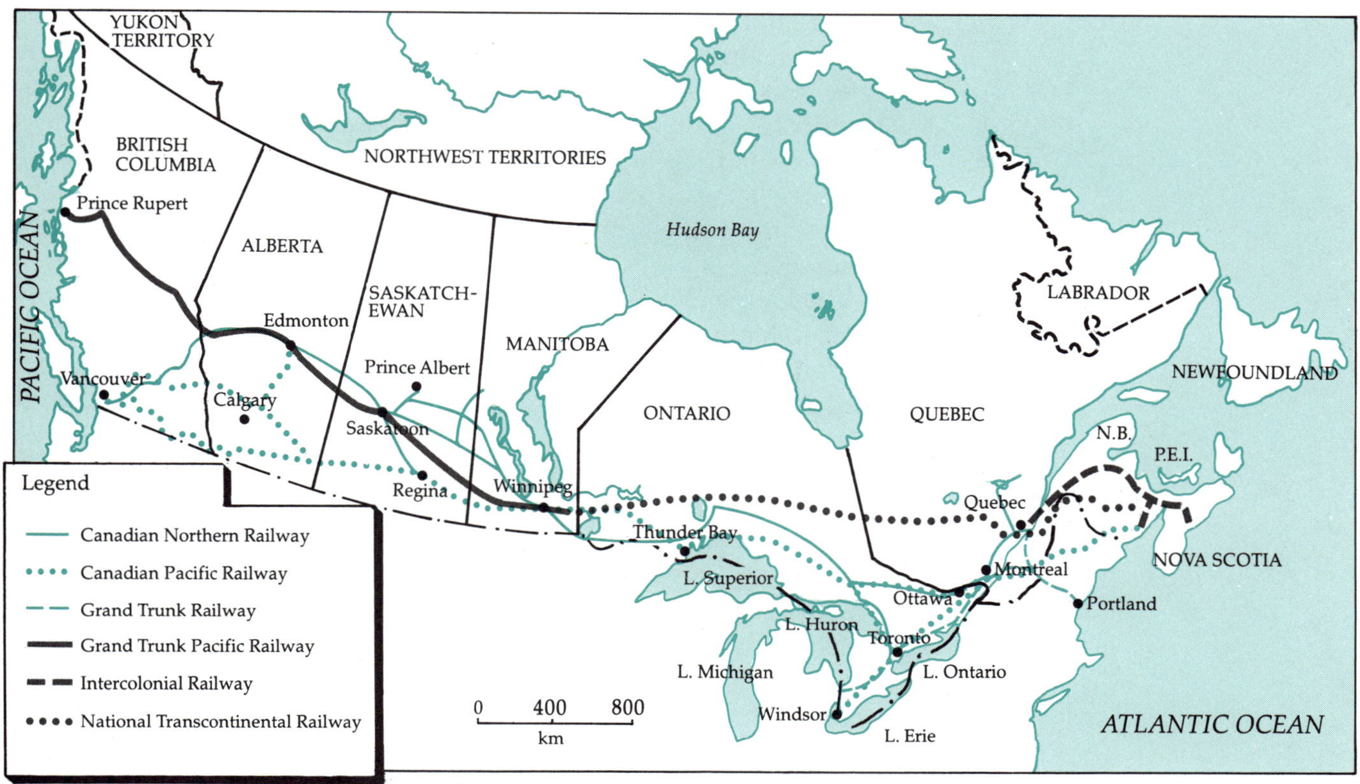

many lines in Ontario and Québec, while the Canadian Northern, owned by William Mackenzie and Donald Mann, had started (in 1896) to create a network from the Lakehead to Edmonton. A merger seemed obvious. Unfortunately, the owners of the Grand Trunk and the Canadian Northern regarded each other with contempt and refused to work together. As a result, Laurier decided, each contender would build a railway across Canada. Both the government and investors had money available for the project, he believed.

Laurier's railway minister resigned in protest at such extravagance, and the Conservatives complained about it. They remembered the building of the first transcontinental line, the CPR. Most Canadians, however, did not. Farmers who resented the CPR were enthusiastic, as were land speculators, railway contractors, factory owners who would sell materials, and anyone else who stood to make a profit. The two lines rolled ahead.

The boom of the Laurier years continued. In 1901, Canada had 5.1 million people; ten years later, there were 7.2 million. Of the 2.1 million people who made up the difference, 1.75 million were immigrants. Wheat production, the best basis for judging the prairie economy, rose from 55.6 million bushels (2.0 thousand million litres) to 132.1 million bushels (4.7 thousand million litres) during the same decade.

Certainly there were hardships. Pioneering was hard, lonely, frustrating work. It was particularly so for women, who often paid the price with a shorter life. Unlike earlier Canadian pioneers, the prairie homesteaders could seldom be self-sufficient. From the first, they had to raise cash crops to pay for shelter, fuel, and even food. They had to look to British Columbia's lumber to build permanent homes, to mines in Alberta for fuel, and to both East and West for furniture, a stove, clothing, shoes, tools, and certain foods. Thus, as Macdonald had hoped, the settlers provided a rich market for Canada's expanding industries.

The Laurier boom made Macdonald's strategy work. But it was not perfect. Many homesteaders lacked the skills or the capital to succeed; even if the land was free, the necessary tools, livestock, shelter, and seed were not. Despite Sifton's wishes, some immigrants went to the cities, drawn by booming industries which had to hunt for enough skilled workers. From 1901 to 1911, the urban population increased twice as fast as the rural population. Montréal, the centre of transportation and finance for the boom, almost doubled in size, to close to half a million people. Vancouver served as the terminus for two of the transcontinental railways and as headquarters for the newly-important forest industry. During the same decade, it grew from a town of 27 010 to a small metropolis of 100 401. Winnipeg, the gateway for immigrants to the Prairies and for the stream of golden wheat which returned, expanded fourfold between 1901 and 1911 to become Canada's third-largest city, after Montréal and Toronto.

Macdonald had envisioned a Canadian economy founded on mutual support between manufacturing and farming. The Laurier era saw the dramatic growth of a new element: resource industries. A large contributing factor was hydroelectricity. The new energy source was inexpensive, and liberated Canada from its dependence on coal, much of it imported from the United States. In Ontario, a new Conservative government began to take over private power companies after 1905. Most people supported the new Hydro-Electric Power Commission, whose slogan was "Power at cost". Hydro from Niagara Falls helped expand manufacturing in southern Ontario. So did the growth of heavy industry in the neighbouring American states. The tariffs imposed on goods imported from the United States made it profitable for American companies to build branch plants in Canada. It made sense, thought such industrialists as Henry Ford, to locate them close to both the United States and the source of electric power.

Hydroelectricity also shaped the new frontier of Canada, along the Canadian Shield in Ontario and in the B.C. interior. For all its drama, the Klondike gold rush was soon over, leaving little of permanence in its wake. Elsewhere, however, mining and forestry became big business, thanks to hydroelectricity. Harnessing the power of the rivers made it possible to smelt ore or turn trees into lumber and pulp and paper. In British Columbia, jobs in mining more than doubled between

1901 and 1911, while jobs in the forest industry, long stagnant, grew by 156 percent.

Like so much else in Canada, business changed during the boom years. Big companies hired professional managers and talked of "scientific" approaches to industrial problems, whether labour conflicts or quality control. Canada had looked to Britain for ideas and capital during the nineteenth century. Now, more businesses began to look to the United States for both.

Prosperity won Laurier re-election in 1900 and a larger majority in 1904. "Let me tell you, my fellow Canadians," he addressed a packed Toronto audience, "that all signs point this way, that the Twentieth Century shall be the century of Canada and of Canadian development. For the next seventy-five years, nay for the next hundred years, Canada shall be the star towards which all men who love progress and freedom shall come."

QUESTIONS

1. **(a)** How did Canada's fortunes change after 1896?
   (b) Why did these changes occur?
2. Why did immigration to Canada increase so rapidly after 1896?
3. How did prairie settlers support industry in British Columbia?
4. What was the significance of the growth of hydroelectric power in the early 1900's?

What Kind of Canada?

In 1920, a Manitoba author described Canada as a "mosaic". She meant that a great many different people can make a beautiful whole without losing their differences. Today, we call her idea "multiculturalism". As

"One hundred and sixty acres of free land for all settlers" is the message on this Department of Immigration poster, written in Ukrainian. About 170 000 Ukrainians settled in Canada between 1891 and 1914. Why did they choose Canada?

"Galicians" is what the Department of Immigration photographer called these people, since the Ukraine was not recognized by either the Austrian or the Russian Empire—or, therefore, Ottawa. Such people could expect a thin welcome from more established Canadians. Was Sir Clifford Sifton right? Would they succeed?

you will see in a later chapter, the concept of multiculturalism is enshrined in the Constitution of Canada.

Laurier's generation, however, did not see Canada in the same light. In 1901, more than 90 percent of all Canadians were of either British or French ancestry. Confederation had already been torn by conflicts between francophones and anglophones, Protestants and Roman Catholics. Now, hundreds of thousands of immigrants poured into the cities and "The Last Best West". Most Canadians wanted immigration; newcomers became producers, consumers, and workers at such arduous tasks as building railways, mining, and tree-felling. But Canadians also worried about adjusting to people with unfamiliar languages and cultures. They wanted newcomers to have the same background as themselves, if possible. If not, they wanted immigrants to adapt to the dominant culture. "If we do not Canadianize and Christianize the newcomer," warned the *Canadian Courier*, "he will make us foreigners and heathens on our own soil and under our own flag."

Clifford Sifton and his immigration officials agreed; they preferred settlers from the United States, Scotland, Germany, and Scandinavia, because they were most likely to adjust to Canadian ways. However, Sifton also knew that people from what we now call the Ukraine had the special experience needed to farm the prairie drylands. When he was later accused of bringing "quantity", not "quality", to Canada, Sifton responded with his most famous lines:

> I think a stalwart peasant in a sheepskin coat, born on the soil, whose

> forefathers have been farmers for ten generations, with a stout wife and a half-dozen children, is good quality. A Trade Union artisan who will not work more than eight hours a day and will not work that long if he can help it, will not work on a farm at all, and has to be fed by the public when work is slack, is in my opinion quantity and very bad quality.

Sifton's opinion was obviously not flattering to working people, but it was shared by many powerful business leaders. For example, Sir James Dunsmuir, a wealthy British Columbia mine owner, hated unions. He soon found that Chinese immigrants would work longer and harder for lower wages than other miners. Instead of trying to organize them, the unions wanted to drive the Chinese workers out. Dunsmuir did not care who dug his mines as long as no-one questioned his authority and the profits rolled in. Many employers in the Laurier era agreed.

In fact, Sifton took the longer view. He thought that a single system of "national schools", taught in English, would make loyal Canadians out of all children. In 1905, however, Laurier insisted on creating a dual system of Protestant and Roman Catholic schools in the new provinces of Saskatchewan and Alberta. He wished to ensure that francophones would have an equal right to their own educational system. Sifton resigned in protest. Laurier gave way and allowed the single system.

Whatever he might say about "quality", Sifton's policies were not welcomed by most Canadians. *Canadiens*, in particular, protested that immigration would make them an even smaller minority in Canada. Few of the new immigrants came from France, and most non-anglophone immigrants were assimilated into the English language community. Liberal Member of Parliament Henri Bourassa bitterly denounced his former friends for trying to "drown" *Canadiens*. His supporter, the Québec politician Armand Lavergne, stated the *Canadien* view as follows:

> In constituting the French Canadian, who has lived in the country since its discovery, the equal in rights and privileges to the Doukhobor or the Galician who has just disembarked, we have opened a gulf between the Eastern and Western sections of Canada, a gulf that nothing will ever be able to close.

One point on which Canadians were almost unanimous was that Canada must be a "white man's country". Native people were pointedly overlooked in this view of Canada. At the time, poverty and sickness seemed to promise an end to Canada's original people. Few Canadians seemed concerned. In addition, Sifton's officials discouraged Black Americans from joining the thousands of American farmers who moved north to the Canadian Prairies. The race issue was most bitter in British Columbia, and focused on the immigration of Asians. The battle lines were drawn between employers who wanted cheap labour, and workers who feared that Asian immigrants would throw them out of work. The workers got plenty of support from other British Columbians. The federal government's failure to exclude Chinese,

Discrimination against Chinese and Japanese immigrants took a violent turn in 1907, with the anti-Asiatic riots. Canadians from Asia were denied the right to vote, and were not allowed to teach, work in the civil service, or practise many professions until the 1950's.

Japanese, and East Indian immigrants became one of British Columbia's most bitter grievances against Ottawa.

Why did Laurier not respond to the trade unionists, politicians, and leaders of the Vancouver-based Asiatic Exclusion League? The matter was complex. East Indians, who worked mainly in the sawmills, were fellow citizens of the British Empire. Japan, a growing military and naval power, was Britain's most powerful ally in the Pacific. Chinese immigrants were sponsored by the most powerful employers in B.C., and Laurier did not wish to antagonize big business.

On September 7, 1907, matters came to a head when 30 000 people gathered in Vancouver at an overflow meeting of the Asiatic Exclusion League. Inflamed by angry speeches, mobs spilled out of the meeting and raced through the Chinese section of town, smashing and looting. Forewarned, the Japanese immigrants in the neighbouring part of the city armed themselves and held off the gangs, though not before shop windows were smashed.

Laurier finally acted. He apologized to the Japanese Emperor for the treatment meted out to the Japanese immigrants, then concluded an agreement virtually to end immigration from Japan. Ottawa also arranged some meagre compensation for the victims of the riot. The incident convinced the transcontinental railway companies that they would get along without Chinese or Japanese workers.

To limit the immigration of East Indians, the government ruled that immigrants must come to Canada by "continuous passage". Since no shipping line sailed directly between Canada and India, would-be immigrants found it almost impossible to meet the requirement. The same regulation effectively barred immigrants from other "undesirable" locations, such as the southern Mediterranean.

There was little that Asian Canadians or their few sympathizers could do, especially since only whites could vote in British Columbia. Immigration to Canada from Asia slowed to a trickle. Then, in 1914, Sikh nationalists in India's Punjab region decided to test the Canadian law. Nearly 400 Sikhs, many of them veterans of British wars, chartered a Japanese ship, the *Komagata Maru*, and sailed directly from Calcutta to Vancouver. The citizens of Vancouver protested, and Ottawa listened. The *Komagata Maru* swung at anchor for weeks in the hot summer sun. Finally, immigration officials decided to force the ship to return. Their first attempt failed when the Sikhs drove off the Canadian boarding party. Finally, the *Komagata Maru* was escorted out of the harbour by the Canadian cruiser *H.M.C.S. Rainbow*. In 1914, Canada remained a "white man's country".

Like Canadians, Sikhs were British subjects. In 1914, these Sikhs hired a ship to make a "continuous passage" to Canada, carefully obeying Canada's own Immigration Act. *Why, then, were they rejected?*

QUESTIONS

1. What attitudes towards immigration were held by each of the following groups in Canadian society: English Canadians, *Canadiens*, employers, workers?
2. From where did most immigrants come before 1896? After 1896?
3. Why did Canadian immigration officials "welcome" people from the Ukraine?
4. What was the purpose of the Asiatic Exclusion League?
5. Why is it ironic that Laurier apologized to the Japanese Emperor after the riots of September 7, 1907?
6. **(a)** What was the real purpose of the "continuous passage" rule?
   (b) In view of this, why did the arrival of the Sikhs on board the *Komagata Maru* pose a special problem for immigration officials?

Stephen Leacock put Orillia on Canada's literary map with Sunshine Sketches of a Little Town.

Living in Laurier's Canada

> "On Main Street itself are a number of buildings of extraordinary importance—Smith's Hotel and the Continental and Mariposa House, and the two banks. . .McCarthy's Block. . .and Glover's Hardware Store with the Oddfellow's Hall above it. Then. . .there is the Post Office and the Fire Hall and the Young Men's Christian Association and the office of the Mariposa Newspacket. . .On all the side streets there are maple trees and broad sidewalks, trim gardens with upright calla lilies, houses with verandahs, which are here and there being replaced by residences with piazzas."

In *Sunshine Sketches of a Little Town*, from which this excerpt is taken, Stephen Leacock wrote a loving fictional portrait of Orillia, Ontario. "Mariposa" might have been any small town in the Canada of the day. Like Leacock's account, many writings of the period are filled with a warm, nostalgic glow. It is as if Canadians knew Laurier's era to be a refuge from the wars and renewed depression which awaited.

What Leacock shows us is Orillia as seen by hotel owners, clergy, bank clerks, and the county court judge. He never reminds us that in 1911 Orillia was a lumbering town, noisy with sawmills, machine shops, and even an automobile factory. In his daydream of the past, Leacock wished to take us into a comfortable, conservative world.

Laurier's Canada certainly had wealthy people, some of whom had started with nothing. One of the owners of the Canadian Northern Railway, William Mackenzie, began as a school teacher; the other, Donald Mann, as a penniless farm boy. The railway and a dozen other ventures in Canada and abroad made them multi-millionaires. Richard Bennett, who would one day become Prime Minister of Canada, escaped poverty and failure at home in New Brunswick, moved to

Calgary, and became a millionaire lawyer for railways and banks. In Laurier's time, no-one paid income tax or inheritance taxes. The rich could well afford to build palatial homes in Vancouver's Shaughnessy Heights or on Winnipeg's Wellington Crescent, or to buy one of the new "horseless carriages" which cost as much as the Prime Minister's annual salary.

But millionaires and their families were a tiny portion of Canada's population, then as now. The great majority of Canadians, both rural and urban, lived lives which we would consider hard, narrow, and uncomfortable. Men and women wore heavy, tight-fitting clothes year-round. The manners of the day allowed little concession to the heat of summer, while a coal furnace or wood stove did not keep homes very warm in winter. Although Canadians ate more than Europeans, food was starchy and monotonous. The season for fresh fruit and vegetables was short, canned food was a luxury, and refrigerators (actually "ice-boxes") would be a dream for most Canadian families until after 1945.

Hard manual labour filled most people's lives. Farmers and their sons worked from dawn till dusk; for their wives, as the saying goes, the work was "never done". Farm work was seasonal for the men; in winter, and sometimes between planting and harvesting, they worked in lumber camps or on the railway. Railway owners Mackenzie and Mann won popularity by fitting construction time into those months when prairie homesteaders were free to work off the farm. The cash from their wages helped families survive the hard early years of homesteading. Later, it allowed them to purchase farm machinery and more land.

In the cities, factory workers worked long hours in noisy, dirty, often dangerous conditions. Those with jobs considered themselves lucky; many found their hard-earned skills being replaced by new machinery. The 1901 census reveals that the average annual wage for a man in

Doukhobor women winnowing grain

Switchboard operators work under the close scrutiny of their supervisors.

industry was $403; for a woman, $193. Wages did increase during the Laurier years, but inflation soon followed, for the first time in decades. From 1901 to 1913, average living costs for an average family of five rose 18.4 percent. Rents rose 35.9 percent during the same period, as a growing population hunted for homes. Working men and women coped by labouring longer hours. Child labour laws passed in the 1880's were often ignored by families and inspectors alike. Officially, only 13 percent of the work force was female. However, many of the women who stayed home earned money by taking in boarders, or laundry, or sewing—or all three.

Profiteering

Profiteering was a charge that businesses took advantage of their customers and workers by asking unfair prices and paying low wages to get large profits.

The commentators of the time often pointed out how many of Canada's very rich had begun as immigrant labourers. But how many people failed to get rich? Life for ordinary Canadians at the turn of the century was a matter of constant worry. Statistics show that, even on $800 per year, a family of five could just meet the cost of rent, food, clothing, and fuel. If anything went wrong—if someone fell ill; if one of the parents drank; if the mother stopped working to have a baby—basic necessities had to be sacrificed. The family would drink hot water instead of tea, the landlord would be put off as long as possible, the children would not attend school because they had no shoes. In times of depression or crop failure, starvation became a reality. Old age meant dependence on children or the discomfort and humiliation of the municipal poorhouse. This constant anxiety explains much that may puzzle us about the attitudes of the Canadians of the period. Living so close to the edge made them fear any possible competition for jobs and housing from immigrants.

Many working Canadians turned to fraternal orders or national societies, such as the Orange Lodge or St. Andrew's Society, for security. In the time before government social security and medicare plans, these helping organizations often paid sickness and death benefits in return for membership dues. When unions developed in Canada, they first took the form of fraternal orders. During the Laurier era, union membership soared from under 20 000 in 1901 to 160 000 by 1911.

Although union membership was legal, unions had few rights; employers could fire workers at will, and they often asked the government to send in troops in case of a strike. William Lyon Mackenzie King, appointed Laurier's Minister of Labour in 1908, realized that, in general, unions simply wanted a share of prosperity, though their leaders were sometimes radicals.

Not all Canadians could afford the dues of fraternal orders or unions. The increasing urbanization brought about by industrial development created a growing class of Canadians who lived on the edge of starvation. On the farm, the ill and helpless would have received food and care. In the cities, they depended on charity and on pittances from municipal relief officials. In his book *My Neighbour*, Winnipeg Methodist clergyman J.S. Woodsworth describes this side of urban life:

> One of our workers went to a home where father, mother and five children were living in two rooms. One child was tubercular. They were sleeping four in one bed, and the sick child was on a couch. . .(In) another case. . .the mother was in an advanced stage of tuberculosis, and father, mother and four children slept in a room 10 ft. by 12 ft. (3.5 m x 4 m).

Still, the Laurier boom did bring relative prosperity to Canada. In doing so it provided an opportunity to try to solve some of the problems of society. Many people had come from Europe or the United States hoping to find a better way of life in their new country. Social and political critics saw the plight of the poor as evidence that the social order and capitalism were not working. Few Canadian reformers were political activists, however. The National Council of Canadian Women (NCCW), 250 000 strong, campaigned against drinking, profiteering, slums, and "the modern cult of self-indulgence and its god, pleasure".

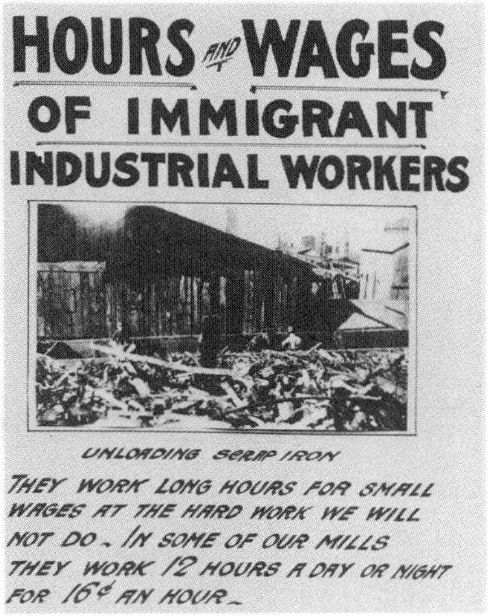

HOURS AND WAGES
OF IMMIGRANT
INDUSTRIAL WORKERS

UNLOADING SCRAP IRON

THEY WORK LONG HOURS FOR SMALL WAGES AT THE HARD WORK WE WILL NOT DO. IN SOME OF OUR MILLS THEY WORK 12 HOURS A DAY OR NIGHT FOR 16¢ AN HOUR.

This placard helped to instruct Methodists about conditions they had never remotely experienced. It was part of the equipment of lecturers in the informal "social gospel" movement in pre-1914 Canada. Did the lectures lead to changes?

Such harsh conditions, as those pictured below, during the Laurier boom shocked a more humane age, and encouraged much-needed social reforms.

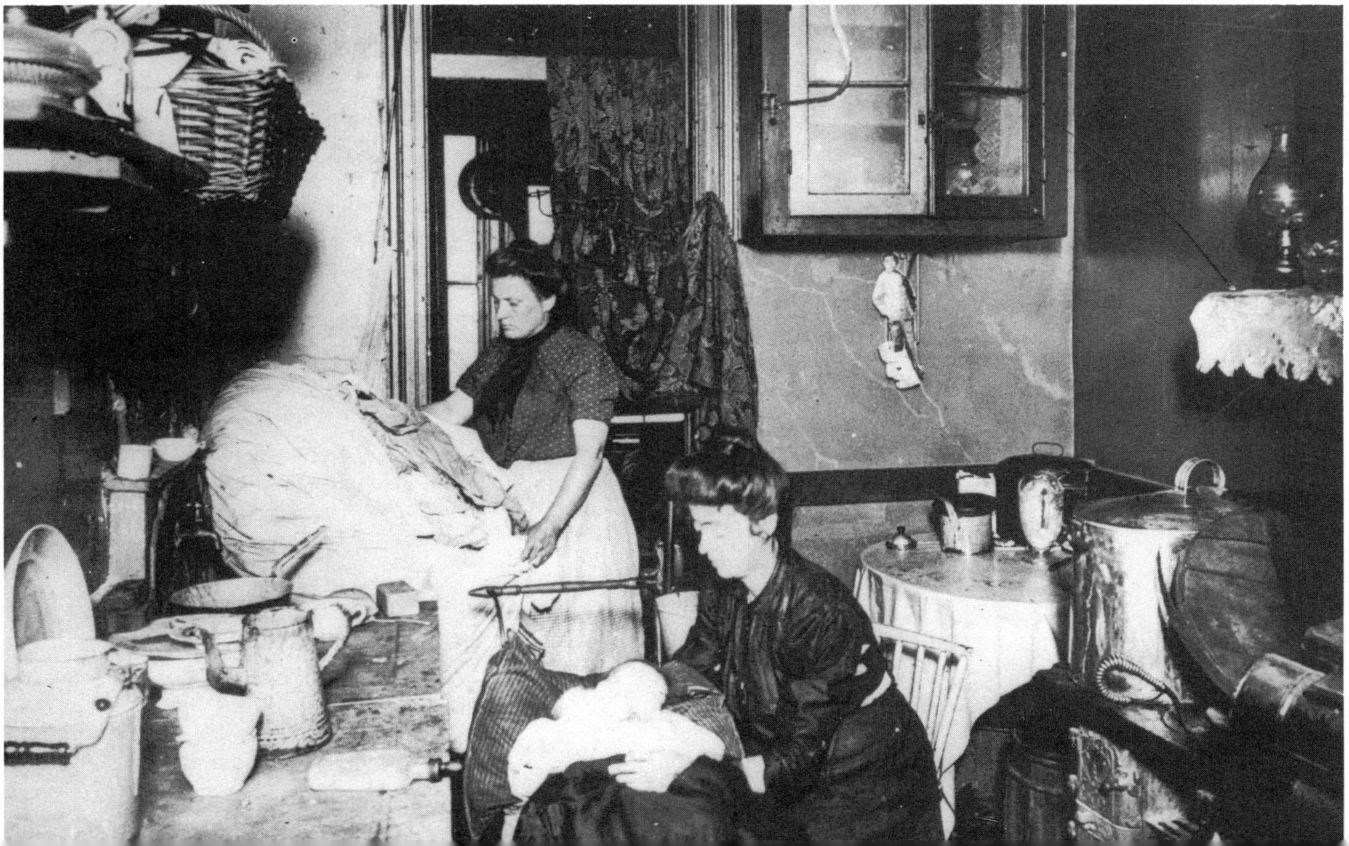

Although they opposed the vote for women at first, in 1910 they adopted a policy of female suffrage. Many Protestant churches were closely allied with the NCCW and other women's groups in the cause of social reform. One of the main concerns of the churches was declining attendance. Supporters of the "social gospel", including J.S. Woodsworth, insisted that the poor would come to church only when the churches took up the fight for justice and morality.

QUESTIONS

1. **(a)** Find evidence in this section that life in the Laurier era could be "hard, narrow, and uncomfortable".
   (b) Did this description apply equally to men and women? Rural and urban populations? Explain your reasoning.
2. During the Laurier era, some women's groups opposed votes for women. What arguments do you think they used? What arguments would pro-suffrage women have used?

A Nation, an Empire—or Both?

At the turn of the century, the most exciting news in Canadian papers came from Africa, where Britain was battling two small South African republics, the Transvaal and the Orange Free State. Britain asked its colonies for assistance. The Canadian and Australian contingents sent in response adapted quickly to the fast-moving guerrilla war. Between 1899 and 1902, 6000 Canadian soldiers and nurses served in Boer War. Of this total, 1800 belonged to official contingents, while the rest were recruited by the British.

Canadian soldiers in the Boer War. Why is this action recorded by a drawing, not a photograph? Do you think the artist saw the battle?

FIGURE 1.3 *The British Empire (1900)*

Their deeds gave many Canadians a sense of pride. They also started a long and sometimes bitter debate about Canada's role in the twentieth century world. Over the succeeding decades, such debates would come close to tearing the country apart.

What was Britain's motive for inviting the colonies to send troops to South Africa? No-one doubted that Britain could win the Boer War and avenge its earlier defeat of 1880. What Britain wanted was to impress potentially hostile nations with proof that the Empire was a strong, voluntary alliance. Writers and politicians promised that Canada would show loyalty by deeds, not words. The Laurier government, reluctant at first, surrendered to the pressure and agreed to send volunteers to Cape Town. Once in South Africa, the British would pay for their keep. Parliament need not be called, nor would the decision be considered "a precedent for future action". Canada had responded as Britain wished.

Despite Laurier's words, the emotional loyalty that led Canada to join the Boer War would make that war a precedent for joining two world wars. Many Canadians felt a deep kinship to Britain and loyalty to the Empire. There was, at the time, no Canadian citizenship; Canadians were British subjects. Some Canadians looked forward to the day

When Laurier visited Britain in 1897, he was acclaimed as a hero. Here, the cartoonist compares his behaviour in 1899, when he did not want Canada to share in a British war. Do you feel this is a fair comment?

when Canada would become the leading nation in the largest empire the world had ever seen. Sir John A. Macdonald expressed the view of many Canadians when he said that, in negotiations with other countries, Canada enjoyed "the prestige inspired by a consciousness of the fact that behind us towers the majesty of England".

Not all Canadians agreed. Laurier had not wanted to call Parliament to make the decision about the Boer War because he wanted to delay an angry debate. Even some who sympathized with the British wondered why Canadians should be sent to a war that did not endanger Britain, much less Canada. Macdonald himself had refused to send troops to Egypt in 1884 when a similar situation arose. As for *Canadiens*, very few felt any enthusiasm for the country which had conquered Québec in 1760. Their view was that Canada had enough domestic worries without engaging in foreign quarrels. Henri Bourassa, the rising star of *Canadien* nationalism, warned that, in fact, the decision *would* be a precedent. The next time, Canadians might even be conscripted for battles on distant shores.

FIGURE 1.4 *The Alaska Boundary Dispute*

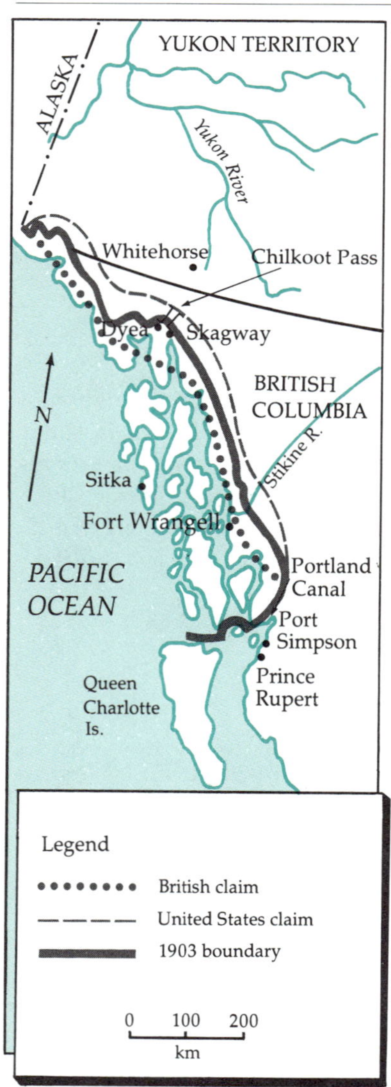

In 1903, a dispute over Canada's boundaries reminded Canadians of their humble place in the Empire and the world. The Alaska Panhandle, a long, narrow strip of land along the Pacific Ocean, had been claimed originally by Britain. A treaty made in 1825 gave it to Russia. When the United States bought Alaska from Russia, they acquired the Panhandle as well. Canadians could therefore reach the Yukon only by crossing American territory, or by enduring a long, arduous overland route. Canada asked a tribunal to rule that the heads of some of the fjords extended into Canadian territory. The British judge on the six-man tribunal sided with the three Americans against the two Canadians.

Canada felt betrayed; was this the reward for helping Britain in South Africa? Laurier criticized the United States, but blamed mainly Britain. He hinted that colonial status might no longer be enough: "The difficulty as I conceive it is that so long as Canada remains a dependency of the British Crown, the present powers that we have are not sufficient for the maintenance of our rights." Why did Britain support the United States? It is true that the Canadian claim was weak, and the case badly prepared. What mattered more was that Britain owed the Americans thanks for their support during the Boer War, in the face of sharp criticism from European countries.

The dispute was soon overshadowed by events in Europe, where the German Empire was becoming a threat to Britain. The German army, the most powerful in the world, presented no direct danger. However, its existence prompted France and the vast Russian Empire to make an alliance. Germany had already found an ally in Austria-Hungary. What alarmed Britain was Germany's sudden decision to build its own fleet and carve out its own colonial empire. Such a rivalry could only bring conflict.

How would Canada respond? "If Britain is at war," Laurier told the House of Commons in 1910, "Canada is at war. There is no distinction."

If anything, ties with Britain were even closer in that year than during the Boer War; many immigrants had arrived in Canada during the decade, and most of them were British. Nevertheless, Laurier hoped that Britain (and therefore Canada) would remain neutral in a European war. He knew that one way to avoid the overseas commitment which so alarmed Québec was to take on the full burden of defence at home. In 1905, Canada agreed to replace the British army garrisons which defended the naval bases at Halifax and Esquimalt. Defence spending increased fivefold between 1897 and 1911. Cadet training was introduced into the high schools in many provinces, including Québec.

CLOSE-UP

A Canadian Navy?

Laurier was a master of compromises. In the early years of the twentieth century, his establishment of a Canadian navy seemed to be the best of them.

To its proponents, a Canadian navy seemed logical and inevitable. Canada's coastline was the second longest in the world. Thousands of Canadian fishing vessels navigated both oceans, an enormous fleet of merchant ships was registered at Canadian ports, and Canadian seamen served around the world. In 1905, Ottawa took over the naval bases at Halifax and Esquimalt from the British—but where were the Canadian warships to defend them? If Canada took over the rest of its own defence, who would protect that long coastline, the fishing vessels, and the merchant fleet? Clearly, Canada needed its own navy.

Opponents of the idea quickly pointed to the fact that the Royal Navy, the most powerful in the world, protected Canada's coasts and shipping at no cost. Moreover, they argued, a tiny colonial navy would be expensive, inefficient, and absurd.

Britain's new naval rivalry with Germany swung the argument in favour of the scheme. New technology—better guns, steel plate, and engines—had transformed naval warfare, and Germany led the world in the production of these items. The British tried to maintain their naval primacy in 1905 by launching the *Dreadnought*, by far the largest and best-armed battleship made till that time. German industrial might was hardly fazed; the Germans built their own dreadnoughts and the arms race continued.

The Royal Navy also responded by strengthening home defences. It started to bring home the warships it had scattered around the world. An Anglo-Japanese alliance in 1902 allowed Britain to cut its fleet in the Pacific. Canada saw the growing strength of the Japanese navy and the lessened defence of its Pacific shore as a threat. It was suggested that Canada and Australia should band together to form a Pacific fleet.

Laurier saw the idea as having imperialist overtones, and was not enthusiastic. Yet surely it was the right moment to create a Canadian navy to defend both coasts. There would be many advantages. Victoria and Halifax would benefit from increased government business; shipyards would profit from the building of warships; and nationalists and advocates of the navy, who had organized themselves into a Navy League, would be pleased. The idea became so popular that it was actually the Conservative opposition who on March 22, 1909 called for the creation of a Canadian navy. Laurier agreed willingly.

Yet just one year later, when the Liberals introduced the Naval Service Bill, the public mood had utterly changed. One reason was that the naval race between Britain and Germany had suddenly accelerated. British spies had found out that Germany was building four dreadnoughts. The Royal Navy, whose building program had been cut back, would be left far behind. "We want eight and we won't wait" became a popular cry in Britain. Imperialists in Canada insisted that the government send help.

If the ten warships which were to be Canada's naval fleet seemed feeble and unnecessary to imperialists, they were perceived as a menace by *Canadiens*. Henri Bourassa told his followers that, whatever Laurier might be pretending, the warships would launch Canada—and *Canadiens*—into a British war. In September, 1910, Laurier called a by-election in a rural Québec riding. Québec nationalists dressed up as recruiting sergeants and went from door to door, counting young men. The voters got the message, and the Liberals were defeated.

But by then, Canada's navy was afloat. The Royal Navy had sold Canada two cruisers, and loaned some of its finest officers and men to help the new service start at Esquimalt and Halifax. The Conservatives were not pleased. When they came to power, they warned, Canada's navy would be sunk.

QUESTIONS

1. How did Anglo-German naval rivalry lead to the idea of a Canadian navy?
2. Who originally supported the creation of a Canadian navy? Who eventually opposed it? Why did the plan go sour?
3. Why do you think Laurier chose to take a middle course on the navy issue?

HMCS Rainbow *arriving at Esquimalt, Nov. 7, 1910. This ship was brought from Britain to become part of Canada's new navy.*

At the same time, a peace movement developed, backed mainly by farmers, labour unions, and some church groups. They welcomed William Lyon Mackenzie King's assertion that the methods he used for settling arguments between management and labour could also prevent wars between nations. Spending money on armaments seemed a waste; many Canadians hoped, like Laurier, that Canada could avoid "the vortex of militarism which is the curse and blight of Europe".

Though imperialists and nationalists had very different views of Canada's future, both had faith and pride in their nation, buoyed by the boom of the Laurier years. If anything, the vision of some imperialists, that Canada (with its barely seven million people) would be the leading nation of the British Empire, was bolder than that of nationalists whose goal was a "Kingdom of Canada". At the very least, imperialists wanted Canada to have an active voice in the defence and foreign policies of the Empire.

Laurier, as a Canadian from Québec, worked for compromise. In public, and particularly for British audiences, he could clothe imperialism in magnificent eloquence. In private, he was wary of making commitments and suspicious of British statesmen. Laurier was aware that Liberal support depended both on Québec and on imperial-minded voters in Ontario and British Columbia and on the Prairies. Like anyone who makes compromise a way of life, Laurier was at various times condemned by imperialists, nationalists, and fellow *Canadiens*. His answer to them all was a fair measure of the man:

> I am a Canadian...I have had before me, a pillar of fire by night and a pillar of cloud by day, a policy of true Canadianism, of moderation, of conciliation.

Pressure to help Britain keep pace with German production of Dreadnoughts *almost put an end to Laurier's dream of a Canadian Navy.*

QUESTIONS

1. Why did "many Canadians (feel) a deep kinship to Britain"?
2. Why did Britain ask for Canada's help in the Boer War?
3. How did *Canadiens* view Canada's involvement in the Boer War?
4. (a) Why do you think there was a Briton on the tribunal which was to decide Canada's Pacific coastline?
   (b) What did his presence say about Canada's sovereignty at that time?

The End of the Laurier Era

Laurier was not worried about the outcome of the general election which had been called for 1911. It helped that the country was prosperous, and that nearly all civil servants and government contractors owed their positions to patronage. They would do anything in their power to keep the Liberals—and their jobs. Laurier also knew himself to be a powerful factor. Robert Borden, the Conservative leader, was conscientious but lacked Laurier's elegance and charm. Moreover, Laurier had been in power for 15 years, and it was hard to imagine anyone else as Prime Minister.

This float built by workers on an experimental farm advertises Canada's prosperity.

Borden, a lawyer from Nova Scotia, had done his best in the two previous elections, denouncing Liberal patronage and urging new ideas for honest, efficient government. He had, however, been defeated. The main opposition to Laurier came from the provincial premiers. Québec had been Liberal since 1897, but Ontario, formerly a Liberal stronghold, had elected a reform-minded Conservative party in 1905. Manitoba was Conservative, too, as was British Columbia. Each premier found Ottawa a convenient scapegoat for provincial ills. Whatever the problem, whether poor roads or Asian immigrants, the Liberal government got the blame for failing to recognize special provincial needs.

The creation in 1905 of two new provinces, Saskatchewan and Alberta, added to the Liberals' troubles. As in Manitoba, the federal government kept control of the land and mineral resources, so that nothing might interfere with the prairie settlement program. In future years, this would cause strife between the federal and provincial governments. A more immediate problem had to do with Laurier's desire to build guarantees for French and Roman Catholic rights into the constitutions of the new provinces. As a *Canadien*, Laurier saw this as important. To his dismay, his ministers disagreed. As you read earlier, Clifford Sifton resigned, and others threatened to do so. Laurier backed down, leaving Alberta and Saskatchewan free to make their own arrangements about schools and language.

Most of Canada soon forgot the matter, but not Québec. *Canadiens* had received the message that, if they left their province, they would have to accept the language and customs of the majority. "I regret every time I go back to my province," Bourassa wrote, "to find developing that feeling that Canada is not Canada for all Canadians. We are bound to come to the conclusion that Québec is our only country because we have no liberty elsewhere." Moreover, few in French Canada had received much of the benefit of the Laurier boom. Perhaps their sons and daughters only had to go as far as Montréal or Valleyfield to work, instead of New England, but they still had to leave home to make a living. Prosperity had passed rural Québec by. Some *Canadiens* did profit from the boom, but most of the gains went to the anglophone industrialists and investors. It was hard for Bourassa and other Québec nationalists to see what they had gained from having a *Canadien* Prime Minister.

Nor did Laurier's problems end there. On a journey to the Prairies in 1910, he found homesteaders demanding that the Liberals return to free trade. Why, they asked, should Canadian farmers pay high tariffs on farm machinery made in Minneapolis, just across the border, in order to provide work for Ontario labourers and profits for Ontario factory owners? Like most people in those days, Laurier had travelled little; he had not seen the West since before the huge waves of settlement had swept in. This trip convinced him that the West was the new power centre of Canada. Its wishes had to be considered.

The opportunity presented itself in the same year. The new American Congress, elected that year, was full of proponents of free trade. The President, William Taft, also believed there would be no harm in reviving the old reciprocity agreements of 1854 with Canada, since they posed no threat to the largest American industries. Laurier was delighted when the Americans offered to sign an agreement. A leading Conservative later confessed that his heart sank to his boots when he heard of the American offer. Here was the pact that Canada had sought to re-establish for generations, and Laurier had delivered it. The Liberals would remain in power forever.

Both parties had misjudged the public mood. Reciprocity had many enemies. Workers in the branch plants of American companies knew their jobs depended on a tariff wall. Canadian businesses and industries were horrified at the prospect of American competition. Surely, the politicians thought, the farmers had always wanted free trade. Some, however, did not. From British Columbia there came reminders from apple growers as well as sawmill operators that their livelihood, too, was protected by the tariffs. Ranchers and meat packers also feared American imports. Still Laurier remained confident. For much of the summer of 1911 he was in England, defending Canada's interests in the Empire. When he returned, he called an election for September 21.

In Québec, the navy was an election issue, and Québec nationalists broke up a Liberal rally in Montréal. Elsewhere, the Liberals and

Reciprocity

"Reciprocity" refers to the elimination of tariffs by Canada and the United States on goods traded between the two countries. This arrangement, a more limited version of free trade, was favoured by consumers, who would benefit from lower prices on imported goods. It was also supported by businesses which wanted a chance to sell in the large American market. It was opposed by business (and workers) who feared losing customers to stronger competitors from the south.

In 1854, an agreement to end tariffs on many products traded between the United States and Canada led to 12 years of prosperity. The Americans cancelled the agreement when Britain aided the Confederates during the Civil War. Since that time, Canadians have frequently debated whether they would be better off economically under a free trade arrangement with the Americans or under a system of tariff protection. The free trade issue was revived again in the late 1980's, when the Conservative government of Brian Mulroney negotiated a trade deal with the United States.

What connection does the artist make between reciprocity and annexation?

Conservatives wrangled over the free trade issue. "No truck nor trade with the Yankees," was the slogan of George Foster, one of Robert Borden's lieutenants. The crowds loved it. The American Senate was showing reluctance to sign the agreement. Americans who favoured the deal added fuel to the anti-reciprocity fire by boasting that it would lead to the Stars and Stripes waving at the North Pole. The Conservatives used such wild talk to embarrass the Liberals. Eighteen wealthy Toronto Liberal supporters abandoned the party over the free trade issue; their action signalled a general movement to the Conservative side by businesses. Suddenly the Conservatives had all the campaign funds they needed. One of their main aims was to break the Liberal hold on Québec. To this end, Conservative money was spent on Henri Bourassa's nationalist newspaper *Le Devoir*.

On election day, the Laurier era ended. In Québec, Laurier's support fell from 54 seats to 38. Borden owed 28 of his Québec seats to Bourassa's fiery editorials in *Le Devoir*. The Conservatives also made a near-sweep of British Columbia, Manitoba, and Ontario. Thus, they needed only four of their Québec seats for a clear majority. For the first time since Confederation, Québec was not a major power in Ottawa.

As so often happens, winning the election proved easier than running the country. Borden wanted the clean, progressive government which he had promised in the campaign; his followers wanted vengeance for years of Liberal power and patronage. All Conservatives, however, agreed on putting an end to the 1910 *Naval Service Act* which had established the tiny Canadian navy. On the next step, there was again furious dissent. Borden and the majority of his party pledged $35 million, the price of building three dreadnoughts, to Britain. The Québec members opposed any aid at all. In Parliament, the Liberals stalled the Naval Aid Bill endlessly, until, for the first time in Canada, the Conservatives cut off debate with a motion of closure. The bill was passed in the House of Commons but was defeated by the huge Liberal majority in the Senate. The idea of a Naval Aid Bill was quietly dropped, and Canada's fledging navy survived.

As early as three years before the Laurier era ended, the Laurier boom had been slowing down. European investors in Canada were made cautious by the threat of war. Just when the two new transcontinental railways were completed and might have started paying off their debts, the world slid into a new depression. By 1913, thousands of Canadians were once again hunting for work, competing with the immigrants who continued to pour into the country. The winter of 1913–1914 brought more misery than any in over two decades. The Liberals—and perhaps other Canadians—blamed the new government and waited confidently for its early defeat. Borden and his government laboured to solve the problems, but many of their causes were beyond the borders of Canada. As the country sweltered through the unusually long, hot summer of 1914, the main distraction was offered by the news of events in Europe.

QUESTIONS

1. Why did some people in Québec feel that Laurier had ignored their interests in leaving to Alberta and Saskatchewan the right to devise their own school systems?

2. Free trade was a political issue in the early 1900's (as it was in the late 1980's). Name two groups who favoured free trade at the turn of the century, and two groups who opposed it, and explain why each group adopted its position.

3. Why would Canadians from different areas of the country have differing views on tariff policies?

Chapter Summary

The Laurier boom was a time of nation building. Economic prosperity allowed Laurier to continue and strengthen Macdonald's National Policy. New transportation systems, including two new railways, were completed. Canada's population increased from 4.8 million in 1891 to 7.2 million by 1911. Many of these new immigrants settled in the Prairies, forming two new provinces, Saskatchewan and Alberta, in 1905.

During the Laurier years, Canadians developed a new sense of nationality. For the first time, immigration policies welcomed immigrants from Eastern Europe. Americans who could not find good land in the United States were attracted to the Canadian Prairies. Immigrants from Asia arrived, settling mainly on the Pacific coast. Being Canadian no longer meant being a transplanted Briton; Canadian society was becoming multicultural.

On the political front, Laurier, like his predecessor Macdonald, was forced to contend with the divisions between Canada's anglophone and francophone populations. His attempts to solve each crisis with compromise eventually lost him support within both groups. It would now be up to his successor, Robert Borden, to attempt to govern Canada without dividing the Canadian people.

IN REVIEW

1. "The Laurier boom made Macdonald's strategy work." What was Macdonald's strategy? Why did it work under Laurier, and not under Macdonald?

2. After the CPR was built, rates for all wheat going east were fixed at a low level, while rates for wheat going west fluctuated and were usually higher. Suggest why British Columbia protested against this policy.

3. What was the basic difference in attitude between imperialists and nationalists?

4. It is 1900. You have been asked to take part in a public discussion on Canada's participation in the Boer War. Give three arguments for and three arguments against sending Canadians to help the British in South Africa.
5. What were some issues that divided English and French Canadians during the Laurier era?

APPLYING YOUR KNOWLEDGE

1. How did life in Laurier's Canada differ from life today?
2. In dealing with immigration from Asia, Laurier had to worry not only about opinion in Canada but also about the reaction of Britain and Japan. Why? Could he have ignored foreign opinion? Do you think Canadian governments should worry about what other countries think of their policies?
3. Why was the *Komagata Maru* incident an important event in the history of Canadian immigration? Can you think of a more recent, but similar, occurrence that was also significant in Canadian immigration history?
4. Laurier was called a "forger (maker) of compromises". Do you think it is justifiable for political leaders to make compromises? Refer to one of Laurier's compromises to support your point of view.
5. What do you suppose Henri Bourassa meant when he said, "...Canada is not Canada for all Canadians"?
6. Did the Laurier government's policies build a stronger Canada? Give specific examples of policies carried out by Laurier's Liberals to support your answer.

FURTHER INVESTIGATION

1. **(a)** The reporting of history can be affected by the reporter's personal point of view. Find a newspaper or magazine article on a current issue (such as trade, immigration, or Native land claims). Read the article carefully, and decide whether it is biased or neutral. Give reasons for your assessment.
   (b) Try to rewrite two or three sentences in the article to introduce a bias, or to change any bias already present.
2. Clifford Sifton appeared to favour "stalwart peasants" over "trade union artisans" as immigrants to Canada. If you were asked about which occupations you would favour for people immigrating into Canada today, what research would you carry out before giving your opinion?
3. If your public library has microfilms of old issues of the *Vancouver Sun, Province,* or *World*, read the reports of the riots in the editions for September 8, 1907 (the day after the events). What happened? How did the riots start? Can you find evidence of bias in any of the accounts?

CHAPTER 2

A Nation Steeled in War

By the summer of 1914, the European powers were positioned for war. In Canada, opinion was divided on Canada's role in any prospective conflict. Those with close ties to Britain believed it was Canada's duty to support the British war effort. Other Canadians viewed the conflict as a European war in which Canada had no part.

Robert Borden was Canada's Prime Minster through the war. During those years, he had to balance Canada's new sense of "imperial nationalism" with its desire to avoid deadly entanglements. As the war dragged on and the number of Canadian dead and wounded increased, this balancing act grew ever more difficult, and Canadians became more bitterly divided.

As you read through this chapter, you will find answers to the following questions:

- *What events led to World War I?*
- *How did Canadians respond to Britain's declaration of war against Germany?*
- *Why did participation in the war effort change the Canadian way of life?*
- *Where did Canadian troops make a significant contribution to winning the war?*
- *How did World War I differ from any previous war?*
- *Why did the need for recruits create a political crisis in Canada?*
- *How did World War I force Britain and the world to change their view of Canada?*

The International Background

In the hot summer of 1914, Canada wrestled with the problems brought by renewed depression. The news from Europe added to Canadians' disquiet. No one in Canada understood the European situation fully; only a handful of European statesmen knew what was really happening. None of them imagined that the crisis would bring the downfall of four empires and the death of 20 million people.

By 1914, the great powers of Europe were divided in two alliances. Great Britain was linked to France and Russia in the *Entente Cordiale*, although Britain's government tried to avoid committing itself to fighting in Europe. Germany was allied to Italy and Austria-Hungary. Its leaders had little faith in the armies of the Hapsburg Emperor, Franz Josef. However, they also believed that Russia's huge, ill-managed forces would take months to organize. In the event of war, victory would depend on defeating France and then Russia. First would come a huge flank attack, sweeping across neutral Belgium into northern

FIGURE 2.1 *Europe (1914) Alliance System*

France and surrounding the main French army. Then Germany would have time to move its army east to confront the Russians. The actions might bring Britain into the war, but the British field army was tiny.

But would such a war come? Experts doubted it. Europe was too civilized. After a series of war scares faded, people were reassured. Some were even disappointed; war would be such a splendid adventure. Everyone was wrong. On June 28, 1914, Emperor Franz Josef's heir was murdered by a terrorist at Sarajevo, Bosnia (Yugoslavia). On evidence that the terrorist had been encouraged by Serbians, Austria was determined to punish Serbia. Russia, as Serbia's protector, threatened to go to war. Germany was obliged to back its Hapsburg ally. That meant launching the war plan designed to attack France. When German armies invaded Belgium, Britain felt bound by an old promise to defend Belgian neutrality. In a few days, the alliance systems had clicked into place. All the pledges of common sense were forgotten and in every European capital, rejoicing throngs applauded marching soldiers. The nightmare of Europe began with celebration.

QUESTIONS

1. What is an alliance?

2. **(a)** List the members of both the *Entente Cordiale* and the German alliance. **(b)** Why might this system have presented a threat to European stability?

3. Why did Britain declare war against Germany?

The War Measures Act

What powers would a wartime government need? For a few days after the declaration of war in Europe, lawyers prepared long lists. Then one of them, W.F. O'Connor, had the answer: a single, short law that gave the federal Cabinet any power it might ever need to preserve "...the security, defence, peace, order, and welfare of Canada". This was the **War Measures Act**, *the justification for thousands of wartime regulations. Under the* Act, *Cabinet did not have to submit its proposals to Parliament for approval. The government could therefore act rapidly in an emergency rather than wait for Parliament to meet, discuss, and approve measures.*

Canada's Response

The news reached Ottawa on August 4, at 8:55 p.m. Cheering crowds filled the streets—in Montréal and Québec as in Vancouver and Toronto. Henri Bourassa, who had been vacationing in Germany and got out just before war was declared, said that the war might bring about a union of French and English. When Parliament met on August 18, Laurier, the leader of the opposition, pledged a truce between his Liberals and the Conservatives: "When the call comes, our answer goes at once, and it goes in the classical language of the British answer to the call of duty, 'Ready, aye, ready!' " When Borden's Conservative government drafted a *War Measures Act* to do anything necessary "for the security, defence, peace, order and welfare of Canada", a Liberal Member of Parliament asked whether it went far enough.

Colonel Sam Hughes, Borden's Minister of Militia, was the man of the hour. Before the war, his enthusiastic militarism had caused the government embarassment. Some people, for example, had criticized

Colonel Sam Hughes, Borden's Minister of Militia returns the salute of his passing troops. Despite his popularity early in the war, he was fired by Borden in 1916. Was it a good idea to have a keen amateur soldier as a defense minister?

compulsory military training for high school students. The new depression had made Hughes unpopular because of the millions he spent on weapons and training. Now his actions were justified. Hughes immediately created a huge new training camp at Valcartier outside Québec City and called for 25 000 volunteers. By early September, 32 000 had poured in. Borden, like most Canadians, was impressed. What people did not know was that the contingent was neither efficient nor representative of the whole country. When the Canadians sailed for Europe on October 3, no single battalion represented *Canadiens*, or any of the Maritime provinces.

Few people would have thought that the inequality of representation mattered; everyone expected the war to be over by Christmas. On both sides, war plans were based on gaining a quick victory, with the loser paying the costs. But by October, the French alone had lost half a million soldiers in mass attacks on German defences. German attacks were somewhat more successful, conquering France's richest industrial region, but they failed to achieve victory. By November, the Germans were locked in combat with the French and British all along the western front. The foes faced one another across lines of trenches that ran from Switzerland, through France and a corner of Belgium, to the English Channel. After months of terrible losses, compromise had become impossible and defeat unthinkable for both sides. Nor would the war on the eastern front end any more quickly. There, the Russian armies suffered catastrophic defeats at the hands of the Germans. When Turkey joined Germany in December, it blocked the last convenient route for providing the Russians with vital arms and equipment.

Christmas came and went, with no end in sight. The world settled down to a long war. In Canada, Hughes' chief military advisor urged him not to promise too many volunteers. Bourassa, too, recommended that the government make a long-term plan before committing itself too deeply. But few Canadians shared their caution. Whether Canadians were fighting for Britain or for Canada, the struggle was worth it. Even those who before the war had been pacifists, including members of the clergy and leading feminists, now spoke at patriotic rallies. The few pacifists who remained, such as J.S. Woodsworth, Canada's best-known social service worker, eventually lost their jobs. Defeating German militarism was regarded as a patriotic, moral crusade.

Patriotic feelings could turn to intolerance. In 1914, more than 100 000 Germans, Austrians, and Hungarians lived in Canada. They included business people, homesteaders, scientists, and labourers who had struggled to help build the railways. In the early days of the war, those who wished to fight for their homelands slipped across to the United States and returned to Europe. But soon public opinion insisted that all **enemy aliens** be fired from their jobs. By the summer of 1915, over 6000 enemy aliens of military age had been interned in camps and prisons across Canada. The old Ontario city of Berlin changed its name to Kitchener in 1916, to honour a British general who died in the war. Orchestras stopped playing music by German composers; universities and schools fired German-speaking teachers; children pelted dachshunds with stones. One reason for the bitterness against enemy aliens was the depression which still gripped Canada. When jobs were scarce, patriotism was a good excuse for getting a rival for work fired. Another reason was violent propaganda, which both sides used to portray their enemies as inhuman monsters.

Enemy Aliens

An enemy alien was anyone from an enemy country who had not sworn an oath of allegiance to the government of the country he or she lived in. Male enemy aliens of military age could be interned (confined). Some Canadians, including the great musician Sir Ernest MacMillan, spent the war as enemy aliens in German camps and prisons.

Though the first response of all Canadians was enthusiastic, *Canadiens* soon showed reservations about the war. They had no more loyalty to France than to Britain. Attempts to persuade *Canadiens* to enlist fell on deaf ears. Even mass recruiting rallies and Laurier's speeches did not prevail. When a second Canadian contingent was approved in October, 1914, it included just one francophone battalion, the 22nd. A major grievance of Québec remained the battle over French-language education in Ontario and the West. Disillusioned, Bourassa claimed that the "Boches" (Germans) of Ontario were as bad as the "Boches" of Germany. *Canadiens* preferred to let the English fight if they chose.

QUESTIONS

1. How did Britain's declaration of war affect Canada?
2. Why might it be surprising that a Liberal would ask whether the *War Measures Act* written by the Conservatives "went far enough"?
3. How did Canadians react to being at war?

CLOSE-UP

What Is Patriotism?

The dictionary defines "patriotism" as "love of or devotion to one's country". In the violent debate over Canada's war effort, both sides described themselves as patriotic, and suggested that the other side was not.

Early in the war, Henri Bourassa was twice scheduled to speak in Ottawa on his viewpoint that Canadians should all think seriously before committing themselves to an all-out war effort. The first time, threats of violence persuaded his hosts to cancel their invitation; the second time, Bourassa was hooted down by opponents in the audience. Part of Bourassa's speech, which was printed as a pamphlet, read:

> To some, the empire is all and everything; others think of France only; another category, logical but narrow in their Canadian exclusiveness, see nothing beyond the borders of Canada: they seem to ignore our most conspicuous world responsibilities.
>
> These various feelings indicate a singular absence of true national patriotism.... Since the outbreak of war, the country has been flooded with 'patriotic' speeches and writings; but these words have been followed with very few deeds for the good of Canada.
>
> This marks all the differences between the thoughtful action of sovereign peoples...and the thoughtlessness of a child nation... Everyone speaks of the duties of Canada to Great Britain or France. Who has thought of the duties of Canada to herself?

Those who kept Bourassa from speaking published a handbill which read, in part:

> The Bourassa factions have cast contempt and defiance in the faces of the loyal citizens of Ottawa. They are well aware of his outrageously false and treasonable utterances since the outbreak of war. They know his presence in Ottawa is objectionable, offensive and exasperating to all loyal citizens, which means the overwhelming majority of our population, yet these abettors of treason and rebellion are determined to flaunt before us this arch traitor of Canada under the hypocritical pretense that 'freedom of speech' demands the sound of Bourassa's voice and no one else will do...they're seeking trouble and they will find it.

–both excerpts from *The Duty of Canada at the Present Hour*, Henri Bourassa, Montréal: *Imprimerie du "Devoir"*, n.d. pp. 6-7.

An appeal for recruits from Québec

QUESTIONS

1. How did the coming of the war affect English-French relations in Canada?
2. In your opinion, was either side in this confrontation unpatriotic? If so, which one, and why?
3. Write one or two sentences that give your definition of "patriotism".

How the War Changed Canada

The First World War was waged very largely on European territory; Canada was utterly remote from it. Nevertheless, Canadians expected the worst. At the outbreak, British Columbia premier Richard McBride purchased two submarines from the United States to protect his province. Throughout Canada, guards watched bridges, railway stations, and the Welland Canal. Such disasters as the burning of the Parliament Buildings in Ottawa in 1916 and the terrible Halifax explosion of 1917 were immediately (and falsely) blamed on German agents. In fact, the Germans did no direct damage in Canada at all. Yet the war left almost nothing in Canadian government, business, or daily life untouched.

If the war had ended as quickly as first predicted, it would have changed little. Even as the struggle dragged on into 1915 and 1916, Borden and the Conservatives tried to avoid deep changes. As much of the war effort as possible was left to volunteer groups. Even the

Over 1600 people died and 9000 were injured as a result of the Halifax explosion, the worst human-caused explosion before Hiroshima. The blast occurred when a Belgian relief ship collided with a French munitions carrier, the Mont Blanc, *in the narrowest part of Halifax harbour. The* Mont Blanc's *cargo ignited and exploded. This picture shows part of the devastated north end of the city.*

military hospitals for the sick and wounded were made the responsibility of a committee of private business people. When the British, desperate for ammunition, looked to Canada for help, Sam Hughes summoned industrialist friends to form a Shell Committee. Canadians wished to "do their bit" for the war. The Canadian Patriotic Fund (CPF) was created as a national charity whose purpose was collecting money to support soldiers' families. A soldier's pay, $1.10 per day for a private, was not raised during the war. Businessmen and school children collected money to buy machine guns. Women spent any spare hours knitting socks and rolling bandages for the war effort.

Most of these efforts were failures. The CPF allowances did little to help soldiers' families cope with rising prices. Hughes himself cancelled the machine gun fund, because governments had already ordered all the guns North American factories could produce. The Shell Committee received $170 million in orders, but delivered only $5.5 millions' worth on time. Prices for the shells were high, but quality was low. Some manufacturers faked inspection stamps, and filled pinhole faults in shells with paint. They ignored the fact that faulty shells could blow up guns—and the soldiers who used them.

In Britain, the need for armaments grew desperate. David Lloyd George, a fiery Welsh radical, took over munitions supply. By the end of 1915, an Imperial Munitions Board had been set up in Canada under British control. Millionaire bacon exporter Joseph Flavelle was put in charge. Flavelle collected able managers who had learned their skills during the Laurier boom, and backed them up when they slashed the prices of shells and enforced quality standards. When western Canadians demanded more contracts, Flavelle declared that they had not even met the orders they had already received. When unions demanded higher wages for their members in munition factories, Flavelle retorted that they were lucky to have jobs after a three-year depression. By 1917, the Imperial Munitions Board was the largest business Canada had ever seen, with a quarter of a million workers, including 40 000 women, in 600 factories. By the end of the war, the Board had produced cargo ships, aircraft, chemicals, and explosives, in addition to millions of artillery shells. It had taken a war to show that Canadians could run a huge, complex industry.

Older industries also profited from the war. The conflict ended western Europe's wheat imports from Russia, and cut off lumber and paper supplies from Scandinavia. Canadian fields and forests could fill both these needs for western Europe. For farmers, the situation created a dangerous temptation. Prewar droughts had shown that much of the Prairies was too dry for anything except cattle ranching. However, the wartime demand and government appeals to grow all they could encouraged farmers to plant on unsuitable land. Perfect growing conditions in 1915 gave the West its biggest grain crop ever. After 1915, prices climbed, but a return of the usual dry weather made yields fall sharply. By the end of the war, even Canadians had a taste of famine as

Food shortages brought on by the destruction of European farmland and declining Canadian production made food scarce in Canada by 1917. This World War I poster urges housewives to "waste not" by preserving food for the winter.

Why do you think issuing bonds was a popular means of raising money to finance Canada's war effort?

they chewed on tasteless "war bread" and endured "meatless Mondays". On the Prairies, overcropping and "grain mining"—doing nothing to improve the fertility of the soil—created the conditions that would lead to the "dustbowl" of the 1930's.

The strain of financing the war brought profound changes to Canada's government. In 1913, the federal government's total expenditures were $184.9 million. In 1917, the total was $573.5 million, $344 million of it for the war effort. If Sir Thomas White, Borden's Finance Minister, had tried to raise such sums through taxes, both rich and poor would have protested. His solution was to borrow the money. "We are justified in placing upon posterity the greater portion of the financial burden of this war," White explained, "waged as it is in the interests of human freedom and their benefit."

But who would lend Canada the money? Britain had none to spare, and American interest rates were high. Joseph Flavelle suggested what to do: borrow the money from Canada's own citizens by selling them government bonds which would pay them interest until the government bought back the bonds at some future date. Such a scheme had never before been tried. In 1915, White asked Canadians for $50 million; he got $100 million, and even more in 1916. In 1917 the government issued special Victory Bonds, hoping to sell $150 millions' worth; it got almost $500 million. Much of the extra money was made available to Britain to buy Imperial Munitions Board products.

The government found itself reluctantly participating in more and more areas of business and family life. With not enough business to make either of them profitable, the two new transcontinental railways were verging on bankruptcy. Borden did not wish to let them fail, since this would have frightened away investors and given the unpopular

CPR a monopoly. The solution was public ownership, which Borden himself had always believed in. However, many of his colleagues favoured private enterprise instead. It took the crisis of war to convince them that there was no other way to save the vital service and keep such investors as the Canadian Bank of Commerce from falling into bankruptcy along with the railway.

The wartime mood also brought major changes in the expectations of Canadians. For decades before the war, demands for the prohibition of liquor had thundered from the pulpits and echoed across meeting halls. Women's groups had always been avid supporters of prohibition, and one argument for giving women the right to vote was that they would use it to ban alcoholic beverages. Surely, prohibitionists argued, when soldiers were giving up their lives for Canada, civilians could give up a harmful pleasure for their country. Beginning on the Prairies, province after province ended the sale of liquor. Finally, only Québec remained "wet". Patriots pointed out that *Canadiens* and "foreigners" were the chief opponents of prohibition, and that King George V and Queen Mary had long since set an example by making Buckingham Palace "dry". In 1918, the shortage of grain—the constituent of most liquor—added the conclusive argument. Ottawa used the *War Measures Act* to impose nation-wide prohibition.

Prohibition

At the turn of the century, over one-half of all criminal offences were linked to the consumption of liquor. Social reformers had urged drinkers to practise moderation. However, they finally decided that only a total ban on drinking—prohibition—would end "the liquor evil".

A prohibition parade in Toronto. Why might being at war win supporters for the prohibition movement?

When Manitoba women finally got the vote in 1916, a proud Nellie McClung could pause to consider her next challenge.

Women had led the prohibition campaign, and the prairie provinces had led the movement to prohibition. It was no surprise, then, that the western provinces also led in giving women the right to vote. On January 26, 1916, Nellie McClung, Francis Beynon, Lillian Thomas, and other suffragists won their valiant struggle in Manitoba. Saskatchewan gave women the vote two months later; Alberta, in April; and British Columbia, in 1917. Ontario followed suit, also in 1917. On May 24, 1918, all female citizens over the age of 21 received the right to vote in federal elections.

None of this was related directly to the war effort. However, the war helped women's cause. It created an atmosphere of change and expectation. In addition, the shortage of men made it more necessary than ever for women to work outside the home. Their successes in leading the prohibition campaign, running farms, working in factories, and converting others to their cause all contributed to bringing women the vote.

Another social change came in response to Canadians' expectations of the postwar world. In return for wartime sacrifices, Canadians wanted postwar rewards. A flood of books and pamphlets offered Canada visions of a better tomorrow. An example was Stephen Leacock's essay "The Unsolved Riddle of Social Justice". It presented a point of view surprising for such a conservative writer—that the government should "supply work and pay for the unemployed, maintenance for the infirm and aged, and education and opportunity for the children".

Some Canadians would not wait until after the war. Canada had prospered during wartime, at least after the winter of 1914–1915. The sales of government bonds also brought more money into circulation. Wages rose, and even poorer people found they had money to spend and save. The wealthy did even better. At a time when a modest

The women who replaced men in factories during World War I did the same jobs as their predecessors, but were often paid considerably less.

automobile cost far more than a worker's annual salary, car ownership soared from 45 716 in 1914 to 196 367 in 1919. However, because of the war effort, factories made mainly war products, not goods for consumers in Canada. The inevitable result of too much money chasing too few goods occurred—inflation. In 1917 and 1918, prices took off, and wages in some industries followed. In other industries, wages remained low, membership in unions increased, and workers struck for higher pay. In the autumn of 1918, the government reacted by banning strikes and lockouts. An "anti-loafing" law under the *War Measures Act* made it a crime for males over 16 to be unemployed.

The heightened expectations of ordinary Canadians also made them feel that the rich were not contributing equally to the war effort. The government's first reluctant response to this viewpoint came in 1917, with the introduction of a small Income War Tax. The first collection of the new tax netted a mere $8 million from 31 130 affluent Canadians. The Finance Minister, Sir Thomas White, pledged that the income tax would be a temporary, wartime measure. Canadians are still filling out the forms for their oldest "temporary" tax.

QUESTIONS

1. In what ways was Canada unprepared for war?

2. How did the attitudes and responsibilities of the government change during the course of the war?

3. **(a)** What is inflation?
(b) What were the effects of inflation on the economy and the populace after 1917?

4. How did the Canadian government raise money to pay for the war?

5. During the First World War, the vote for women grew to be an important political issue. What connection was there between the issues of female suffrage and prohibition?

Canadians at War

Nearly 425 000 Canadian men and women served overseas in the Canadian Expeditionary Force (CEF), while 35 000 joined the British services. Some of these were recent British immigrants to Canada. Others were men who wished to join the new warfare in the skies. They had no choice but to join the British naval and army flying services, since Canada waited until the end of the war to create its own air force. Some recent immigrants were required by the laws of their former homelands to return to the army in time of war. Of the Canadians who went overseas with the CEF, close to 60 000 never returned.

Almost 2000 women served overseas in Canadian military hospitals. Their presence reassured Canadians that their sick and wounded would receive caring treatment.

Most Canadians knew nothing of war beyond the heroic stories they had read in schoolbooks. When they arrived at the front, they realized that the instructors who had trained them in "modern" warfare knew little more. This war was like nothing anyone—from general to private—had expected. In the 1890's, a Polish banker, Ivan Bloch, had predicted that future wars would stagnate into opposing trench lines made impregnable by machine guns and artillery. Hundreds of thousands would die before generals would admit the futility of attack. Wars would end only when the strength and resources of one or both sides were utterly exhausted. Military experts dismissed Bloch's nightmare vision, but it had come true.

A no-man's-land, blasted with shells and strewn with barbed wire, wreckage, and corpses, separated two trench systems. The soldiers crouched in ditches or dugouts as hidden snipers waited to kill the unwary. Night was turned into day, as soldiers worked feverishly after dark to rebuild trenches, collect food and ammunition, or scout enemy lines. Thanks to the new air war, men in aircraft could see the enemy beyond their lines and hail down merciless artillery fire. At dawn and dusk, every soldier stood on guard, since those were the best times for an attack. Then, in daylight, the exhausted men might be allowed a few hours' sleep. Rain and cold left soldiers soaked and shivering, ready for a daily tot of S.R.D.—"service rum, diluted".

If all went well, every few days the men in the firing trenches and those in supporting trenches changed places. After about a week, both groups retired to base camps and new troops took their places. Away from the front lines, the men might get a chance for a bath, but the body lice which plagued them soon returned. Awash in filthy mud, the wounds of the injured frequently became infected. Antibiotics were a generation away, and blood transfusions were still experimental. Food was a major topic of interest; the coarse, monotonous army diet of corned beef, bread, and tea made anything else seem a luxury. Canadian troops took any opportunity they could to purchase such delicacies as eggs, fried potatoes, and French red wine at *estaminets* or taverns behind the lines.

New arrivals from Canada soon found out that much of the war propaganda was nonsense. The Germans were neither starving nor cowardly; in fact, they were well-fed, highly trained, and often chivalrous. The Canadians had much else to learn as well. They did so the hard way. At Ypres, France, on April 22, 1915, the 1st Division held the British line in the face of the first poison gas attack and waves of enemy troops. The cost was 6035 casualties, some of them due to inexperience and poor weapons. At St. Eloi in April, 1916, the new 2nd Division was driven from key positions because its commanders could not locate their men to send help. In June, 1916, the 3rd Division lost its general and many men when the Germans pulverized Mont Sorrel with shell fire. After a first attempt failed, the battle-hardened 1st Division carefully rehearsed, then recaptured the position.

Canadian Army Structure

A Canadian infantry division had about 20 000 men, including infantry, artillery, engineers, and supporting troops. It was divided into three brigades, each with four infantry battalions. A battalion had 1000 fighting men at full strength, but usually had far fewer. Each battalion had four companies; each company, four platoons. A platoon was commanded by a lieutenant, the lowest rank of officer.

To a soldier, his battalion was almost a family. He returned to it from hospital or another posting, wore its badges, and shared its successes and failures.

A trench on the Canadian front. Soldiers served two or three days in the front lines, a similar period in support trenches, then withdrew to rest areas.

CLOSE-UP

Words from the Front

A poem written by a Canadian soldier in the trenches and a different soldier's letter home after a battle are quoted below.

Yes the rats do roam and make their home
In the fields where the dead men lie.
Yes, the lice do bite all day and night
And never quit till you die.

Here the human moles from their stinking holes
Crawl up through the muck and slime
To hide all day, then work all night
Till there is no sense to time.

The great shells roar through the leaden skies
As their targets crouch in the drains,
Then burst with a roar and the shrapnel flies,
And it rains and it rains and it rains.

When the great green mass of chlorine gas
Drifts down from the eastern sky,
You choke and spit till your lungs are split
And you hear your best friends die.

In the stinking stench of a rotten trench
Mid the swarms of filthy flies,
Some men get caught so their bodies rot,
And the maggots eat their eyes.

In that sea of mud you can feel your blood
Go cold as you shake with fright,
And among the dead you raise your head
To stand to your post to fight.

–Robert Swan, as quoted in the *Great War and Canadian Society*, Toronto: New Hogtown Press, 1978, Daphne Read, editor, pp. 141-2.

Never shall I forget the look on the faces of the men who in providence came out unscathed. It was a look of distress mingled with pride—distress for their fallen comrades, pride when they remembered what they had accomplished...You would naturally think that, after what they endured, nothing could save them from nervous collapse. Nothing of the kind. Over all is the spirit of cheerfulness and pluck which never deserts them. As one fellow said to me, "There is no time for the pulling of long faces."...The tales of heroism I have listened to would fill a column—the wounded helping the wounded and dying; officers mortally wounded buoying up the men to victory...it was victory and

This painting, by Canadian artist H.J. Mowat, shows a trench battle during World War I.

although we mourn for those who have fallen on sleep, we do not mourn as those who have no hope. The Dominion who sent them will send others unto them. It was just our gift to the Empire.

–Letter from the front, May 19, 1915, as quoted in *With the First Canadian Contingent*, Toronto: Hodder and Stoughton Limited, the Musson Book Company Limited, n.d., pp. 93-4.

QUESTIONS

1. (a) What do you think was the purpose of the poet in writing these verses?

(b) Quote the two lines which you feel convey the poet's message most effectively.

2. (a) Refer to the letter. What difference is there between its message and that of the poem?

(b) What, in fact, was "...our gift to the Empire"?

3. Which quotation more closely describes your personal views on warfare?

That autumn, Canadians learned their bitterest lessons in the Somme offensives. "If hell is as bad as what I have seen..." wrote a *Canadien*, Lt. Colonel Thomas Tremblay, "I would not wish my worst enemy to go there." His battalion, the 22nd, known as the "Vandoos" (from the French for "22"), the 25th Battalion from Nova Scotia, and other units of the three Canadian divisions carried the line forward at incredible cost. In October, it was the turn of the raw 4th Division. Twice it failed; then with bitter desperation the survivors reached the goal. The Somme cost Canada 24 029 dead and wounded—for a few dozen hectares of shell-blasted mud.

The four divisions formed the Canadian Corps. By the end of the Somme offensive, its soldiers had become able veterans. In this war without precedent, the Canadian volunteers could be just as proficient as the professional soldiers of other nations.

Early in 1917, the Canadian Corps showed what it could do. The British front was mainly a flat plain dotted with mining villages. Only the whale-shaped Vimy Ridge broke the French skyline. The French had been driven from Vimy two years before. Sir Julian Byng, the Canadian Corps' British commandeer, vowed to win it back. He went about his plan with care. At dawn on Easter Sunday, April 9, 1917, months of preparation and rehearsal ended. By noon, the ridge was taken, though it took four more days of fierce fighting before the last Germans had given up. Every division of the Corps took part in this first truly Canadian victory.

As a reward, Byng was appointed to a higher command. His successor was Arthur Currie, a former insurance and real estate broker from Victoria, B.C., now a cool, resourceful field commander. Canadians now felt that the Corps was really theirs. The British, too, realized that the Canadians had developed into a unique fighting force. That summer, at Arleux, Fresnoy, and Lens, the Corps proved that the victory at Vimy was no fluke. In October, the Canadians were to be part of the first "modern" battle of the war—fought with tanks. Their former commander, Byng, had assembled hundreds of the new machines. Equipped with tracks, gun turrets, and armour plate, they could wade through machine gun fire, barbed wire, and trenches. At Cambrai, tanks would smash the German line, and the Canadians would follow up.

But there was a change in plans. The commander-in-chief, Sir Douglas Haig, ordered the Canadians to rescue the failing British assault on Passchendaele. For months, wave after wave of British attackers had been mowed down in a sea of mud by the Germans who held the high ground. Six hundred thousand men had been killed or wounded. Currie protested: The objective was useless and would cost his Corps 16 000 casualties. Haig insisted; there were reasons, he confided, that he could not explain. Currie demanded time to prepare. The roads and platforms constructed over the waterlogged soil at his

Passchendaele. Canadians protested at having to fight in a useless battle but, once committed, they used their new skill to limit casualties. Why did the battle mean so much to Haig?

command, the supplies, the guns brought in to replace those drowned in mud—all made a difference to the battle. Step by step, and at terrible cost, the Canadians crept closer. Finally, on November 6, 1917, Passchendaele—by now little more than brick dust in mud—fell, at a cost of 15 654 Canadians killed and wounded.

The Canadians had won their worst battle of the war, but to what purpose? Later, Haig insisted that the Canadian attack had been necessary to keep the Germans from attacking the collapsing French army. He also wanted to capture German submarine bases in Flanders, and to ward off defeatism in Paris and London. But redirecting the Canadian Corps away from Byng's offensive at Cambrai guaranteed that British tanks had too little support to hold the 10 km gap they smashed in the German line. By the end of November, the Germans had regained their lost ground, wiping out most of a Canadian cavalry brigade and a Newfoundland battalion in the process.

QUESTIONS

1. (a) Name some of the contributions which Canadians made to the war effort.
(b) What, in your opinion, were the three most important achievements of Canadians at war?

2. Compare the actions and achievements of the three commanders—Byng, Currie, and Haig—as described in this section.

3. (a) Why was the battle at Passchendaele an important Canadian victory?
(b) What effect, if any, did the victory at Passchendaele have on the outcome of World War I?

A Crisis of Commitment

After 1916, it became harder and harder to recruit volunteers. Do these posters present a realistic view of a soldier's life?

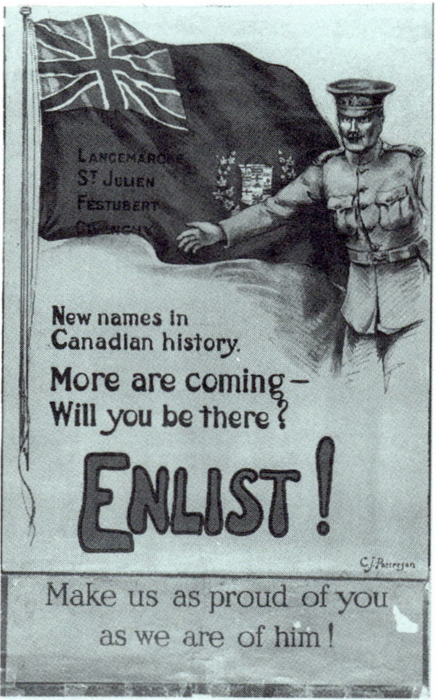

By mid-1916, 351 617 Canadians had enlisted for service overseas, including 1491 nursing sisters. As the war dragged on, enthusiasm evaporated. The lack of volunteers alarmed the government. Even those who volunteered preferred the Forestry Corps or battalions of railway builders. Only a few thousand now chose the infantry—not enough to replace the losses.

Things had been different earlier in the war. In 1914, so many volunteers appeared that Minister of Militia Sam Hughes rejected married men who had not brought their wives' written permission. Nearly 160 000 young Canadians enlisted in 1915, and over 170 000 in 1916. Militia regiments and patriotic leagues recruited battalions for overseas. Cities and counties competed for volunteers. Recruiters offered Highland kilts or the pleasure of being among fellow "sportsmen". One battalion, the Bantams, took men below the height limit. Borden declared publicly that conscription would never be necessary.

Why did Canadians volunteer? For the unemployed in the 1914 depression, it was a chance at a job. Others saw it as an opportunity to return to their homelands. For young Canadians of the day, war was an adventure, a test of manhood, or an escape from farm work or small town life. Most volunteered because it was expected of them and, as their diaries and letters reveal, because of a strong sense of duty. None knew what awaited them. Few of the wounded returned to Canada before 1917, and even the politicians and generals did not know the full horror of trench warfare.

How many men could Canada afford from its population of only eight million? The experience of 1916 showed that the Canadian Corps needed 20 000 replacements every year for each of its four divisions. In the summer of that year, Hughes created a new 5th Division. Yet at the same time, the number of volunteers tailed off. In the first half of 1916, the CEF recruited 134 000 men; in the last six months, only 36 000. There were several causes for the decline. Most of those who were willing to volunteer had already done so. Munitions factories clamoured for workers at wages unimaginable in peacetime. Farmers, seeing the best prices in history, wanted their sons at home to help grow grain. By late 1916, no-one would say that the war was an adventure, or that it would be over quickly.

Another problem with recruiting bothered Canadians: French-speaking Québec was not pulling its weight. There were various reasons for this reluctance. The province had fewer people of British origin, and its young men tended to marry and settle down earlier. The main reason, however, was that *Canadiens* had no interest in participating in the war. Bourassa and other Québec nationalists made no bones about it. They believed that, some day, Canada as a whole might welcome their warnings against becoming involved in Britain's wars.

The slowdown in the recruitment of volunteers and the slow progress of the war distressed the Prime Minister. Borden was deeply committed to the war effort. A summer visit to England in 1915 convinced him that, among British leaders, only David Lloyd George shared his earnestness. In his New Year's message of 1916, Borden announced that Canada would send half a million men to the war. The announcement produced some shock but little concrete effect.

A year later, Borden was pleased to hear that Lloyd George had become Prime Minister. Among his first acts was to summon the dominion Prime Ministers to London to form an Imperial War Cabinet. Between sessions, Borden visited the hospitals, with their endless rows of Canadian wounded. He learned that, because there were too few replacements, these men would be sent back to fight until they were killed or terribly disabled. He was in England when the Canadian Corps took Vimy Ridge, and learned the cost: 10 602 casualties, 3598 of them fatal. That month, only 4761 Canadians volunteered. Borden also learned that, two days before Vimy, the United States had finally declared war on Germany. Congress had immediately imposed a *Selective Service Act* to raise two million soldiers. Could Canada's contribution be allowed to falter?

Borden made his case before Parliament in May, 1917. "All citizens are liable for the defence of their country," he declared, "and I conceive that the battle for Canadian liberty and autonomy is being fought on the plains of France and Belgium." A month later, he introduced into Parliament a *Military Service Act* which would permit conscription.

Borden was well aware of the political risks. In Australia, voters had rejected conscription. Farmers feared that their farms would fall into ruin if their sons were conscripted. Labour unions were afraid that

Sir Robert Borden believed that it was his duty to visit wounded Canadians during his trips overseas. Their suffering steeled his resolve that Canada must do everything possible, including imposing conscription, to help end the war.

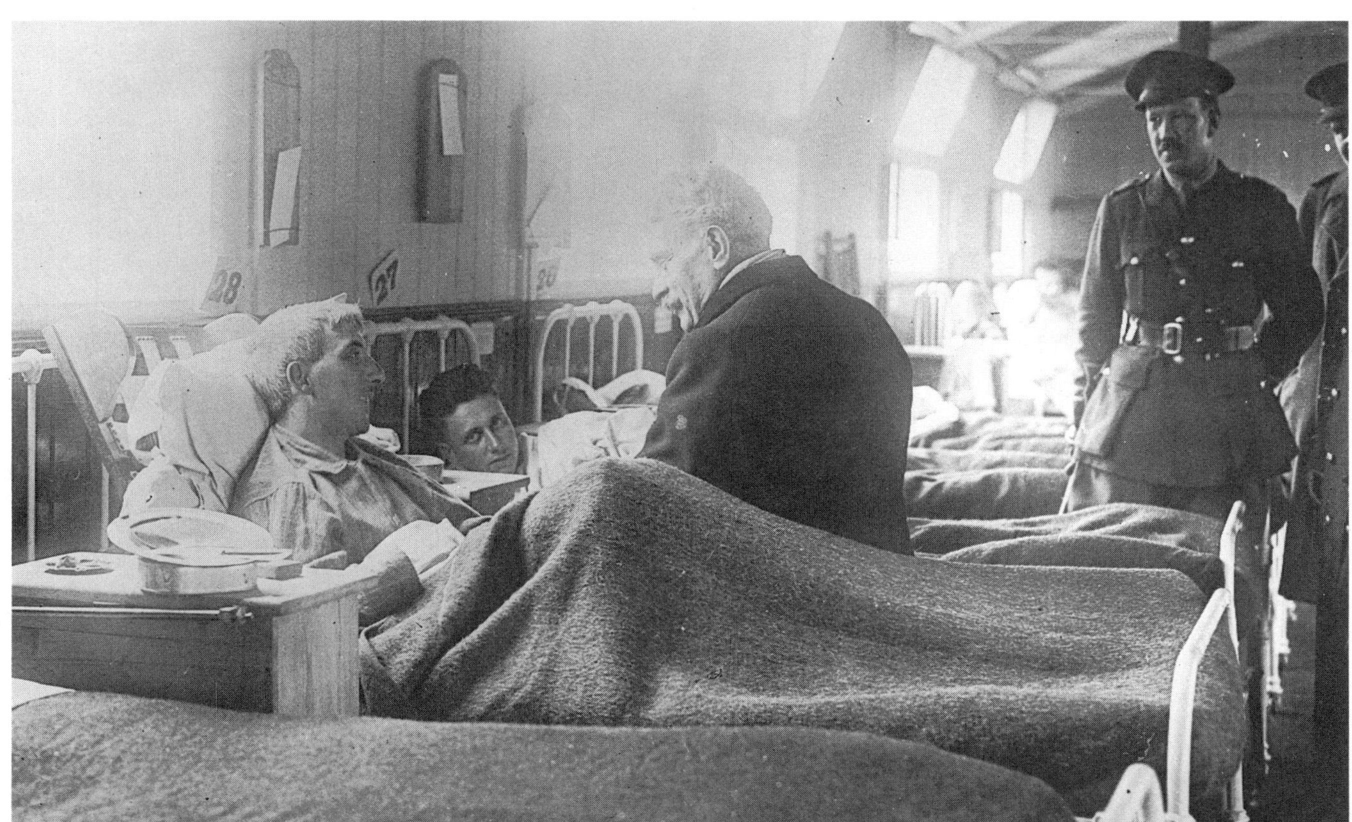

An anti-conscription march in Montréal in 1917. The real fascination of this picture lies in how little in evidence the francophone majority seems to be. The photo could be of Toronto or Vancouver.

conscription would be used to break strikes. But the main opposition, as always, came from Québec. To Borden, Canada was fighting for civilization and against militarism. Bourassa's answer was that Canada should keep its men home to grow food and make munitions for the war, and profit from it. Borden saw such arguments as unworthy; Bourassa believed that the Prime Minister was sacrificing Canadian lives and wealth at Britain's command. The two men's views were irreconcilable.

Laurier agreed with Bourassa in opposing conscription. "If this military service bill is passed," he said, "we will face a cleavage which may rend and tear this Canada of ours down to the roots." The Liberal party leader was sure that his party shared his views. But in British Columbia, the prairie provinces, and Ontario, the war had become a crusade shattering party loyalties. Reforming Liberals such as Newton Rowell, the Ontario Liberal leader, and J.W. Dafoe, the editor of the *Manitoba Free Press*, saw that Borden was committed to the war, while Laurier was not. Borden contacted some of the reforming Liberals and found them nervous, but willing to support him. Ironically, it was easier to persuade them after the government forced through two laws that hurt Laurier's chances of election victory. The *Military Voters' Act* allowed all soldiers to vote, while the *Wartime Elections Act* took the vote from citizens born in enemy countries and gave it to the wives, mothers, and sisters of soldiers. In early October, 1917, a large number of English-speaking Liberals indicated to Borden that they were willing to discuss entering a coalition with the Conservatives. On October 6, Parliament was dissolved; five days later, a delighted Borden announced a new "Union government". Its pledge was to win the war through conscription, wartime prohibition, cooperative management of the railways, and an end to party patronage.

Victory for the Unionists looked easy at first, since eight out of nine provincial premiers—all except Québec's Sir Lomer Gouin—endorsed Borden's government. Then trouble arose. In riding after riding, Liberal and Conservative candidates wrangled over who would be nominated. In Kitchener (formerly Berlin), Ontario, an anti-conscription crowd drove Borden from his platform. Unionist candidates in Québec needed police protection. His nervous ministers persuaded Borden to promise exemptions from conscription for farmers' sons and soldiers' brothers.

On December 6, Canadians were appalled by news from Halifax. A French ship carrying explosives had caught fire and exploded, wrecking much of the seaport and killing 1630 people. Shocked survivors were left to seek shelter in the worst winter storm in years. The war had come to Canada. Eleven days later, the election shattered the country. Borden's majority—162 seats to Laurier's 82—looked bigger than it was. Only 3 of Borden's seats were in Québec. Without the soldiers, 90 percent of whom voted for the Union government, Borden's lead was barely 100 000 votes.

After the election, the *Military Service Act* was enforced. Of the 404 395 men called for the first group of conscripts, 380 510 found some reason to appeal. In Québec, local tribunals exempted *Canadiens*, but, as Mr. Justice Lyman Duff later wrote, "applied conscription against the English-speaking minority. . .with a rigor unparalleled." When Duff's appeal court reversed the tribunals, an explosion was inevitable. It came on the Easter weekend of 1918 in Québec City, when a man was arrested for not having his exemption papers. A furious crowd destroyed the military service office and tossed the records into the snow. Mobs roamed the streets, destroying the premises of anglophone business people. Ottawa sent the only available troops, 700 men from Ontario. On Easter Monday, April 1, soldiers caught by crowds in a square opened fire, killing four people. The riots ended as Roman Catholic clergy ordered the faithful to obey the law. But the bitterness remained.

The contention over conscription had not ended. On March 21, 1918, massed German forces struck the Fifth British Army, still recovering after Passchendaele. The British line dissolved into pockets of desperate resistance. Far away, in Ottawa, Borden concluded that the Canadian Corps would need more men. The exemptions and appeals must end. After acrimonious Cabinet debate, on April 19, Ottawa announced that all exemptions were cancelled.

To many who had supported the Union government in the election, this was betrayal. Deprived of their sons and labourers, farmers struggled to finish the spring seeding as best they could. On May 15, many of them invaded Ottawa. Borden listened politely but ignored their complaints. The Canadian Corps needed men; women, children, and the elderly would have to harvest the crops.

CLOSE-UP

How Did Conscription Work?

When he announced the *Military Service Act*, Prime Minister Borden declared that the Canadian army urgently needed 100 000 men. He also promised that conscription would respect religious beliefs and disrupt families, businesses, and farms as little as possible. Did the government succeed in all it set out to do?

Arthur Meighen, Borden's most capable minister, was put in charge of conscription. The new *Act* divided all Canadian men between 20 and 43 into six classes, beginning with those 20 to 24 who were single, and ending with those 40 to 43 who were married. It also set out who could be exempted and where they could make their case. Men who were needed to support their parents or families, those employed in essential jobs or in farming, those with special skills, clergymen, and conscientious objectors on religious grounds, were all exempt. In each province, selection committees which were equally split between government and opposition chose officials for local tribunals and appeal courts. A final court of appeal was instituted. Lyman Duff of British Columbia, a Supreme Court Judge, was put in charge. In addition, 200 medical boards were appointed to decide whether conscripts were fit to serve.

Registration began in January, 1918, because the government had promised to hold off until after the election of December. It started with Class I, young, single men. Soon it became obvious that nearly everyone would ask for an exemption; of 405 395 who reported, only 24 115 agreed to serve. In Québec, 115 000 out of 117 000 who reported asked to be exempted; in Ontario, the figure was 118 000 out of 125 000. In Manitoba, every student at the agricultural college asked for an exemption; in Québec, every student at Laval University did likewise. Some tribunals asked no questions, while others were very strict. Montréal's tribunals dealt with 2595 conscripts in two days and exempted 2021. In St.

Catharines, on the other hand, exemptions were so rare that an army officer watching the proceedings said, "I believe even a dead man would have to show good reason."

A major problem was draft evasion. Even when men were ordered to appear, many simply vanished. In Québec, the police refused to help locate draft evaders. The attempt by military authorities to enforce conscription was one of the factors leading to the bloody Easter riots of 1918 in Québec City.

By April 1, only 20 025 "MSA men" had reported, while another 6775 had volunteered. Nearly 4500 evaders had been arrested. Borden was far from achieving his goal of 100 000 men. English Canada represented another problem; the supporters of the Union government had believed that conscription was not for them or their sons but for "slackers and French Canadians". The fierce German offensives of late March, 1918 made Borden's mind up for him. All exemptions for Class I men would be cancelled. Frantic appeals won a few concessions; for instance, soldiers' brothers and some conscientious objectors would remain exempt. The latter group included Mennonities and Doukhobors, but not Jehovah's Witnesses and Plymouth Brethren. All others must serve.

Surprisingly, the cancellation brought no renewal of violence in Québec. The Easter riots had released much of the tension. The clergy advocated order and obedience to the law. It was, in fact, farmers in Ontario and the West who were most furious. They saw the cancellation as a breach of trust. They, too, won one concession; drafted men would be granted leave during seeding and harvest times.

Even though both the Departments of Justice and of Militia and Defence kept records, accurate statistics on the number of conscripts are hard to find. The Justice Department claimed that the *Military Service Act* made a total of 121 124 men available; the army claimed 124 588. Over one-fifth of these—24 745 or 24 937, depending on the source—had to be discharged as unsuitable. By November, 1918, the CEF calculated that it had received 99 651 conscripts. Yet even this number is an estimate, since the army did its utmost to prevent distinctions being made between conscripts and volunteers.

Did the government succeed in its plan? There are those who point out that in 1914 Borden had said publicly that conscription would not be necessary. But no-one could have expected the war to last as long as it did, or to be as brutal. Borden's *Military Service Act* did provide the army with its 100 000 much-needed men—though he had to cancel most exemptions to do it. If the war had lasted until 1920, as many believed it would in the summer of 1918, all those men, and more, would have been needed.

Conscription was a voter's issue during the 1917 federal election campaign. For which party would you have voted?

QUESTIONS

1. What is conscription?
2. (a) Which groups were exempt from conscription?
   (b) Why were they given special consideration?
3. (a) Under what circumstances, if any, would you support conscription?
   (b) What groups, if any, would you exempt from conscription?

QUESTIONS

1. "In the first half of 1916, the CEF recruited 134 000 men; in the last six months, only 36 000." What reasons were there for the decrease?
2. Why was Borden so determined to commit Canada to sending a large number of soldiers to the war?
3. What were the arguments for and against conscription in 1917?
4. Why was conscription particularly problematic for farmers?
5. What brought about the cancellation of most conscription exemptions?
6. What were the causes behind the Easter Riots of 1918?

Canada's Role in the Postwar World

The war years propelled Canada towards an independent role in the world. In 1914, Canadians had gone to war as Imperials in the British Army; by 1917, they were members in spirit and law of a Canadian army. By 1918, Sir Arthur Currie knew he could appeal to Canadian authorities against British orders he regarded as unwise.

The war showed both the strengths and weaknesses of the British Empire. Every part of the Empire, from India to Newfoundland, contributed soldiers and resources. Britain was far stronger than if it had stood alone. But there were difficulties—even one so simple as getting all the leaders of the Empire together at a time when Canada was a week from Britain by ship, and Australia and New Zealand were a month distant. There was also the greater problem that Britain's leaders were not eager to share their power in making decisions with the leaders of the dominions.

If the war changed Canada, it also changed Canada's Prime Minister. At the outset, Borden was an "imperial federalist", anxious that Canada should have a voice in the Empire's foreign and defence policies. After his visit to Britain in 1915, he thought that Canada's contribution to the

The women of Fenelon Falls, like others all across Canada, celebrated the end of World War I and the return of the troops. These women prepared a pageant showing the flags of the Allied countries.

war effort should be rewarded with some influence. However, Borden's proposals were politely dismissed by Britain's colonial secretary. Borden was furious. He wrote to a friend, "It can hardly be expected that we shall put 400 000 or 500 000 men in the field and willingly accept the position of having no more voice and receiving no more consideration than if we were toy automata." Then Borden's temper cooled, and he turned to getting Canada's war effort in order and encouraging the United States to join the war.

Borden was pleased when David Lloyd George, newly elected Prime Minister, called the dominion Prime Ministers to form an Imperial War Cabinet in 1917. It was Lloyd George's intention to involve the dominion leaders in foreign policy. But Borden wanted even more, and thought he had it in the War Cabinet's Resolution IX. Though the details were to be worked out after the war, the resolution stated that the dominions would henceforth be equal to Britain in status, with the right to "an adequate voice in policy and foreign relations".

In June, 1918, Borden returned to Britain, furious once again. He had learned of the string of disasters that included Passchendaele, and of the German offensives which had shattered the British and French armies. Sir Arthur Currie had told him of the incompetence of the British generals, who built tennis courts instead of barbed wire fortifications. "Let the past bury its dead," Borden stormed at Lloyd George, "but for God's sake let us get down to earnest endeavour." Lloyd George listened, and forced his generals to come in and listen while Borden repeated his angry charges. Then they and the other Empire leaders sat down to plan Britain's strategy for the coming years of the war. On the western front, the British and French armies had to be saved in order to allow the United States to build up its enormous strength. In the east, where Russia had been forced into a costly peace with Germany, resistance had to be revived. What Borden recommended, Canada would help to do.

FIGURE 2.2 *World War I Engagements (1914-1917)*

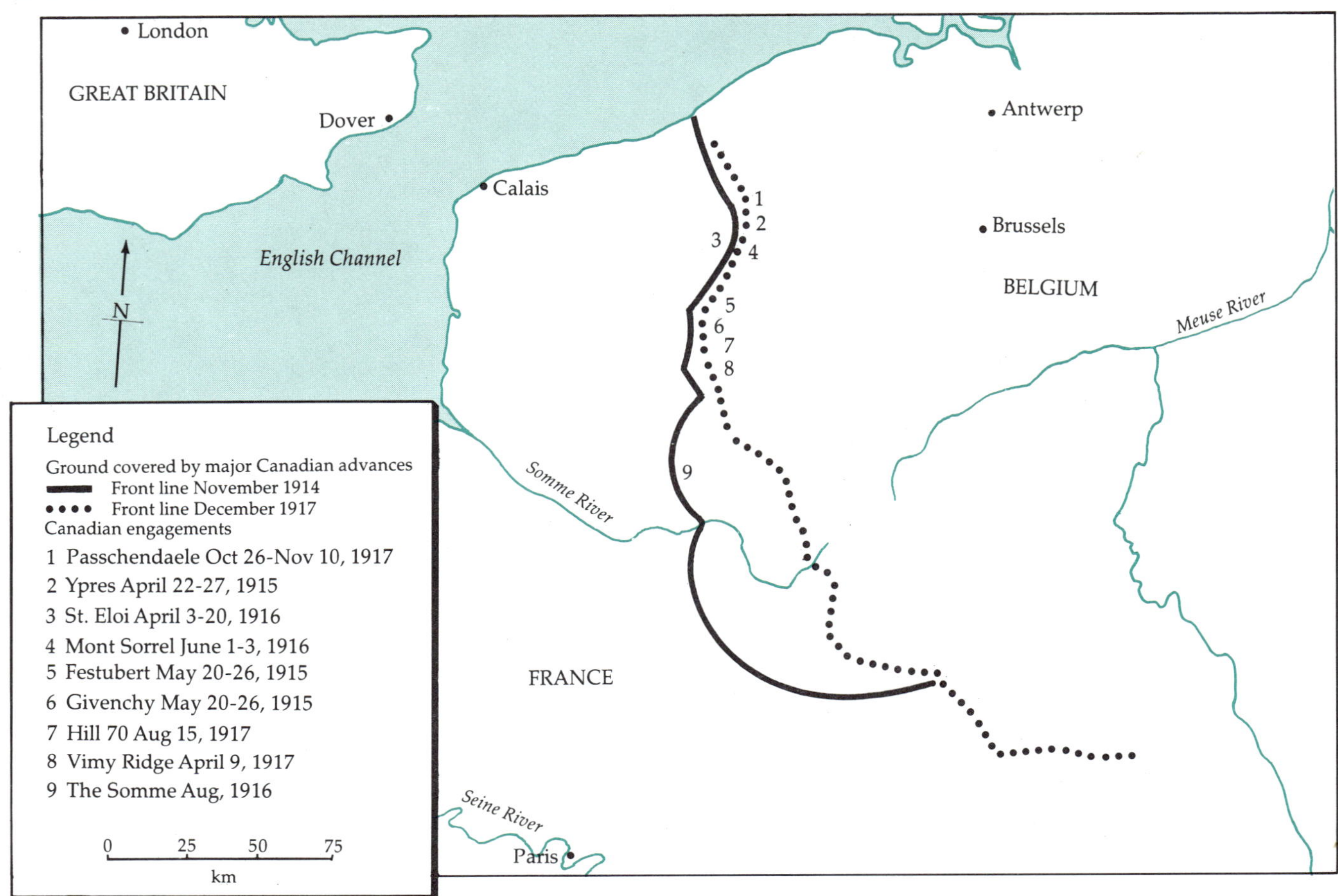

Borden returned to Canada in mid-August. The long conference had shown the dilemma of imperial association; endless talk was needed to achieve consensus. How much easier it was, Borden thought, to deal with the Americans. It was an unsettling idea.

Before leaving London, Borden had learned of the plans for a surprise attack by the Canadian Corps and the Australians. The Canadians had escaped the German attacks from March to June, 1918. They were rested and ready for action. The new offensive was intended to push the Germans back from their recent gains near the key railway town of Amiens. While their wireless sets chattered from the old, abandoned positions, the Canadians secretly moved south. On August 8, the Canadians, together with Australian troops, raced for the German line. With them came masses of tanks and clouds of aircraft. Losses were high, but the bewildered Germans surrendered. In a single day, the Canadians had advanced 13 km.

As German resistance reformed, Currie changed his tactics. He stopped, changed fronts, and this time used artillery to batter a way through the German fortifications on the Drocourt-Quéant line. Then the Corps rested and took in the first drafts of conscripts. Their next task was a seemingly impossible obstacle, the Canal du Nord. Currie managed it by forcing a narrow gap in the German line and pouring his troops through. Only first-class troops and competent officers could have done it; Canada now had both. Elsewhere, British, French, and fresh American divisions assaulted the German lines. By the end of September, the German army was in retreat all along the western front. By October 11, the Canadians were in Cambrai. A month later, exhausted, footsore, and far ahead of their supply wagons, they fought their way into Mons, the Belgian city where the British army had first

FIGURE 2.3 *World War I Engagements (1917-1918)*

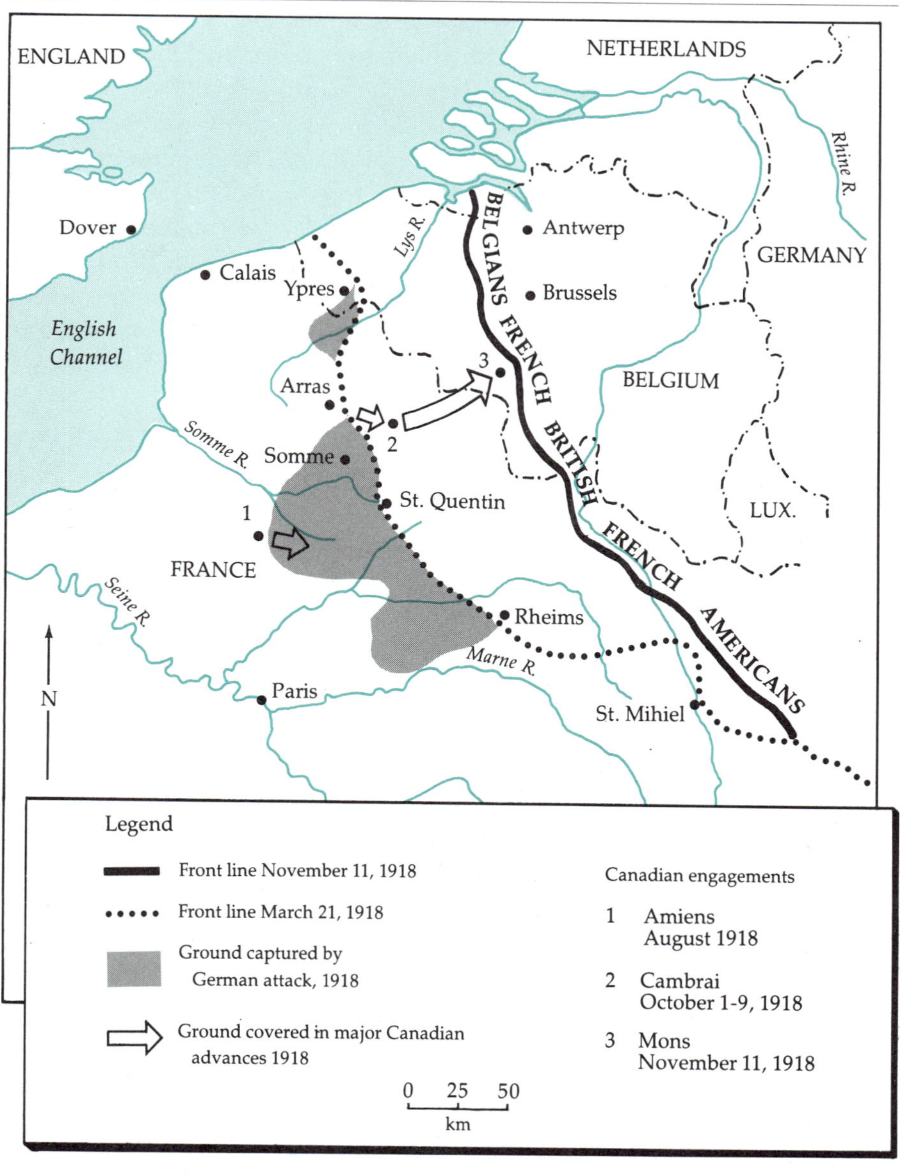

met the Germans in 1914. It was there, on November 11, 1918, that the First World War ended. The battles from Amiens to Mons had cost Canada 46 000 dead and wounded, but they had helped end the war.

Across the Atlantic, Canadians were facing another type of battle on the home front. A world-wide influenza epidemic which had begun in India in 1917 had reached Canada in September, 1918. It struck the young, the old, and the weak. The war had taught Canadians to look to the government in any crisis. But the response from Ottawa and the provinces was slow. Finally, schools, hotels, and even provincial legislatures were turned into hospitals. In Canada, the epidemic claimed between 30 000 and 50 000 lives. In the midst of the agony came a rumour of peace. Canadians surged into the streets on November 9 to ask for news. Early on November 11, the true good news finally arrived. The "war to end all wars" was over.

What would Canada gain from a war which had cost more than 60 000 Canadian lives and quadrupled the national debt? It was a question Borden could ponder as he journeyed to Versailles to share in postwar decisions. American President Woodrow Wilson had expressed idealistic hopes in his Fourteen Points. The document stated his view that lasting peace depended on freedom of the seas and of trade, self-determination for small nations, and a world association of nations with the power to stop aggression. Not everyone shared the American idealism. The French wanted Germany humiliated and its army eliminated. Britain wanted Germany's navy and colonies. Both countries insisted on German payment of huge reparations for the cost of the war.

Woodrow Wilson's Fourteen Points

In a bid to set idealistic postwar aims, U.S. President Woodrow Wilson announced the American peace terms on January 8, 1918. His Fourteen Points included the following:

- *freedom of the seas*
- *an end to secret treaties*
- *self-determination of nations*
- *the establishment of a permanent League of Nations to protect all countries from aggression*

Publicly, Wilson's allies were delighted; privately, they thought he was naively idealistic. Why Fourteen Points, asked French Prime Minister Georges Clemenceau; "the Good Lord only had ten."

November 11, 1918. Toronto residents take to the streets to celebrate the end of World War I.

This photograph shows the leaders of the four major allied countries at the end of World War I. They are, from left to right, Vittorio Orlando of Italy, David Lloyd George of Britain, Georges Clemenceau of France, and Woodrow Wilson of the United States.

Canada, too, wanted a share in reparations, but the real reward Borden sought was world recognition that Canada was a sovereign nation. The British had no objection—or interest. The French and Americans felt otherwise. They suspected that giving Canada and the other dominions national status was a British trick to gain more votes at the peace conference. Perhaps, they suggested, Canada and the other dominions could each have one vote, while sovereign nations such as Belgium and Portugal—and, of course, France and the United States—would have two. Borden answered angrily that Canada had lost more men in the war than Portugal had sent! Finally, the Americans gave way. Seats did not mean votes, President Wilson was reminded.

What seats did mean was status. Borden's insistence on having a separate seat at the peace conference brought Canada the much more important distinction of a seat in the new League of Nations. Once again the Americans objected that the dominions would be British puppets; once again, Wilson gave way. Borden signed both the peace treaty (the Treaty of Versailles) and the League of Nations covenant on behalf of Canada.

Back in Ottawa, the Prime Minister presented both documents to Parliament for approval. Some critics worried that Article X of the League covenant, which pledged every member to defend the boundaries established at Versailles, would cost Canada any freedom it had gained from Britain. Now France, Italy, or even Germany might force Canada into a war. Borden could only reply that an imperfect League was better than none. As a member, Canada would try to change Article X. To his relief, Parliament agreed.

In fact, few Canadians cared about Borden's achievement. The war had exhausted idealism. Even Borden's colleagues felt that he had been enjoying himself in Europe while they wrestled with more important domestic crises. As far as many Canadians were concerned, Canada was in the League because it was too much trouble to get out. Americans, however, felt differently. Upon Wilson's presentation of the

League covenant for approval, the American Senate rejected membership in the League of Nations. Among their objections was Wilson's grudging decision to let the dominions have their own seats. Canada may have reached towards independence, but in American eyes, it remained a British colony.

QUESTIONS

1. How did Prime Minister Borden's views on Canada's role in the Empire change over the course of the war?
2. What did Resolution IX of the Imperial War Cabinet state?
3. **(a)** What strategy did Borden recommend for the last part of the war? **(b)** What events led to his making these recommendations?
4. At the end of the war, what did each of the following nations want: Britain, France, the United States, Canada?
5. Why was it important to Borden that Canada should have its own vote at the Versailles peace conference, and its own seat in the League of Nations?
6. What was the response of (a) other politicians and (b) Canadians in general to Borden's achievements immediately after the war?

Chapter Summary

In 1914, Europe and the British Empire were plunged into a war that lasted over four years. The war brought many changes to Canada. Perhaps the most immediate was that nearly half a million Canadians fought in the war; of them, 60 000 were killed, and thousands more injured.

Canada's ability to raise troops and run war industries successfully made the country more self-confident and resulted in increased independence. At the same time, however, disagreements about the war effort deepened the division between Canadiens *and English Canadians. The Canadian government acquired more powers and became increasingly involved in business, finance, and social services. At the end of the war, Canada got its own voice in the world, in the form of a seat in the League of Nations.*

One group obtained an indirect benefit from the war. Women, who helped sustain the war effort, demanded and won the right to be more involved in running the country.

IN REVIEW

1. Create a timeline for important events of World World I, starting with Canada's declaration of war and ending with Canada's membership in the League of Nations.
2. Henri Bourassa described himself as a Canadian patriot. His opponents described him as disloyal, a traitor, and a rebel.
   - **(a)** Which group of Canadians would have agreed with Bourassa's description of himself? Why?
   - **(b)** Which group of Canadians would have seen Bourassa as disloyal? Why?
3. **(a)** How did the war in Europe change the lives of Canadians?
   - **(b)** Which of these changes do you think was the most significant? Give reasons for your choice.

APPLYING YOUR KNOWLEDGE

1. What does Laurier's use of the phrase "ready, aye, ready" to the expected call to war from Britain reveal about Canada's independence in 1914?
2. During World War I, over 6000 enemy aliens of military age were interned. Do you feel this action was justified? Could it be justified today if Canada were at war?
3. Do wars create special circumstances that demand special powers for governments, even though these powers may restrict individual freedom? Why or why not?
4. Sir Thomas White claimed that it was justifiable to borrow to pay for Canada's war costs, even though future generations would have to pay the money back.
   - **(a)** Do you agree or disagree with White's viewpoint?
   - **(b)** Can you suggest other means of raising the necessary money?
   - **(c)** How might the public of White's time have felt about your suggested solution?

FURTHER INVESTIGATION

1. **(a)** Alliances are agreements for mutual defence and protection. In what way can they also be a danger to peace?
   - **(b)** What two major alliances exist in the world today? Do you think these alliances are more likely to safeguard or endanger peace?
2. Collect a sampling of writings and art from World War I. What can you learn about people's attitudes towards the war from the material you have collected?
3. Compare a map of Europe in 1914 with a map of Europe in 1919. What major changes had taken place? Research the process by which they occurred.

CHAPTER 3

A North American Nation

After four years of war, the world had changed. The boundaries of Europe were redrawn, creating new nations. Revolution in Russia had placed a new communist government in control of the country. The United States' role in the war had proved that country to be a major world power. Britain's Empire, too, was changed: The dominions now wanted complete autonomy, and the remaining colonies would soon begin to seek independence. Canada would have to live in a world in which its traditional protector, Britain, was weaker, while Canada's huge neighbour grew more wealthy and powerful.

For many of those who fought in Europe, the end of the First World War meant the beginning of a new society. Canadian veterans returned home, but both home and the veterans had changed.

In this chapter, you will examine society and events in postwar Canada in light of questions such as these:

- *How did the end of the war affect the Canadian economy and the lives of Canadians?*
- *How did Canada's relations with Britain and the United States change in the postwar era?*
- *What was the Great Depression? How did it affect Canadians?*
- *What new political solutions did Canadians suggest for Canada's problems?*
- *What course did Canada's foreign policy follow in the 1920's and 1930's?*

Growth and Discontent

The First World War was over—but Canada's troubles were not. The years which followed the war brought some of the worst crises in Canadian history. The problems that had simmered during wartime, such as inflation and regional division, boiled over. They combined with new difficulties, labour unrest and railway bankruptcy among them.

With the armistice, the munitions plants were shut down. Suddenly, a quarter of a million workers had to hunt for jobs. They were joined by the 350 000 Canadian veterans who returned to civilian life. Upon their return, the veterans received $250 million in back pay and allowances. The average payment of just under $715 per person was not enough to keep an unemployed man for long, and certainly no compensation for a soldier's meagre wartime pay. In 1919, jobs were, in fact, plentiful. The real problems came later.

During the war, when work was abundant and profits were high, membership in unions had increased from 143 000 in 1915 to 378 000 by 1919. Now the workers faced employers whose profits had dropped and who wanted to restore their prewar authority. The Russian Revolution of 1917 and political unrest in postwar Germany encouraged radical unionists' ideas. At a meeting in Calgary in March, 1919, union members talked of a workers' revolution in Canada like the one in Russia. The leaders pledged to create One Big Union (O.B.U.) for all workers. Another sign of the mood of the time came in May of the same year. A general strike that began in Winnipeg when 30 000 workers walked off the job on May 15 spread across Canada, from Vancouver to Amherst, Nova Scotia. Most of the Winnipeg strikers—half of whom

A streetcar burns as strike sympathizers gather in the streets of Winnipeg. Even police and firemen joined the general strike to protest poor working conditions and employers' refusal to negotiate with unions.

were not even union members—wanted the right to bargain with employers, not a revolution. But the rhetoric of the radical minority alarmed employers and middle class Canadians alike. Even as the strike ended, Parliament made it a criminal offence merely to talk about revolution. The government ordered the police to seize the strike leaders. Strike sympathizers protested in a mass rally. On June 21, 1919, mounted police charged the crowds on Main Street in Winnipeg, in a confrontation which became known as Bloody Saturday.

Employers saw the government's actions as the signal that they could drive out unions wherever possible. From Vancouver dockers to Cape Breton miners, unions fought wage cuts and harsh new rules. Usually they lost. By 1924, union membership in Canada had slipped to 240 000.

The returning veterans were no happier with their treatment than the unions were with theirs. Many of them united in a demand for a $2000 bonus. They and many other Canadians, from women's groups to the opposition Liberals, saw the payment as overdue justice for men who had fought for their country. The government counted the cost—one thousand million dollars—and refused. Most veterans condemned politicans and their own leaders for the defeat. Their divided, shrunken organizations dug in for a long struggle to improve the lot of both disabled veterans and dependent pensioners. Only in 1925 did the Canadian Legion emerge as a voice for returned soldiers.

Farmers in the West, too, were discontented. Since 1917, their wheat had been marketed by a government board which set the price for the crop. The farmers wanted the board to keep wheat prices constant, to protect them in the event of a decrease in the world price. In 1919, the board set the price at $2.15 per bushel ($79 per tonne), just when the world price rose to $3.15 per bushel ($115 per tonne). The next year, the government dissolved the board—just as the bumper crop in Europe made prices tumble as low as $1.11 per bushel ($41 per tonne). Farmers who had borrowed money on the strength of the old price faced bankruptcy. They naturally blamed the government for their plight.

Inflation was another serious problem which plagued postwar Canada. It had reappeared in 1917, after the prosperity of 1915-1916. The cause was an excess of money accompanied by a scarcity of goods. After the war, common sense might have urged the banks to charge low interest rates, in order to encourage business to expand and create jobs. However, the banks saw inflation as the main threat to the economy. They raised interest rates to make money more scarce and thus defeat the foe. As a result, small businesses went bankrupt, and jobs disappeared along with them. By 1921, Canada—indeed, much of the western world—was deep in depression.

The banks also insisted that their huge investment in the two transcontinental railways should be protected. One way to do so, according to the CPR, was to give it both lines to manage. Arthur Meighen, Prime Minister Borden's Minister of the Interior, refused. He

During the 1920's, rail travel in Canada reached its height of luxury and convenience. Why do railroads no longer provide the quality of service that they once provided?

was too good a westerner to give the CPR back its monopoly, against the wishes of western farmers. Meighen's solution was the Canadian National Railway (CNR). It incorporated the two bankrupt lines (the Canadian Northern and Grand Trunk Railways) as well as the government-run Intercolonial line, which served the Maritimes. The CNR started existence with an enormous load of debt from two of its main components.

One result of the creation of the CNR was a disaster for the Maritimes. For years, the government-owned Intercolonial had kept the freight rates from the Maritimes to the rest of Canada low. Because the volume of shipping was so high, the line broke even or turned a profit despite its low rates. The Intercolonial was controlled in the Maritimes, through its head office in Moncton. To reduce its huge debt, the new CNR closed down the Moncton headquarters, transferring control—and jobs—first to Toronto, then to Montréal. Although the Intercolonial had prospered under the old rates, the CNR decided that rates must be raised: by 40 percent in 1920, and later by as much as 110 percent. By 1925, the prices of goods from Nova Scotia and New Brunswick had been boosted so much by the freight increases that they were no longer competitive in the national market. Cape Breton's coal and steel industries headed for ruin amidst bitter, violent strikes and savage wage-cutting. Within five years, 150 000 Maritimers fled the region. The Maritimes, like the West, had good reasons for postwar discontent.

The year 1921 brought not only depression, but also a general election. Borden, the creator of the Union, would not run for Prime Minister again. He had quit as party leader in 1920, after failing to persuade Québec Premier Sir Lomer Gouin to take over the Unionist party. The wartime issues which had brought about the Union government were gone. Some Unionists returned to the Liberal Party; most renamed themselves Conservatives, and chose the skilful Arthur Meighen as their leader. Since the aged Laurier had died in 1919, the

Arthur Meighen, Minister of the Interior under Robert Borden, and later Prime Minister of Canada. Meighen was a brilliant debater who took on the hardest tasks, from defending conscription in 1917 to justifying high tariffs to pro-free trade farmers.

Liberals, too, needed a new leader. In August, delegates gathered in Ottawa for the first leadership convention in Canadian history. The victor was William Lyon Mackenzie King, the former Minister of Labour and consultant to the Rockefellers. King was picked because his knowledge of labour issues made him seem modern, while his loyalty to Laurier in 1917 won him backing in Québec.

Both the government and the opposition faced discontent across the land. Many rural anglophone voters wanted neither man, neither party. In the years after the war, farmers had run as candidates in several federal by-elections, and won. By 1921, the provincial governments of Manitoba, Alberta, and Ontario were dominated by members of the United Farmers. "Honest John" Oliver, the premier of British Columbia, was a Liberal—but also a farmer. At the federal level, the farmers were known as the Progressives. However, they did not see themselves as a party in the traditional sense, but rather as a group of like-minded individuals.

For the first time, therefore, Canadians had three choices in the 1921 general election. The Progressives campaigned on issues important to the rural populace: free trade, lower taxes, cheaper freight rates, and greater power of the voters over Parliament through increased use of referendums. The Liberals also campaigned on the free trade issue in British Columbia, the Prairies, and Ontario. In Québec, King's strength lay in the fact that Québec Liberals knew he had supported Laurier in the 1917 election. The Conservatives, on the other hand, wished to retain the tariffs between Canada and its trading partners. Their opposition to free trade and their association with the 1921 depression cost them the election. On December 7, after the longest election campaign in Canadian history, the Liberals swept Québec and the Maritimes with 116 seats. The Conservatives won only 50. Their strongest bastion of support was Toronto. The real surprise, however, came from the Progressive coalition, who won 65 rural seats in the West. Winnipeg and Calgary each elected one Labour M.P.

King's skills at conciliation were urgently needed. As leader of Canada's first minority government, he had to unite Québec and the West. It would not be easy. On tariffs, railways, and much else, Québec Liberals had more in common with the Conservatives than with the Progressives. Shrewd negotiator that he was, King found the common denominator. Both Québec and the West opposed militarism and imperialism. King slashed the defence budget and, once again, Canada's tiny navy almost vanished. He also appointed O.D. Skelton, a sworn enemy of imperial schemes, as his Undersecretary of State for External Affairs. Skelton would ensure that Canada would oppose any plans for a united Empire.

In 1922, Britain nearly went to war with Turkey. As Conservative Toronto cheered, Meighen responded with the traditional "Ready, aye, ready". King remained silent. In the following year, he announced that Canada would henceforth sign its own international agreements independently of Britain. The first, in 1923, was the Halibut Treaty with the United States. So it was that Canada joined the ranks of sovereign nations.

Between the general elections of 1921 and 1925, the depression eased. Automobile factories in Ontario and new mines in the north created jobs. For two reasons, King was sure that he would win the 1925 election: Business had picked up, and the members of the Progressive coalition had begun to bicker among themselves. However, he had overlooked some reasons for Liberal unpopularity. First, his government had accomplished very little. Second, King had not kept the promises he made in 1921 to the Maritimes. In the Conservative campaign of 1925, Meighen played on the unhappiness of Maritimers. As a result, King lost all three of the eastern provinces. Nor did British Columbia or Ontario admire King's record. On October 29, 1925, the Conservatives won 116 seats to the Liberals' 99 and the Progressives' 24.

No party had a majority, and King refused to resign as Prime Minister. His disillusioned party failed to oust him. The Progressives, forced to choose between the two traditional parties, reluctantly preferred King. King promptly gave the voters a "prosperity budget" full of tax cuts and giveaways, calculated to increase his popularity throughout the country.

But King's problems were not over. Although prohibition had been abandoned by most provinces by 1924, it continued in the United States. In early 1926 evidence surfaced that a thoroughly corrupt Customs Department was helping to smuggle liquor into the United States, and that some of King's Québec ministers were protecting the offenders. King faced a vote of censure in Parliament that he would surely lose. He managed to obtain a weekend reprieve, and appealed to the Governor General, Lord Byng. King's request was simple—though the previous election had been scant months before, Byng must dissolve Parliament and call a new election. Byng was horrified. King was refusing to face his responsibility as the head of a corrupt government. Moreover, he was depriving Meighen, leader of the largest party, of the chance to form a government. Faced with Byng's resistance, King resigned.

Meighen took office with deep misgivings, since he himself would have preferred a new election. At once, the Liberals alleged that Meighen (and Byng) had twisted the Constitution. Today, constitutional experts might well argue that Byng was right in law. Politically, however, he was unwise. King managed to convince the Progressives, with their strong faith in the power of the voters, that the Governor General, as an appointed official, should have taken the advice of his Prime Minister. The Progressives, who had originally supported Meighen in the affair, changed their minds. Now Byng had to give Meighen the election which he had refused to give King.

To Meighen's mind, there was no abuse of the Constitution, unless it

Lord Byng, Governor General of Canada from 1921 to 1926. A popular general during the war, Byng had won the hearts of Canadian soldiers overseas by his lack of formality and his concern for saving lives.

The King-Byng Confrontation

Was Prime Minister King right in claiming that the confrontation between him and the Governor General, Viscount Byng, was a major constitutional issue? Many lawyers and historians since that time say "no". Their opinion is that Viscount Byng, an upright and honest man, was outsmarted by King, who knew how to appeal to nationalist feelings and to prosperity. Others insist that King established a precedent. It would be a brave Governor General who would refuse a dissolution.

was King's desperate bid to dissolve Parliament. As for Canadians, few of them paid attention to the constitutional details. They were more concerned about getting rich; by 1926, the economy was booming once again. In Québec, voters saw that most of the accused in the smuggling scandal were francophones. Surely that proved that the Conservatives hated *Canadiens*. They also recalled Meighen's backing of conscription and his support of British imperialism. On September 14, 1926, King got the majority he had wanted. The Progressives lost more seats, and Meighen even lost his own constituency.

QUESTIONS

1. Account for the growing discontent of the following groups during the 1920's: veterans, labour, and farmers.

2. What promoted the growth of trade unions during and after World War I?

3. (a) Why were interest rates kept high after the war?
(b) How did the high interest rates affect Canada's economy?

4. What were the major causes of bankruptcy among farmers during the early 1920's?

5. What effect did large freight increases have on the Maritimes in the early 1920's?

6. Why were the Progressives so successful in the 1921 federal election?

7. (a) What constitutional issue was at stake in the King-Byng confrontation?
(b) In your opinion, who was right—King or Byng?

Americanization and Canadianism

The outcome of the 1926 election was due to prosperity. In the industrial cities of Ontario and Québec, workers laboured overtime to turn out cars, clothing, radios, gramophones, and a host of new consumer products. Railways reached their "golden age" as luxury trains crossed the country. In cities and resorts, Canadians built the grandest hotels Canada had ever seen. Immigration flowed as steadily as in the Laurier boom, filling the last of the prairie homesteads. Workers poured into the frontier regions of Canada, felling British Columbia's forests, mining the riches of the Canadian Shield, or laying track for the new Hudson Bay Railway.

The new prosperity came from a new source: the United States. The east-west trade strategy of Sir John A. Macdonald and Sir Wilfrid Laurier fell victim to the war. Postwar Britain, which had long been

Canada's main export market, could not afford to invest in Canada or to buy Canadian products. The United States could do both; it had made money from the war. Since the mid-1880's, Canada had bought more from the United States than from Britain. Now, for the first time, Canada also sold more to the Americans than to the British. From the mines of Anyox and Flin Flon to the paper mills of Powell River and Shawinigan, American companies found what they needed in Canada. And if Canada kept its tariff walls against the United States but lowered them to the members of the former Empire, American companies would simply sell to the imperial market from branch plants inside Canada. Of course, the branch plants also produced goods for the Canadian market and so avoided the tariffs.

The north-south trade axis was strengthened by technology. The developing provincial highway systems were designed to attract American tourists and their cars. To lure Americans, British Columbia changed its driving rules; instead of being driven on the left, as in Britain, cars would be driven on the right, as in the United States. Improved aircraft and telephone service also made links easier between Canada and the United States.

Few Canadians objected to the Americanization of their economy. One reason was that it seemed so painless. British investors had usually loaned money to Canadian businesses; it had made Canadians nervous to think that the money would have to be repaid. American investors didn't lend money; rather, they created branch companies within

A family outing in the mid-1920's. This period of relative affluence saw the work week reduced from 50–60 hours to 44–50 hours. Some of the new leisure time could be spent at the beach, if there was one nearby. The concept of paid holidays for most working people did not yet exist, so vacations had to be taken close to home.

Canada and took their own risks. If they sent home their profits, they also created jobs and development in the process.

Economic prosperity also affected political and social life in Canada. The federal government had less and less to do, since nearly every change during the 1920's added to provincial power. As cars and trucks started to replace trains, the provinces found themselves becoming the key actors in Canadian transportation. Canadians wanted more education; most provinces made secondary education both free and compulsory. Women voters demanded pensions for widows, low-income mothers, and the disabled. Ironically, some provinces ended prohibition and took over liquor sales to finance their new welfare programs. King's government introduced old-age pensions for those over 70 who could demonstrate need, and gave federal grants to those provinces that wished to join the scheme.

In case after case, appeals to the Judicial Committee of the Privy Council in Britain (which was then Canada's highest court) strengthened provincial powers. In addition, since so much of the new wealth was based on natural resources, the prairie provinces insisted that control of resources be transferred to them. As the 1930 general election approached, King agreed. Now all nine provinces could compete independently for American investors.

But prosperity was not shared equally. British Columbia, Ontario, and Québec were the big winners, though little of the wealth trickled down to poorer people. In 1929, after five years of good times, a federal labour department study concluded that $1430 would keep a family at a "minimum standard of health and decency" without holidays, travel, or such new gadgets as radios. The average Canadian wage in that year was $1200. Farmers on the Prairies profited from the advice of an American lawyer, Aaron Sapiro, during the late 1920's. Sapiro persuaded them to pool the annual wheat harvest and use their collective power to bargain with the arrogant brokers of the Winnipeg Grain Exchange. The farmers took Sapiro's advice. By 1928, their new wheat pools had raised prices above $2 per bushel ($73 per tonne). It was the Maritimes that reaped the least benefit from American-based prosperity.

Radio in Canada

A cultural development as important as the invention of writing was the creation of a publicly-owned broadcasting system. In 1929, a Royal Commission made recommendations for a Canadian federal broadcasting system closely modelled on the British Broadcasting Corporation. The commission had been formed in response to disputes over the few available frequencies and worry about the power of American radio stations to mould Canadians' minds. Powerful lobbying helped persuade the Conservative government of R.B. Bennett to act in 1932. However, his creation, the Canadian Radio Broadcasting Commission (CRBC), had too little money to do more than establish five stations and to show what a good public system might do. Only in 1936 was the Canadian Broadcasting Corporation (CBC) created, with a mandate not only to provide a national radio system but also to regulate private broadcasting.

American influence on the Canadian economy and on Canadian culture went hand in hand. There was nothing new about American books and magazines coming into Canada or about Canadians going south for conventions, vacations, and settling. In fact, more people had emigrated to the United States from Canada than from any other country. Canadians joined American-based service clubs such as Rotary, Kiwanis, and Lions, and belonged to American-based unions. Canadian employers borrowed American ideas for dealing with those same unions—whether crushing them or "killing them with kindness" through company profit-sharing and pension plans.

What was new about the influence of American culture was the forms it took. New technology brought new entertainment media,

Technicians with some early radio equipment. The first radio broadcast in Canada took place in 1922. What was the impact of radio on Canadian culture?

from comic strips to moving pictures. In many cases, that entertainment came from the United States. Newspapers found that Saturday circulation doubled when a comics supplement (purchased from an American newspaper syndicate) was added. An American station in Pittsburgh made the first radio broadcast in 1922. A Canadian station, CFCF, in Montréal followed a month later, but by 1930, the Americans had two national networks to lure Canadians. When they weren't listening to the radio, Canadians went to the movies. By 1929, a nation of ten million was buying two million movie tickets a week. Major Hollywood figures such as Louis B. Mayer, Jack Warner, and Mary Pickford might be Canadian-born, but there was nothing Canadian about Hollywood. Broadcast over radio, American professional baseball became a passion across Canada. And by 1928, only two Canadian teams remained in the National Hockey League (though almost all the players were Canadians). They fought four American teams for the Stanley Cup, which had been donated by the Governor General, Lord Stanley, as a symbol of Canadian hockey excellence!

Yet the cultural Americanization of Canada did meet some resistance. The postwar period saw the birth of a powerful, if self-conscious, Canadianism. It could take ugly forms. One was a new immigration law which made it easier to deport "undesirables" who "abused" Canada by uttering radical opinions. Canadianism could also be creative and inspiring. The work of the Group of Seven, who painted stark northern landscapes in their own style, bore witness to the development of a distinctive Canadian culture. So did the art of Emily Carr, who painted the swooping forests and silent Native villages of British Columbia. The rave reviews won by this new style at a major British art exhibition in 1924 advanced the cause of Canadianism. As well, Canadianism could inspire and sustain such talents as poets E.J. Pratt, Frank Scott, and A.J.M. Smith, and novelist Morley Callaghan.

But Canadianism in the 1920's made no effort to bridge what novelist Hugh McLennan would later call "the two solitudes". French and English were deaf to one another. Few anglophone Canadians knew of Jean-Aubert Loranger, Robert Choquette, or Philippe Panneton. Abbé Lionel Groulx, who taught history to generations of Québec's leaders, expressed Henri Bourassa's nationalism even more aggressively. Only in Québec, he insisted, could a French and Roman Catholic nation be saved. Foreign influences must be banned. A tragic fire in a Montréal movie theatre which killed 78 children aided Groulx's fight to bar

Emily Carr's powerful paintings of British Columbia landscapes are examples of the unique painting style that was part of the 1920's new Canadianism.

children from Québec cinemas and hence from Americanizing influences. He was less successful in his campaign to censor books, magazines, and other sources of "cultural corruption".

Groulx spoke for and to a minority. So did the Canadian nationalists who followed the Group of Seven, encouraged Emily Carr, and kept the new magazine, the *Canadian Forum*, alive. In fact, most Canadians hardly noticed these self-conscious efforts to give their country its own culture. Movies, radio, sports, magazines—all were a form of escape. Yet though they indulged in escapism, Canadians did not wish to "escape" to the United States. Poll-takers found that most Canadians had no admiration for the United States, a country they saw through its scandal sheets, gangster films, and sensational news broadcasts. "Canadians," an advertising agency warned American clients, "are apt to be critical of United States political forms, judicial procedure and folkways." "It would seem," an American author concluded, "that Canadians are determined to be both a North American and a British nation, but above all a nation with a distinctive Canadian personality."

QUESTIONS

1. Give two reasons why the United States replaced Britain as Canada's major trading partner in the 1920's.

2. Why did American companies start branch plants in Canada?

3. What situation encouraged the formation of the cooperative wheat pools on the Prairies?

4. Which part of Canada benefitted least from the prosperity of 1920's?

5. Give three pieces of evidence which support the claim that Canada was becoming an "American nation" during the 1920's.

6. **(a)** Give three examples of "Canadianism" that developed in the 1920's to buffer Americanization.
(b) Why did Canadianism do little to unite French and English Canadians?

The Great Depression

Canada's prosperity in the 1920's had two great flaws. First, it was narrowly based; most Canadians could not afford the cars, refrigerators, and radios that poured from the factories. By itself, the Canadian market could not absorb the products Canadians made. This fact led to the second problem. Since 80 percent of what Canada's fields, forests, waters, and mines produced was exported, Canada was heavily dependent upon the world economy. Europe was groaning under a load of postwar debt. America wanted its loans repaid by Britain and France,

Panic on Wall Street on "Black Tuesday". The stock market crash was soon followed by worldwide depression. How did World War I contribute to the Great Depression?

but they could not afford to do so until Germany had paid them the reparations imposed at Versailles. Germany could not afford to do so... and around it went. The Great Depression was born of greed, impatience, and the poverty of most of the world.

In Canada, the first sign that all was not well with the economy came when the wheat pools tried to sell the 1928 crop. The pools felt safe in guaranteeing their members $1.28 per bushel ($48 per tonne); after all, two years earlier wheat had sold at $2 per bushel ($73 per tonne). But the huge harvest now faced competition from other countries, including parts of Europe, Argentina, and Australia. It eventually sold for $1.09 per bushel (under $40 per tonne). A drought killed much of the 1929 crop, but prices still fell. The prairie provinces, whose economies had been on the upswing in the middle of the decade, had to tighten their belts.

The rest of Canada soon followed suit. Europe had no money to buy Canadian goods. Trying to protect its own industries, the United States raised its tariffs to the highest level ever. Canadian factories began to close as their products went unsold, and unemployment rose sharply. Many shareholders in public companies decided to sell while they could still get some money for their stock. As more and more people tried to sell, prices fell swiftly. Optimists ignored the signs and watched their fortunes collapse when stock markets in the United States and Canada crashed in October, 1929.

Economic experts and politicians offered reassurance. Depressions were nothing new; there had been one in 1921, 1913, and so on. The economy, they insisted, was "fundamentally sound". Recovery was just around the corner; economies, like workers, needed a rest now and again. In Ottawa, Prime Minister King was convinced that R.B. Bennett, the new Conservative leader, and the Conservative provincial premiers were blaming the Depression on his government in an attempt to win voters. King announced that Ottawa might give financial aid to hard-hit western farmers, but not even "a five-cent piece" to provinces led by Conservatives. Unemployment, he declared, was a provincial problem.

King's comments were constitutionally correct, but they helped cost the Liberals the 1930 election. The war had shown Canadians that governments could make a difference. Bennett, unlike King, promised to end unemployment "or perish in the attempt". He would use tariffs to "blast a way into the markets of the world". Even Québec listened to Conservative promises. On July 28, 1930, Bennett won 137 seats, 16 of them from rural Québec. The Liberals got 91, the Progressives slipped even farther to 12, and J.S. Woodsworth's Labour Party won 3.

If one man's energy could have beaten the Depression, it would have faded in a year. Bennett called Parliament and forced through the largest tariff increases since 1879. He also sent $20 million to the provinces for make-work schemes intended to end unemployment. He declared that he would never agree to a system such as unemployment insurance, under which the unemployed got money for idleness. Then he was off to England to promote an Empire-based trade system. On his return, he met with American President Herbert Hoover to discuss the proposed St. Lawrence Deep Water Way. The project would create both jobs and a new route to the West. But U.S. senators from the Atlantic seaboard states vetoed it, fearing that the project would take away jobs and money from their region. Bennett promptly offered more money to create jobs. He also aided the wheat pools, now bankrupt. In 1934 he created the Bank of Canada. Although privately owned, it would act as a check on the chartered banks by carrying out government financial policies affecting banks and banking. This was done to encourage investors and depositors, who were nervous in the financial crisis. The money brought by investment and bank deposits would, Bennett planned, create still more jobs.

"Bennett of the booming voice", telling a 1930 election audience how he would "blast a way into the markets of the world". Bennett's energy and self-confidence were a temporary tonic for a nation that still believed in millionaires.

But none of Bennett's actions seemed to lighten the Depression. Instead, it became worse. By 1933, hundreds of thousands of farms and businesses were ruined. From coast to coast, mines, mills, and factories slashed their payrolls, cut wages, or closed down. A quarter of all Canadians were out of work. A few businesses fired married women because men needed the work; far more fired men and hired women and children because they would work for lower wages. The impact of the Depression was felt in every aspect of Canadian life. In 1928, farmers had bought 17 000 tractors; in 1932, 892 were purchased. Construction all but ceased; in Vancouver, the rusted steel skeleton of the "new" Vancouver Hotel became a graphic reminder of bad times.

As in any depression, not everyone suffered. Those who were fortunate enough to have jobs could find comfort in the fact that, until 1933, prices fell faster than wages. In 1931, one-fifth of Canadians earned $1500 a year, or more. An average house cost $6000, while a good car cost $600 and the week's groceries to fill it cost $5. Another effect of the Depression was to increase standards of education; more young people finished high school and university, because the alternatives were so bad. And anyone with $10 for a radio, 25 cents for a movie ticket, or a nickel for a newspaper could find escape. The 1930's were a decade of lush Hollywood musicals, radio comedy, and frantic publicity stunts.

But for many there was no escape. The true horror of the Depression was felt by people who had never imagined that they would lose their jobs, savings, and self-respect. "The difference between a derelict and a man is a job," said the hero of one of the few realistic Hollywood films of the decade. As the economy tightened, society seemed to follow suit. Religious leaders packed revival meetings with claims that the Great Depression was divine punishment for loose living and luxury. Censorship grew stricter. Judges gave harsher sentences. In the struggle for jobs, newcomers often suffered discrimination. Many immigrants who could not get work or who held radical views were deported.

A quarter of Canada's ten million people could not escape the ultimate humiliation—relief. Friends, savings, and sacrifice could often keep a family off relief for a year or so, but the Depression did not end. Finally, hunger became stronger than pride. Municipal officials and public opinion made relief as humiliating as possible. Inspectors snooped to see that recipients no longer had forbidden items such as radios, unnecessary furniture, pets, or family treasures. Winnipeg forbade any lights except a single naked bulb. "Reliefers" were given food vouchers instead of cash, to "save them from temptation". Anyone found drinking or breaking any of the dozens of petty regulations could be deprived of benefits and left to starve. Single men could make no claim for relief at all and were ordered to "get moving", to find jobs somewhere.

CLOSE-UP

The Single Unemployed

For Canada, railways had become the symbol of growth and prosperity. In the 1930's, they became instead the symbol of despair. There were few sadder spectacles of the Great Depression than the young, single unemployed who rode the freight trains back and forth across Canada in a hopeless search for work.

Canada had always had an army of transient workers, heading in the appropriate season for the harvests of the Prairies, the bush camps of British Columbia, or the mines and factories of Ontario. The Depression added reinforcements to this transient army. It

This young man was luckier than some. At least he had a cot to himself for the night.

was a terrible time to be a young man. Single men had no right to relief. Many of those who were old enough to work "hit the road"— or the rails. Once they were on the move, they were nobody's problem. The municipalities looked after their own, but not strangers. Transients were traditionally considered "bums", "hobos", "derelicts". Now these labels were applied to many of the young men of a generation.

Life on the open road might have sounded romantic at first, but the young men soon found it wasn't. Even though train crews often looked the other way when someone jumped a freight, railway police had a reputation for beating non-paying passengers. "Riding the rods" under a freight car could be fatal if a traveller fell asleep; clinging to the roof of a swaying car was not much safer. Freight riders starved on the long sections without stops in northern Ontario, froze in cold weather, and choked on soot and smoke in the tunnels under the Rockies. Most of the travellers were headed for British Columbia. When they arrived, they found no jobs, just hobo jungles.

The fate of the single unemployed worried their families and also the government, which feared that revolution could result.

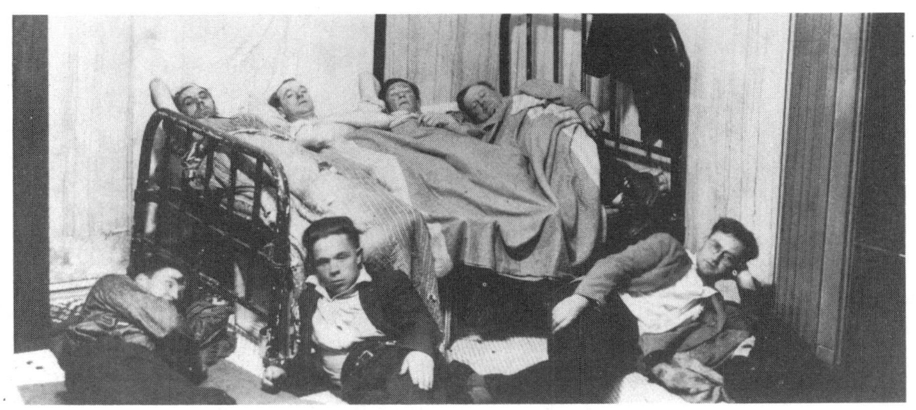

Four men share a bed in a men's shelter, while three others sleep on the floor. Why was the Depression particularly hard on single men?

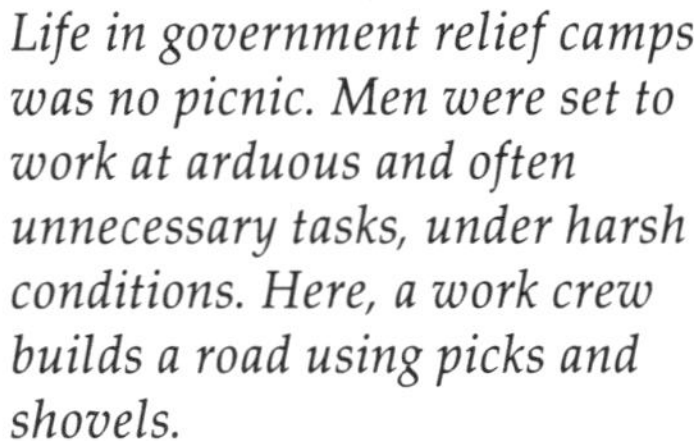

Life in government relief camps was no picnic. Men were set to work at arduous and often unnecessary tasks, under harsh conditions. Here, a work crew builds a road using picks and shovels.

The provinces could not cope, so Ottawa must. Major-General A.G.L. McNaughton, head of the Canadian army, was deeply concerned. He calculated that a man could be fed, housed, and put to work with simple tools at a cost of a dollar a day—including 20 cents' pay. Bennett was delighted with the solution. In 1932, 2000 men were at work in McNaughton's "relief camps"; by 1935, more than 150 000 men had laboured in over 200 relief projects.

At first, everyone, even the unions, welcomed the scheme. But the mood soon changed. The Liberals branded Bennett a dictator; army-run relief camps suited the image. Harold Winch, a British Columbia socialist M.L.A., termed them "slave camps" or "slave compounds". Far from keeping the men from revolution, the camps were an easy target for radical agitators. The men themselves felt bored and isolated. They resented both their meagre pay and doing work that machinery could have done better. Worst of all, as the months turned into years, they felt themselves being cheated of all the possibilities of life. Winch expressed their situation eloquently: "Here are interned the unwanted, not needed, single youth. . . . Able to work; wanting to work; denied the opportunity; wanting to become useful, self-respecting citizens of the community, and destined to wander aimlessly, homeless and hungry, throughout the length and breadth of this country of Canada, wealthiest in natural resources of the entire world."

In April, 1935, communist organizers persuaded half the 7000 workers in British Columbia's camps to gather in Vancouver in a strike for "work and wages". Having had no success in Vancouver, in June the workers decided to appeal to the federal government. The B.C. strikers would lead unemployed people from across Canada to Ottawa to meet the Prime Minister. The 1200 young men who headed east on CPR freight trains were met at many of the stops by local supporters who brought them food.

The government was less enthusiastic. Thousands more unemployed waited at Winnipeg and eastern cities; the trek could be the start of a revolution. Bennett decided that the trekkers must be stopped at Regina, where the RCMP had hundreds of men at its training centre. The leaders would be allowed to continue east to meet with him. At the meeting, Bennett exploded, alleging that the last thing the strikers wanted was to work. The strike leaders answered the insults with insults. Meanwhile, in Regina, the trekkers waited. The police threatened anyone who offered them help. On Dominion Day, most of the strikers went to a baseball game to relieve their boredom. Others attended a rally of sympathetic citizens in Regina's Market Square. Suddenly, violence erupted. By midnight, a policeman was dead, 80 people were injured, and downtown Regina was a shambles.

Bennett later insisted that he had beaten back a communist revolution, but few believed him. The Dominion Day riot helped bring about the Bennett government's downfall in September, 1935. By mid-1936, the Liberals closed the relief camps. This was no solution to the plight of the young unemployed. The Liberals came up with a new idea: subsidizing farmers to hire them as farm labourers. The scheme had the additional advantage that the men would be too scattered for the communists to organize. British Columbia presented a problem; it had too many young reliefers and not enough farms. British Columbia Premier T.D. Pattullo found the answer: setting up forestry camps in the interior. But Ottawa provided too little money for his idea to work, and in April, 1938 Pattullo had to close the camps. Once again, the young

Striking camp workers travelling east during the "March on Ottawa", June, 1935

The RCMP and Vancouver police drive "sit-downers" from the post office in Vancouver. Desperate for remedies when the rest of the country wanted to forget the Depression, the unemployed tried repeatedly to bring their plight to the public's attention.

men flooded into Vancouver to demand work or relief, this time occupying the post office and the art gallery. The premier refused to give in.

On June 19, police hurled tear gas bombs into the post office and drove out the occupants, beating some of them severely. Journalists called the day "Bloody Sunday". At the art gallery, Harold Winch saw to it that there were no beatings. Critics condemned Pattullo, though the federal government was at least as much to blame. Neither Ottawa nor the provinces could solve the plight of the young unemployed. It would take another world war to find them jobs.

QUESTIONS

1. Was the government's decision not to give relief to single men fair? Give reasons to support your point of view.
2. **(a)** What was the purpose of the relief camps?
   (b) Why did Harold Winch call them "slave camps"? Do you agree or disagree with Winch?
3. Why did some Canadians fear the men "marching on" Ottawa in April 1935?
4. Write a newspaper report describing the march on Ottawa. Try to make your article as unbiased as possible, whatever your views on the situation may be.

Municipalities were tight-fisted with the unemployed because they suffered as well. Towns and cities with the worst unemployment and the least revenue faced the heaviest relief burdens. Soon, municipalities and even provinces found themselves going bankrupt from paying relief. Help from the federal government came with many strings attached, and too late for many municipalities. When whole regions were ruined, local relief systems collapsed.

That was what happened on the Prairies. Bennett's tariffs gave some help to manufacturers in eastern Canada. Eastern farmers who could not sell their crops could at least feed themselves and any unemployed relatives who fled the cities. But westerners were out of luck. The 1930's brought natural as well as economic disaster. The drought of 1929 continued. By 1931, the topsoil of southern Alberta and Saskatchewan was so dry that the wind began to carry it away. Great black clouds of fertile prairie soil were swept so far east that ships on the Atlantic were dusted by it. In 1932, a plague of grasshoppers devoured every green living thing. The next year, drought, hail, wheat rust, and frost joined the grasshoppers in wreaking such havoc that it seemed as if Nature had organized its forces to compel humankind to quit the region. Year after year, until 1939, winter and summer brought their miseries.

Many westerners took the hint, heading north to the parkland belt of central Alberta or the Peace River country, or west over the mountains. In 1928, Alberta and Saskatchewan had been second and fourth respectively in *per capita* income; by 1933, they were seventh and ninth. Entire townships were on relief, with families surviving on a bag of flour and a few vegetables. Communities in the East and in British

Packing up their belongings and moving on was the only choice left for many farmers, as the drought on the Canadian prairies turned farms into dust bowls.

Columbia forgot their own problems and loaded railway cars with food and used clothing destined for the Prairies.

The prairie disaster lasted until 1939. Meanwhile, a remarkable partnership of farmers and scientists was learning how to beat back the desert that threatened to engulf the southern Prairies. The developments included new strains of wheat bred specifically for the region, and old methods of soil management borrowed from the descendants of Sifton's Ukrainian settlers. Huge expanses of land on which wheat had been grown were returned to the grazing for which they were more suited. The Bennett government's *Prairie Farm Rehabilitation Act* reversed the disaster through an environmental miracle wrought by human hands.

At the time, such victories seemed scarce. However, statistics would later show that Canada had hit bottom in winter of 1932-1933, was climbing upwards in 1934-1935, slipped in 1937-1938, and was close to 1929 levels in prices, profits, and investment by the end of the decade. As always, some people had profited from the decade of depression. Manufacturers used the benefits of Bennett's high tariffs to pay off their loans and invest in new, labour-saving machinery. The radio business boomed as house-bound people turned to the new form of entertainment. But ordinary Canadians saw little of the recovery. In 1939, 15 percent of them were still hunting for work. The humiliating relief procedures created a body of thousands of people permanently trapped in dependence. They were the casualties of the Great Depression, as much as mentally and physically scarred veterans were the legacy of the "war to end all wars".

QUESTIONS

1. **(a)** How did the raising of tariffs in the United States promote the coming of the Depression to Canada?
(b) How did Canadian manufacturers use "the benefits of Bennett's high (Canadian) tariffs" during the Depression?

2. During the 1920's, most Canadians could not afford to buy the products of Canadian factories. How does the inability of people to buy goods help cause a depression?

3. What steps did Bennett take to end the Depression "or perish in the attempt"? Did they work?

4. Why did the Prairies suffer more than the rest of Canada during the Depression?

5. During the Depression, municipalities and even whole provinces were threatened with bankruptcy because of the need to pay relief to the unemployed. Why did governments not simply raise more money through taxation?

A New Deal?

In 1930, Canadians had turned to the Conservatives because R.B. Bennett claimed to have the "cure" for the Depression. But Bennett failed. By 1932, four provinces were bankrupt, and the federal government might have followed if Bennett had not slashed federal spending and raised taxes. If the Conservatives had no solutions, the Liberals were little better. They called for greater economy and reduced spending. Were Canadians ready for a new approach to the problems of the economy?

One such approach was the economic theory known as "Social Credit". As early as 1922, a Calgary M.P. had spoken of it in Parliament. In 1932, William Aberhart, a Calgary high school principal and radio preacher, turned Social Credit into a political message. In brief, Social Credit theory argued that it was the difference between the price paid to the producer and the price paid by the consumer which created "poverty in the midst of plenty". This difference had to be made up by the government, or people could not afford to buy. It would be paid to the people as a "social credit". Aberhart's audiences, terrified by debt, poverty, and insecurity, believed him when he spoke of the "fifty bigshots" who manipulated the world's economy. The bankers who had sneered at Social Credit in the 1920's, Aberhart claimed, were simply trying to hide the truth. In 1935, Albertans elected Aberhart and his Social Credit Party as their provincial government, in place of the United Farmers of Alberta. There were few followers of Social Credit outside Alberta, however.

"Bible Bill" Aberhart and Social Credit offered hope to desperate Albertans during the Depression. By the end of the 1930's, Aberhart's party had altered or rejected most of the original Social Credit theories.

This cartoonist from the Winnipeg Free Press does not seem to have shared Alberta's faith in Aberhart's Social Credit message. What point is the cartoonist trying to make?

J.S. Woodsworth, first leader of the Co-operative Commonwealth Federation (CCF), had played an active part in the Winnipeg General Strike of 1919. He was also a pacifist in both the First and the Second World Wars.

Another economic and political theory was more widespread in the Depression years—socialism. For years, Canadian socialists had offered Canada a "co-operative commonwealth" to replace the injustice and failure of capitalism. However, socialists themselves did anything but cooperate. They ranged from communists through trade unionists to social service workers, and seldom agreed with each other's views. By the 1930's, socialist ideas had become sufficiently widespread that the time had come for a socialist party in Parliament. A radical remnant of the Progressive Party and local Labour parties formed the nucleus. J.S. Woodsworth, the former Methodist minister, had been a Labour M.P. since 1921. In 1932, he convinced the annual meeting of the quarrelsome western Labour parties and farmer organizations that the Depression called for unity. At this meeting, the Co-operative Commonwealth Federation (CCF), representing Progressives, various Labour parties, and farmers, was born. A year later, the CCF held its first convention and adopted the Regina Manifesto, a lengthy document which set forth its goals.

CLOSE-UP

The Regina Manifesto

The following passage comes from the introduction to the CCF's Regina Manifesto:

> We aim to replace the present capitalist system, with its inherent inhumanity and injustice, by a social order from which the domination and exploitation of one class by another will be eliminated... the present order is marked by glaring inequalities of wealth and opportunity, by chaotic waste and instability; and in an age of plenty it condemns the great mass of people to poverty and insecurity... This social and economic transformation can be brought about by political action, through the election of a government inspired by the ideal of a Co-operative Commonwealth and supported by a majority of the people. We do not believe in change by violence.

The fourteen points of the manifesto called for

1. the establishment of a planned economy
2. control by the people, through the government, of all financial machinery such as banks and currency
3. government ownership of transportation, communications, electric power, and other essential services
4. help for farmers through security of land ownership, crop insurance, removal of tariffs, co-operatives, *etc*.

5. import and export boards to control trade
6. encouragement of producers' and consumers' cooperatives
7. a national labour code to cover such matters as unemployment insurance, old age pensions, accident insurance, *etc*.
8. publicly organized health, hospital, and medical services
9. the amendment of the *British North America Act*, so that the federal government would have the power to deal with crises such as the Depression
10. foreign policy to promote international cooperation and peace
11. changes in the tax laws
12. freedom of speech and of assembly
13. humanization of the law
14. an emergency program to deal with the problems brought on by the Depression

QUESTIONS

1. Write a paragraph which summarizes the policy outlined in the CCF's Regina Manifesto.
2. With which of the manifesto's points do you agree? Disagree? Explain your reasons.

The CCF started strong. In the 1933 provincial election in British Columbia, it came in second. It was just edged out by T. Duff Pattullo, a Liberal who promised "work and wages", as well as the socialist idea of medicare. In 1934, the Liberals won in southern Saskatchewan, but the CCF got enough seats in the north to become the opposition in that province too. The West and Ontario boasted hundreds of CCF clubs. But the party had many enemies as well. Not even the Depression could sway most Canadians towards socialism. The Communist Party saw the CCF as a deadly rival; if the CCF were successful in bringing about economic change, there would be no need for a revolution—nor, therefore, for the Communist Party. Roman Catholic bishops called the CCF's socialist ideas a threat to the faith. By the end of 1934, the CCF's advance had slowed down.

Many owners of small businesses and other victims of the Depression found the economic theories of Harry Stevens more acceptable than those of either Social Credit or the CCF. Stevens, a British Columbia Conservative whom Bennett chose as Minister of Trade and Commerce, was himself a small businessman. He knew that large firms were surviving the Depression by squeezing smaller suppliers and

President Roosevelt's New Deal

The New Deal included many programs to put Americans to work building dams, renewing forests, and erecting public works. New Deal policies raised farmers' incomes, encouraged workers to form unions, and gave many people hope. Some saw it as the hope of America; others hated its reforms. Historians still argue about whether the New Deal actually helped end the Depression in the United States.

retailers. Big companies used their buying power to get lower prices from manufacturers. Small businesses could not get the same low prices and so could not sell for as little as the bigger firms unless they cut wages or lengthened work hours.

Stevens set up a parliamentary committee, then a Royal Commission, to study the situation. Both revealed how badly such famous companies as Eaton's and Simpsons treated employees and suppliers alike. Canadians, though used to the ravages of the Depression, were shocked to hear of the sweat-shop conditions in which women and children worked long hours for meagre wages. Bennett, many of whose other ministers had close connections to big business, forced Stevens to resign. But many Canadians saw Stevens as a hero. In July, 1935, he left the Conservatives and formed the Reconstruction Party, designed to help small businesses and workers.

Still another new approach to the economic woes of the 1930's came from across the border. In 1932, Democratic presidential candidate Franklin Delano Roosevelt swept to power in the White House. As a candidate, he had been anything but a radical. Once in power, however, the new President introduced the policies which he called his "New Deal". The New Deal seemed to accomplish what Bennett's tariffs and other policies could not. Thanks to radio, Canadians were exposed to Roosevelt's ideas when they tuned in to his "fireside chats" with the American people. For the first time, they envied the Americans' political leadership.

Bennett, too, was impressed. With boundless enthusiasm, he had set out to beat the Depression, but failed. The Liberals might portray him as a tyrant, but he was not. The thousands of letters from desperate Canadians which poured into his office affected him deeply. He was in torment when he heard shantytowns called "Bennettburghs", or the horse-drawn cars of those who could not buy fuel called "Bennett

A "Bennett buggy". Horses were cheaper to fuel than cars during the lean years of the early thirties. Many farmers removed the engines of their vehicles, hitched a couple of horses to the bumper, and used horsepower. The man in the driver's seat in the photograph is William Lyon Mackenzie King. Why would Mackenzie King want to be seen in a photograph such as this?

buggies". Bennett had already been an innovator. Now he suggested new reforms, borrowing the "New Deal" slogan to catch attention. On January 3, 1935, Bennett made his intentions known on coast-to-coast radio. "There can be no permanent recovery without reform," he declared, "and, to my mind, reform means government intervention, it means government control and regulation, it means the end of *laissez faire*." That spring, as he had promised, Bennett introduced legislation for unemployment insurance, a minimum wage, maximum hours of work, marketing boards to raise farm prices, and a trade commission to stop the price-fixing discovered by Harry Stevens.

Then Bennett fell ill. Once recovered, he went to England for the silver jubilee of King George V. By the time he returned, Canadians had become convinced that his proposals would never take effect. Critics pointed out that most of the suggested laws were beyond Ottawa's powers. Bennett's new reform image was finally shattered by the 1935 Dominion Day riot in Regina.

CLOSE-UP

Letters to R.B. Bennett

Many Canadians wrote letters to the Prime Minister, R.B. Bennett, during the Depression years. Most described their circumstances or gave their views of the Depression. Knowing that Bennett was a very rich man, some asked for assistance. Bennett saw to it that his secretary answered the letters—and the appeals. Desperate writers often found a $5 bill inserted in Bennett's reply.

> Dear Sir:
>
> I am writing you as a last resource to see if I cannot, through your aid, obtain a position and at last, after a period of more than two years, support myself...The fact is: this day I am faced with starvation and I see no possibility of counteracting it or even averting it temporarily.
>
> I have applied for every position that I heard about but there were always so many girls who applied that it was impossible to get work...First I ate three very light meals a day; then two and then one. During the past two weeks I have eaten only toast and drunk a cup of tea every other day.
>
> Day after day I pass a delicatessen and the food in the window looks oh, so good! So tempting and I'm so hungry!...The stamp which carries this letter to you will represent the last three cents I have in the world, yet before I will stoop to dishonour my family, my character or my God, I will drown myself in the Lake.
>
> Hamilton, Ontario

Dear Mr. Bennett:

I suppose I am silly to write this letter but I haven't anyone else to write to. . . we are just one of many on relief and trying to keep our place without being starved out. . . trying to get a start without any money and 5 children all small. . . I am sure we can make a go of this place. . . if we could just manage until next fall. Just had 70 acres in last year and the dry spell just caught it right along with the grasshoppers.

Please help me by sending me some money and will send you my engagement ring and wedding ring as security. . . My two rings cost over $100.00 15 years ago but what good are they when the flour is nearly all done and there isn't much to eat in the house. . .

Burton, Alberta

Dear Sir:

I wish to give my opinion of relief. First it is a shame for a strong man to ask for relief in this country. . . The best thing that can happen to a young man is to toss him overboard and compel him to sink or swim, in all my acquaintance I have never known one to drown who was worth saving. . . It takes hardship to make real men and women so cut out relief. . . There are some people in this country who are in hard circumstances, but I can safely say there is no one having the hardship that we pioneers had 28 or 30 years ago.

Blaine Lake, Saskatchewan

QUESTIONS

1. Why did some Canadians write to Bennett to tell him how the Depression affected their lives?

2. Write an answering letter from Bennett for any one of the letters quoted.

Change was in the air in 1935. In that year, Harry Stevens formed his Reconstruction Party. It was also in that year that the Social Credit Party's victory in Alberta wiped out the United Farmers of Alberta. Yet another political change was to come. "King or Chaos" was the Liberal campaign slogan for 1935. With Canadian voters split among the new parties or clinging loyally to the Conservatives, the Liberals needed no more votes than in 1930 to win a lopsided majority: 171 Liberals faced only 39 Conservatives, 17 Social Credit members, and 7 CCF M.P.'s. There were also 11 independents, most of them leaning to the Liberals. Harry Stevens's party won almost as many votes as the CCF, but he was the lone Reconstruction M.P.

A political cartoon showing three federal party leaders in 1935. Were they all really playing the same tune?

The new Liberal government soon showed that it had some ideas of its own. In 1938, it put the Bank of Canada, hitherto privately run, under government control. In contrast, it made the Canadian Radio Broadcasting Commission, which had started out as a government agency, more independent and therefore politically neutral. (Its name was changed at this time to the Canadian Broadcasting Corporation or CBC.) The government also launched Trans-Canada Airlines (now Air Canada).

Prime Minister King inherited an improving economy and Bennett's biggest success—"blasting a way" into U.S. markets. In the months before the election, Bennett had negotiated a partial reciprocity treaty with the United States. King went to Washington to confirm the agreement.

King's years in opposition had not changed his opinions fundamentally. He still wished to see low taxes, a balanced budget, and nothing that would divide Canadians. His answer to unemployment was a National Employment Commission which would cut down on excess government spending. To King's dismay, the Purvis Commission reported that unemployment was a national problem. Ottawa must take responsibility for it, instead of leaving it up to the municipalities and provinces. Moreover, its report urged, the government should pour $20 million into the economy to create jobs. King, with his old-fashioned economic views, found these suggestions unacceptable, though some of his ablest ministers welcomed them. In the end, the Commission got $1 million for its policies.

The Purvis Commission's report highlighted a longstanding Canadian problem: the inequality among the nine provinces. How could rich and poor provinces offer their citizens similar levels of service? Could Canadian unity survive the enormous regional differences in wealth, education, and opportunity? Throughout the 1930's, conflict among provinces and between the provinces and Ottawa undermined efforts to cope with the Depression. The creation in 1937 of a Royal

Commission on Dominion-Provincial Relations to investigate the problem infuriated such relatively wealthy provinces as British Columbia and Ontario. Québec, as always, feared for its autonomy. Alberta, whose Social Credit program had angered Ottawa, opposed federal intervention. Furthermore, the courts had ruled in 1936-37 that the federal government did not have the constitutional power to enact Bennett's "New Deal" reforms. The Royal Commission, headed by Newton Rowell and Joseph Sirois, faced enormous difficulties.

Maurice Duplessis waves to his supporters.

Canadians expressed their feelings about the conflict between the provincial and federal governments through the premiers they elected. T. Duff Pattullo of British Columbia, William Aberhart of Alberta, and Mitchell Hepburn of Ontario were all flamboyant figures who defied Ottawa. Their promises of reform gave people hope; their criticism of Ottawa's failure to end the Depression brought satisfaction. In 1936, Maurice Duplessis joined this group of controversial premiers. Though Duplessis was a Conservative, he managed to persuade radical Québec nationalists to join him in the *Union Nationale* Party. Duplessis won the 1936 Québec election from the Liberals, who had been in power for 39 years, by promising to nationalize the privately owned electricity trust headed by Sir Herbert Holt. Once in power, he forgot about the reforms he had promised. Instead, he used his power to focus *Canadien* frustrations against union leaders, communists, and Jehovah's Witnesses. The most controversial of Duplessis' policies was the so-called Padlock Law, which allowed the police to lock any building allegedly used for "communistic" purposes. The law, however, nowhere defined "communistic".

Like Duplessis, once in power, the other provincial premiers tended to forget their radical promises. Instead, they grew less progressive and more authoritarian. The change was in keeping with the spirit of an age in which judges handed down stiff sentences and hungry, frightened people grew intolerant. Mitch Hepburn, who had started political life

Maurice Duplessis' Padlock Law brought protests from both francophone and anglophone citizens of Québec.

as a farmer candidate, now delighted in associating with the rich and powerful. Pattullo told a reporter, "What I say goes in this province." Aberhart proposed forcing Alberta newspapers to publish Social Credit opinions on their front pages. Ottawa, under pressure from bankers and publishers, used its power of disallowance to quash the proposed law. However, it did not interfere with Duplessis' Padlock Law.

In the United States, the "New Deal" had not really cured the Depression. Nor had any of the other new political avenues which Canadians explored during the 1930's. There were ideas that might have helped Canada, but lack of agreement among the provinces and between the provinces and Ottawa seemed to make real change impossible. Meanwhile, Canadians waited and wondered whether the Depression would ever end.

QUESTIONS

1. Why were the policies of William Aberhart and his Social Credit Party popular in the 1930's?

2. **(a)** How was J.S. Woodsworth able to unify various socialist groups?
(b) What name was given to the resulting new party?

3. **(a)** What was U.S. President Roosevelt's New Deal?
(b) How did it influence Bennett's approach to ending the Depression in Canada?

4. Why were the leaders of many provinces "infuriated" by the appointment of the Royal Commission on Dominion-Provincial Relations?

5. Why does the text describe Maurice Duplessis as a controversial premier?

6. Did any of the new political solutions of the 1930's cure the Depression? Explain.

Isolationism or Involvement?

After peace had been made in 1919, Canadians tried to forget about war, diplomacy, and the rest of the world. The rewards of the war had been few: a separate signature on the Treaty of Versailles, and a seat in the quarrelsome League of Nations. Its legacy was bitterness and division among Canadians. In the 1920's, the conciliatory policies of Prime Minister King had managed to bring about some agreement between French and English. Still, King and many others feared that another war would divide Canada even more than World War I had.

King saw a way to avoid the possibility that Britain might involve

Canada in another war. Canada must have more autonomy. It would have helped Britain's recovery to keep the Empire together as a unit in foreign and defence policy, but King had no sympathy for such aims. At the 1923 Imperial Conference, King joined with South Africa's J.B.M. Herzog to win a clear statement that each dominion's foreign policy was a matter for that dominion to decide. Three years later, a report by Lord Balfour confirmed the King-Herzog principle. Britain and the dominions agreed that they would all be defined as "autonomous Communities within the British Empire, equal in status, in no way subordinate one to another in any aspect of their domestic or external affairs, though united by a common allegiance to the Crown, and freely associated as members of the British Commonwealth of Nations." Canada soon opened embassies in Washington, Paris, and Tokyo. In 1931, the British Parliament approved the *Statute of Westminster*, giving its formal agreement to Canada's new status.

By that time, of course, King was not Prime Minister; Bennett was. As leader of the Conservative opposition, Bennett had denounced King's policies and deplored the establishment of Canadian embassies. Yet Bennett's slogan in his victorious 1930 campaign was "Canada first, then the Empire". Once in power, Bennett changed into a nationalist. He shocked British leaders who came to Ottawa in 1932 with his demands. To Bennett, the Empire came a poor second to Canada. Bennett even retained O.D. Skelton, King's Undersecretary of State for External Affairs, who was a strong nationalist. In fact, Bennett's energy might well have given Canada a more active role in world affairs, but the Depression stopped him.

The Depression tempted Canadians to copy the isolationism of the United States. *Canadiens* had long since cut their ties with France. If English Canadians could do the same with Britain, then Canada would be just as free as the United States to turn its back on Europe and its problems. That was Skelton's view, and he did his best to share it with the others in his department, among them a young historian named Lester B. Pearson. Skelton had great influence among those Canadians who paid attention to their country's world role. But so did J.W. Dafoe, editor of the Winnipeg-based *Free Press*, the most powerful newspaper in western Canada. It was Dafoe who called Canada "an American nation". He wanted Canada to uphold the League of Nations and collective security. Others, including J.S. Woodsworth of the CCF and Agnes Macphail, Canada's only woman M.P. at the time, held yet another view. They wished Canada to disarm, renounce war, and set an example to the world.

When King returned as Prime Minister in 1935, he took these opinions into account. They were more in tune with his views than the editorials about Canada's duty to Britain which often appeared in Canadian newspapers. Nevertheless, King recognized, as did most people, that the risks of war were rising. The Depression had helped to bring military rule to Japan. Europe was once more in turmoil. In Italy, the government had dissolved in chaos after the war and had been taken over by a fascist dictator, Benito Mussolini. A harsh Communist dictatorship in the Soviet Union had degenerated into the insane cruelty of Josef Stalin's regime. Under his reign of terror, millions of Soviet people died of sickness and starvation in the Ukraine and in prison camps in Siberia. Adolf Hitler had become chancellor of Germany in January, 1933, and had taken over the presidency in the following year. He soon destroyed resistance to his rule, even among fellow Nazis, defied the Versailles Treaty by launching full-scale rearmament, and began the systematic destruction of German Jews. Britain and France agreed that it would be best not to intervene; after all, the Versailles Treaty had been harsh, and many Germans obviously supported Hitler. The savage treatment of the Jews was "a domestic problem".

CLOSE-UP

The Treaty of Versailles and World War II

Many people have suggested that the terms of the Treaty of Versailles, signed at the end of World War I, led to the rise of Hitler and World War II. Below are some of the terms of the treaty:

1. Germany was to give up all its overseas possessions to the victorious countries.
2. All German overseas investment was to be confiscated and turned over to the allied powers.
3. Germany was to give up land it had taken from France and Denmark, and make room for the new nations of Czechoslovakia and Poland. These areas contained 6.5 million Germans, and over half of Germany's supplies of iron, coal, lead, and zinc.
4. Germany was to give up the rich Saar Valley; in 15 years, a vote could be held to see whether the residents wanted the valley to be returned to Germany. (They did, and the territory was returned in 1935.)
5. Germany was to give up its remaining air force, have a very limited navy and army, and was not to rearm in any way. The Rhineland was to become a demilitarized zone.
6. Germany and Austria were not to join in any form of union.

A later demand by the winning side also required Germany to pay extremely heavy reparations, assessed at $32 thousand million. Interest payments on the debt were higher than the required annual payment.

In fact, no payments were ever made.

After he came to power, Hitler made many speeches attacking the conditions imposed by the victors. The following is an excerpt from one of them:

> When the Fourteen Points of President Wilson were announced Germany believed these assurances and laid down her weapons. And then a breach of faith began such as the world has never seen... The German colonies were stolen from us, German foreign securities were simply confiscated, and our merchant marine was taken away. Then came financial pillage such as the world has never up to this day seen. Reparations of astronomical figures were imposed on the German people about which even English statesmen said that they could be paid only if the whole German nation reduced its standard of living and worked fourteen hours a day. What German spirit and German diligence had created and saved in decades was now lost in a few years. Millions of Germans were torn away from the Reich (Germany)... The League of Nations was made not an instrument of understanding but a guarantor of the meanest dictate that human beings have ever thought of.
>
> –Hodgett, A.B. and Burns, J.D., *Decisive Decade*, Don Mills: Thomas Nelson & Sons (Canada), 1973, pp. 310-11.

QUESTIONS

1. How do the excerpts from the Treaty of Versailles support Hitler's claim that the treaty was too harsh in its treatment of the Germany people? Give your reasons, citing evidence from the excerpts.

2. What connection was there between the Treaty of Versailles and the Second World War?

A rally of Nazi stormtroopers and German soldiers in Nurnberg, Germany, 1937. Why were world leaders reluctant to take action when Germany openly defied the terms of the Versailles Treaty by rearming?

Volunteer soldiers watch the sky from their trench during the Spanish Civil War. About 1200 Canadians went to Spain as part of the communist-backed International Brigade. Many served in the Mackenzie-Papineau Battalion. Their idealism was unpopular in parts of Canada. Why was this so?

Canada considered all these developments to be none of its business. When the Japanese invaded China in 1931, the Canadian government instructed its representative at the League of Nations, W.A. Riddell, to argue that Japan had moved to restore order to a troubled land. But when Canada's government changed hands in 1935, Riddell got a chance to act on his own initiative. As Mussolini prepared to invade Ethiopia, Riddell ignored Skelton's isolationist policy and urged the League to cut off oil supplies—vital to Mussolini's army—from Italy. King first read of this "Canadian Resolution" in the newspapers and was horrified. He promptly repudiated Riddell's proposal, declaring that Riddell had spoken as a member of the Sanctions Committee, not as Canada's representative. A year later, when Hitler and Mussolini backed General Francisco Franco's rebellion against the new Spanish Republic, Canada joined other democracies in neutrality. When hundreds of young Canadians went to fight for the Republic, Parliament responded by passing a *Foreign Enlistment Act* which threatened them with two years in jail.

Most Canadians paid no heed to the world situation. Some, however, sympathized with the new dictators. Roman Catholics approved of the fact that Mussolini had made peace with the Vatican after half a century of bad relations between the Church and the Italian government. Anti-semitism was as common in Canada as in Europe; Canada took in only 4000 of the 800 000 Jewish refugees who fled Hitler's Germany between 1933 and 1939. Those who found dictatorships repugnant usually found other arguments for doing nothing. One of the foremost was that the Treaty of Versailles was cruelly unjust. Who could blame the Germans for ignoring it? That was the view of O.D. Skelton, who said that the League of Nations therefore had no moral stand from which to intervene. Many politically aware Canadians agreed with him.

Despite Canadian isolationism and his striving for national independence, King still believed that if Britain went to war, Canada should follow. His solution was to do everything in his power to avoid war, or, if it came, to limit Canadian participation. A half-hearted rearmament begun in 1937 focused on home defence. The air force and navy were expanded only because they could protect Canada. The army's expansion was limited to a few coastal artillery guns. They were placed largely to reassure British Columbia that it could defend itself against a Japanese attack.

In 1938, Hitler threatened to invade part of Czechoslovakia. As the crisis deepened, Britain's new Prime Minister, Neville Chamberlain, flew to Munich—and agreed not to interfere as Hitler took what he wanted. King and most Canadians rejoiced at Chamberlain's claim that he had secured "peace in our time". Dafoe of the *Winnipeg Free Press* was an exception; he titled his editorial on Munich "What's the Cheering For?"

Europe's slow slide towards war brought Canada closer to the United States. Roosevelt had added a "Good Neighbour" policy to the New Deal; it pleased Canadians that it extended northward. A further trade agreement in 1938 strengthened the partial reciprocity treaty made by King in 1935. King forbade military discussions with the British, but now he sent Canadian officers in civilian clothes to Washington. They had much to discuss. New technology had made it possible that enemy bombers could refuel at some hidden base in the Arctic and swoop down on "Fortress America". At Kingston, Ontario in 1938, Roosevelt promised his Canadian audience that "the people of the United States will not stand idly by if domination of Canadian soil is threatened by any other empire".

The promise comforted Canadians because, by early 1939, Chamberlain's appeasement policy had failed. War seemed inevitable. In March, Hitler ignored his promises to Chamberlain and took over the rest of Czechoslovakia. King was appalled at the failure of Chamberlain's diplomacy. He realized that Canada now had to be prepared for war. Ernest Lapointe, King's lieutenant in Québec, persuaded the Québec Liberal members to back King in supporting Britain. Even the new Conservative leader who replaced Bennett, Dr. Robert Manion, helped King. To build his own support in Québec, Manion pledged that he would never allow conscription. King echoed him: "So long as this government may be in power, no such measure shall be enacted." In a brilliant stroke intended to remind Canadians of their ties to Britain, King arranged the first visit to Canada of a reigning monarch. A shy King George VI and a radiant Queen Elizabeth spent the late spring of

Appeasement Policy

By the 1930's, many people believed that the Versailles Treaty of 1919 had been unfair to Germany. They agreed with Hitler's claims to former territory and his rebuilding of the Germany army. Many also felt that it was preferable to appease Hitler rather than risk the horrors of a new war. British Prime Minister Neville Chamberlain was a leading exponent of this policy of appeasement. Winston Churchill and a few other British politicians who wanted to stand up to Hitler came to power when it was almost too late. When war came, appeasement fell into disfavour.

King George VI and a young Queen Elizabeth on their first royal visit to Canada. Prime Minister King is leaning on his cane at right. What was King's aim in arranging the visit?

1939 bringing glamour and a revival of Commonwealth patriotism to a Depression-weary country.

The glow remained until September 1, when German tanks rumbled into Poland, one of Britain's allies. On September 3, Britain declared war on Germany. By the time Parliament assembled on September 7, Canada's armed forces were mobilizing. Among Canadian political figures, only the CCF's J.S. Woodsworth and a few Québec nationalists opposed the decision to join the war. Canadians had been united as much by world events as by King's conciliation. Hitler's assault on German Catholics had shocked Québec, while his 1939 alliance with the Soviet Union had raised hostility among anti-communists. Still, what mattered most to the majority of Canadians was the single fact that Britain was at war. On September 10, 1939, Canada traded isolationism for involvement and declared war on Germany.

QUESTIONS

1. How did Bennett's attitudes towards nationalism differ before and after he became Prime Minister?
2. Who was the leader of the U.S.S.R. in the 1930's? Of Italy? Of Germany?
3. What event in Europe finally convinced King that Canada "now had to prepare for war"?
4. What arguments did some Canadians give for not interfering in the actions and policies of European countries?
5. How did King gain the support of Québec for his plans to assist Britain in the coming war?

Chapter Summary

The 1920's have been called both "the Roaring Twenties" and "the decade of dead ends". Times were prosperous, and many people believed it was possible to become rich. For most Canadians, that dream died with the stock market crash of 1929. What followed was ten long years of worldwide economic depression. The standard remedy, protective tariffs, only deepened the Great Depression. Drought, combined with low prices for farm produce, made the prairie provinces the hardest hit in Canada.

In a search for solutions, Canadians briefly experimented with new political philosophies. Immediately after the war, some Canadians expected the new communist government in Russia to show the world how to share a country's prosperity fairly among its population. Unions once again tried to organize Canadian labour. Both these movements declined after the depression of 1920-1921. The quest for new political solutions would surface again during the Great Depression. The CCF and Social Credit both owe their beginnings to the hard economic realities of the 1930's.

The 1920's and the 1930's also saw Canada finally gain sovereignty. The Statute of Westminster, *signed in 1931, gave Canada the right to full control over its own domestic and foreign policy. The next time Canada went to war it would go as a nation, not as a part of the British Empire.*

IN REVIEW

1. **(a)** Why did American influence over Canadian society increase during the 1920's?
   (b) What steps were taken to counter this Americanization?
2. During the 1930's, a number of Canadians turned away from the traditional Liberal and Conservative parties. What were the reasons for their rejection? Were their criticisms justified?
3. Why did many Canadians favour isolation from Europe during the 1920's and 1930's?
4. Why was the signing of the Halibut Treaty a milestone on Canada's road to sovereignty?

APPLYING YOUR KNOWLEDGE

1. "Canadians are determined to be both a North American and a British nation, but above all a nation with a distinctive Canadian personality." Is this observation still true? Explain your answer.
2. The *Foreign Enlistment Act*, passed to prevent Canadians from fighting for the Republicans in Spain, was intended to keep Canadians from participating in any war in which Canada was not officially involved. Do you think the law was fair? Why would Canadians want such a law?
3. Britain declared war on Germany on September 3, 1939. Canada did not do so until September 10. What is significant about the fact that Canada declared war a week later than Britain? (Think back to the start of World War I.)

FURTHER INVESTIGATION

1. Canadians are still divided on whether American investment benefits Canada. Offer as many reasons as possible for (a) encouraging such investment and (b) discouraging it.
2. Is the Americanization of Canada still occurring? If so, do you feel it matters?
3. Give both the benefits and the drawbacks of government-owned media (such as the CBC). With which position do you agree, pro or con?
4. Do research to find out what terms Germany would have imposed on its enemies if it had won World War I.

CHAPTER 4

Canada's World War

Canada was not prepared for war in 1939. The long years of economic depression had closed down many of the industrial plants of the 1920's. Those which had remained operating were in need of modernization. The Canadian forces had been cut, and between 1919 and 1937, almost nothing had been spent on military equipment. Memories of the conscription crisis of 1917 made some Canadians anxious about the effect of war on French and English relations at home.

In this chapter, you will discover the answers to the following questions:

- *What were the main causes, events, and turning points of World War II?*
- *What were Canada's contributions to the war effort?*
- *How did the war affect the lives of Canadians on the home front?*
- *What effect did the war have on the role of the Canadian government?*
- *Why did this war, like the previous one, create a political crisis in Canada?*

"This Is Not Our War"

When Canada entered the Second World War, no cheering crowds filled the streets as they had in 1914. Most of the young men who lined up to enlist were looking for jobs, not glory. Later generations might agree that Nazism was an evil that had to be stopped, but such views were scarce in the Canada of 1939. The horrors of World War I and the hardships of the Depression had soured Canadians on the world outside their borders. Prime Minister King spoke for many Canadians when he agonized publicly: "The idea that every twenty years this country should automatically and as a matter of course take part in a war overseas for democracy or self-determination of small nations, that a country that has all it can do to run itself should feel called upon to save, periodically, a continent that cannot run itself. . . seems to many a nightmare and sheer madness."

King had nevertheless made some effort to prepare Canada for the inevitable. He also wanted to accept as small a wartime burden as possible. When the heads of the Canadian navy, army, and air force prepared a $500 million mobilization plan, the government cut it in half. King intended most of the money to be spent in Canada. Isolationists could be told that it was actually for home defence.

The primary concern of King's government was always to avoid any policy that might help to split Canada. Conscription was the most obvious danger. Inflation, profiteering, and hoarding were other threats to unity. The government revived the *War Measures Act* and created a Wartime Prices and Trade Board (WPTB) to control prices and profits. King knew that the borrowed money which had financed the First World War had resulted in inflation. The Board would help in the fight against inflation. So would King's Finance Minister, J.L. Ilsley, who intended to run the war on a "pay-as-you-go" basis, avoiding massive borrowing. Above all, King did not intend to repeat Borden's policy of putting the cause of allied victory ahead of Canada's economic and political well-being. The government intended to be cautious.

Just how cautious became clear when the British asked Canada to help train pilots and navigators. Canada's open spaces and safe skies were ideal for training, as the British had found during the previous war. King was delighted: Canada could make a contribution at home. His only regret was that the offer had not come in time to forestall

Winnipeggers wait for news of the declaration of war outside the Free Press *office on September 10, 1939. Why was the mood different from that in 1914?*

Canada's promise to send troops overseas. Nonetheless, King bargained hard with the British over costs, control, and a statement that this would be Canada's "most effective contribution to the war effort". He was not upset that most of the Canadians who graduated from the program would join the Royal Air Force (RAF), or that Canadian Air Force (RCAF) squadrons overseas would be paid for by the British.

"This is not our war," King burst out during one of the bargaining sessions with the British. Such sentiments did King and the Liberals little harm. In October, 1939, Maurice Duplessis tried to use the war as a chance to win an easy victory in a Québec provincial election. Federal Liberal ministers countered by warning that, if Duplessis won, they would all resign, and no-one would be left in the Cabinet to oppose conscription. Québec voters believed the Liberals and remembered Duplessis' harsh policies and broken promises. The Liberals won the province.

Not all Canadians approved of King's reluctant approach to the war, however. Mitchell Hepburn, the premier of Ontario, forced his Liberal-dominated legislature to condemn the federal Liberals for being unprepared. The Conservative leader of the federal opposition, Robert Manion, joined the fray. He demanded a "National Government" ready to wage a real war. King met Parliament and presented a speech from the throne in response to the criticisms. Then he asked the Governor General to dissolve the House and call an election before the opposition could answer. In vain the Conservatives protested that it was unfair. Election day, March 26, 1940, showed that most Canadians did not agree. Voters gave King the biggest victory in Canadian history: 178 Liberals to only 39 Conservatives, 10 Social Credit, 8 CCF members, and 10 others. Manion himself lost his seat in Parliament.

Montréal's mayor, Camillien Houde, at an anti-conscription rally in 1939. Was King right to have him interned for four years for his opposition to the National Resources Mobilization Act?

Barely two weeks after the election, the full fury of the storm broke in Europe. On April 9, Germany struck at Denmark and Norway. In the following month, as the world realized the meaning of *blitzkrieg* or "lightning war", the Germans smashed their way across the Netherlands and Belgium into France. Eleven days later, German troops reached the English Channel. On June 17, France surrendered. Suddenly Canada was Britain's largest remaining ally.

Months before the war, King had promised Parliament and Adolf Hitler himself that if bombs rained down on London, Canada would be at Britain's side. The disaster of early 1940 made Canadians eager to take action, but there was little they could do. The 1st Infantry Division had reached Britain in 1939, and was now one of the few army formations available to defend England. Canada's four destroyers and the single RCAF squadron with modern airplanes were sent to Britain's aid. The government passed the *National Resources Mobilization Act* in order to conscript manpower—though only for home defence. When Montréal's mayor, Camillien Houde, urged people not to register under the *Act*, he was arrested and interned for the next four years.

The full significance of Britain's desperate plight took time to dawn on Canadians. With Germany in control of most of continental Europe, dozens of ports could serve as bases for German submarine attacks. Britain's Atlantic lifeline was in danger. The Royal Canadian Navy would need every escort vessel it could get to protect convoys bearing vital food, supplies, and military aid to Britain. To maintain the Air Training Program, the RCAF would have to obtain equipment from the United States or from Canada's own tiny aviation industry. Four more divisions would be added to the one that already served in Britain.

Britain's danger was also Canada's. Canadian senator Raoul Dandurand, President of the League of Nations, had claimed in 1924 that Canada was "a fire-proof house, far from the sources of conflagration". The first six months of 1940 destroyed that illusion. If Britain fell, Canada would face Hitler almost alone. Washington understood all too well what that would mean for the United States. On August 17, 1940, King met U.S. President Roosevelt in Ogdensburg, New York. There the two men approved a Permanent Joint Board of Defence which would "consider in the broad sense the defense of the northern half of the western hemisphere". King returned to Ottawa very pleased with himself; he felt that he had succeeded in linking the neutral United States with Britain. But Winston Churchill, the experienced politician who had become Britain's Prime Minister, was not grateful. He did not need King as a go-between. What the Ogdensburg agreement did, in fact, was to make Canada a junior partner in American plans to defend the continent.

Roosevelt would do everything in his power to save Britain. In an isolationist America, and in an election year, his power was not great. Besides, the threat most Americans feared was not Germany, but its ally, Japan. Japan's war in China and its plans for a "Greater East Asian Co-prosperity Sphere"—essentially, a Japanese Empire—endangered American influence in the Far East, particularly in the United States' own "dominion", the Philippines. American fears were realized on December 7, 1941. In a surprise attack, Japanese bombers devastated the naval base at Pearl Harbour in Hawaii. Then they destroyed American bombers at Clark Field in the Philippines. The Americans immediately entered the war.

Canada was far less involved with events in the Pacific than with those in the Atlantic. Still, it had sent two inexperienced infantry battalions to Hong Kong to join the small British garrison there. Perhaps their presence would somehow deter the Japanese from attacking. The hope was futile. On Christmas Day, after bitter fighting, the survivors surrendered. Of the 1975 Canadians who had left Vancouver, the horrors of battle and Japanese prison camps would leave only 1418 survivors.

For both Canadians and Americans, it was no longer somebody else's war.

The Battle of Britain

In September, 1940, as the Germans collected barges to ferry invading troops across the English Channel, Hitler's Luftwaffe struck from the air. For a few weeks, they concentrated on radar stations, air bases, and naval bases; then they returned with high explosives and fire bombs to devastate London and other British cities. But they had moved on to civilian targets too quickly. The RAF had survived. Radar located the invaders. Hurricane and Spitfire fighters strafed German bombers in huge aerial battles. Polish, Czechoslovak, Free French, and Norwegian pilots joined airmen from Britain and the Commonwealth to drive back the German bombers. Narrowly, and only after months of struggle, the Battle of Britain was won. Hitler had suffered his first defeat.

Canadians troops march through Hong Kong on November 16, 1941. Much of their equipment was still at sea when the Japanese attacked. Why were Canadians in Hong Kong?

CLOSE-UP

The Days of War

1931	• Japan takes over Manchuria (northern China).
1933	• Adolf Hitler seizes power in Germany; begins campaign against "non-Aryan" peoples of Germany.
1935	• Hitler begins German rearmament.
1935	• The people of the Saar vote 90 percent in favour of once again being part of Germany. • Mussolini sends Italian troops into Abyssinia (now Ethiopia).
1936	• Germany reoccupies the Rhineland.
1938	• Germany invades and annexes Austria. • Hitler's hate campaign against Jews, Marxists, and non-Aryans intensifies. • German troops invade and take over the Sudetenland. • British Prime Minister Neville Chamberlain announces he has negotiated "peace in our time" with Hitler.
1939	• *March 14*: Germany takes over the rest of Czechoslovakia. • *August 23*: Germany and the Soviet Union sign non-aggression pact. • *September 1*: Germany invades Poland. • *September 3*: France and Britain declare war on Germany. • *September 10*: Canada declares war on Germany. • *September 17*: Russian troops move into eastern Poland.
1939–40	• Soviet Union occupies Finland, Baltic states, part of Romania. • *September, 1939–April, 1940*: "Phoney war"; little happens.
1940	• *April*: Germany invades Denmark and Norway. • *May 10*: Germany launches *blitzkrieg* against Netherlands, Belgium, Luxembourg, France. • End of May: Belgium and the Netherlands surrender. • *May 27–June 4*: Allied troops evacuate Dunkirk. • *June 17*: France surrenders.

- *September*: Battle of Britain; Italian troops attack Egypt.
- *December*: The London Blitz.

1940–43
- Battle of the Atlantic.

1941
- *January*: U.S.A. begins lend-lease program to supply war materials to Britain.
- *June*: Germany repudiates non-aggression pact and invades Soviet Union.
- *December 7*: Japanese attack Pearl Harbour; U.S.A. joins Allies.

1942
- Soviet troops stop German advance at Stalingrad.
- *October on*: Allies force Germans and Italians back across North Africa.

1943
- *January 31*: Soviets defeat Germans at siege of Stalingrad and begin to push them back.
- *May*: German and Italian troops surrender in Africa.
- *July*: Allies invade Sicily, then mainland Italy.
- *Mid-year*: Losses caused by German U-boats in the Atlantic greatly reduced.

1944
- *Spring*: Allies do heavy bombing of German industrial centres and French rail lines to prepare for invasion.
- *June 4*: Rome falls.
- *June 6*: D-Day—British, American and Canadian troops invade Normandy, in northern France.
- *July 20*: German generals, blaming him for their losses, try to kill Hitler and fail.
- *July 25*: Free French march back into Paris.
- *August*: V1 and V2 rocket bombs launched against Britain.

QUESTION

1. Use an atlas to determine why Germany chose to conduct its invasions of European nations in the order in which it did.

At Dunkerque (Dunkirk), a French sea port, British and Allied troops were cut off by German forces and faced almost certain death or imprisonment. British naval vessels and hundreds of civilian craft crossed the English Channel under German attack to rescue them. The town was liberated in May, 1945, but more than three-quarters of its houses were destroyed in the fighting.

QUESTIONS

1. Why did news of the start of the war in 1939 bring out no "rejoicing throngs"?
2. What policy towards World War II did King initially advocate?
3. What do the results of the March, 1940 election indicate about King's policies towards the war in Europe?
4. **(a)** How did Canada suddenly become Britain's biggest ally in June, 1940? **(b)** What changed as a result?

Total War

C.D. Howe speaking in Sudbury during a 1942 Victory Loan Campaign. Howe was responsible for meeting Canada's commitment to manufacture war supplies for Britain—but first he had to find the men, the machines and the money.

The British described their desperate struggle against Hitler as "total war". The phrase did not describe Prime Minister King's attitude to the war once the crisis of 1940 was over. While Canadians were urged to give everything, including their lives, to the war effort, King hoped that Canada's main role would be as an "arsenal for democracy". Expanding Canadian industry to help the allied cause would help pull the economy out of the Depression. It might also distract those who wanted Canada to send more soldiers to Europe.

The symbol of Canada's war effort on the home front was Clarence Decatur Howe, an American-born engineer who was King's Minister of Munitions and Supply. At first, business people were suspicious of his abrupt manner; other ministers criticized his extravagance. In 1940, Howe travelled to Britain to obtain orders for war materials. His ship was torpedoed. Howe survived and became a hero, coming home with orders for almost anything Canada could produce. By helping manufacturers get large orders, Howe made patriotism profitable. Canada's large automotive industry switched to making army vehicles. By 1943, much of the British army rode in Canadian trucks. Other factories made guns, radios, radar sets, aircraft—almost anything the war required. When existing companies could not meet Howe's varied demands for war materials, he created Crown corporations—28 of them in total.

Canada's Finance Minister, J.L. Ilsley, had to pay for Howe's expenditures. He recycled the ideas of the First World War: war bonds, war savings stamps, and higher income tax. Ilsley talked the provinces into handing over their main taxing powers to Ottawa in return for a guaranteed income. Most corporations and ordinary Canadians had to pay much higher taxes as a result. Full employment, regular paycheques, and rising profits eased the financial burden. The export of Howe's war materials also helped Canada pay its war costs. Thanks to Howe and Ilsley, Canada's economy was far more efficiently geared to war then it had been in 1914–1918. Even so, Canada's national debt skyrocketed from about $3 thousand million to $11 thousand million by the end of the war.

Canada shared one acute economic problem with Britain. By the end of 1940, the British had run out of American dollars to buy arms and airplanes from the United States. Canada was in a similar situation, and Canadian production depended on American imports. Roosevelt helped Britain through "lend-lease". The agreement allowed Britain to borrow money on the promise of paying it back at the end of the war. Canada could not obtain a similar deal, since it was not bankrupt. Clifford Clark, the Deputy Minister of Finance, found the answer. If Canadians needed American goods, the United States needed Canadian military supplies for their own rearmament. In April, 1941, King and Roosevelt negotiated an agreement under which each country would produce the armaments it was best at producing. The agreement linked the economies of the two nations for the period of the war.

An aircraft assembly worker putting together the "fishbowl" nose of a DeHavilland Mosquito. As during the First World War, women took over jobs for men fighting on the front.

If the government solved one problem, there were always more. When a strike stopped work at the aluminum smelter in Arvida, Québec, Howe got the power to use troops against future disruptions. A large aircraft factory near Malton, Ontario, failed to become efficient; Howe seized the plant, brought in new management, and told the new company, Victory Aircraft, to produce Lancaster and Mosquito bombers.

The pride caused by the new industrial developments helped Canadians forget how difficult it was to start from the ground up. It took years for the shipyards, bankrupted by the Depression, to organize and train the skilled workers needed to build good warships. Howe boasted that Canadians could produce anything. Nevertheless, early Canadian radar sets were of poor quality, and some Canadian bombers were heavier and therefore less efficient than British ones. But Howe persevered, and his efforts did as much to modernize Canadian industry as they did to win the war. By 1943, the million and a quarter men and women in Canada's factories had become a skilled, efficient work force. In the postwar world, Canada would be a strong industrial competitor if it chose to be.

One of Howe's biggest problems was finding workers. A country which had had too many people during the Depression now had too few. Howe and the Minister of Defence, J.L. Ralston, were in competition for manpower. In 1941, the government created the National Selective Service (NSS) to manage Canada's work force. In September, 1942, single women aged 20 to 24 were ordered to register. By that time, no able-bodied man aged 17 to 45 was permitted to drive a taxi, sell real estate, or help make such products as beer, toys, or sporting goods. Howe still complained that he had too few people; Ralston, for his part, began to think that conscription would become necessary.

All three branches of the armed forces scrambled for the highly-trained men vital to modern war, competing with each other and with Howe's factories. The navy had no problem getting recruits: men from the Prairies flocked to it. The air force offered the excitement and glamour of aerial combat or the useful skills of ground crew. The army had the hardest time. Whatever the generals might say about the thrill of modern warfare, anyone who had a relative in the First World War knew what to expect from land combat. The army had another problem as well; its generals now realized that soldiers needed particularly high mental and physical standards to stand the strain of battle. The politicians refused to understand. Whenever the generals mentioned "standards", King and his ministers suspected they were trying to bring in conscription.

Some generals did, in fact, want conscription; others did not. The truth is that their opinions did not matter. It was politicians, newspapers and magazines, and the public who settled the issue.

The slogan "total war" was a rallying cry for supporters of conscription. Surely Canada should have conscription if the words were to have any meaning. When France fell, the Toronto-based magazine *Saturday Night* took up the cry. The Canadian Legion rallied 500 other organizations in a "Call for Total War". The Conservatives, who had had no active leader since Robert Manion's defeat in March, 1940, asked Arthur Meighen to come back. He agreed, confident that the conscription issue would unite most of Canada and defeat the Liberals, as it had in 1917. Even two Liberal premiers joined the call. A poll conducted in November, 1941 found that 60 percent of Canadians were in favour of conscription. Early the next month, the Japanese bombed Pearl Harbour. King did not have to be told that support for conscription would be even stronger. The government reacted by creating two new army divisions to protect the Pacific coast, and another for the Atlantic. All three divisions were made up of men recruited under the NRMA. Advocates of conscription were not satisfied.

King thought of a way to defeat the call for conscription. He would hold a plebiscite to allow Canadians to vote on whether to release him from his earlier pledge of no conscription. Much of Canada saw it as a chance to record its patriotism; Québec considered the plebiscite a betrayal. A promise made to *Canadiens* would be unmade by the anglophone majority. The government also denied opponents of conscription the opportunity to make their views public on the CBC. Anger filled the members of Quebec's *La ligue pour la defense du Canada*. They included André Laurendeau of *Le Devoir*, Jean Drapeau, a future mayor of Montréal, and a young Pierre Elliott Trudeau. On April 27, 1942, nearly 3 million Canadians voted "yes" to releasing the government from its promises. Over 1.6 million voted "no". Anglophone voters were four to one in favour; Québec was four to one against. Communities of new Canadians in the West were split more evenly.

There was a price for King's clever solution. The plebiscite left a divided country and a divided government. King set out to reunite both, using his most memorable slogan, "Not necessarily conscription, but conscription if necessary." Critics mocked him, but King insisted that the issue was still open. King's senior minister from Québec, Pierre Cardin, resigned in protest. So did the Minister of Defence, J.L. Ralston, because he believed conscription was necessary. Then, mindful of his duty, Ralston changed his mind. But his resignation letter remained in King's desk.

CLOSE-UP

Japanese Canadians in World War II

Scenes from British Columbia, 1942: More than 1300 fishing boats bob idly on the Fraser River and elsewhere on the west coast, corralled under government order. In East Vancouver, thousands of harried, weeping women and children are herded into trains headed for the B.C. interior. Other trains are crowded with men.

These people were among the more than 21 000 Japanese Canadians who lived in British Columbia. They comprised the vast majority of Japanese in Canada. Before the war, they were treated as second-class citizens, denied the vote and restricted in the jobs they could do and the professions they could enter.

In 1941, Canadians' fear of the Japanese grew stronger. As war approached, the RCMP and the army reassured Canadians and their government that people of Japanese origin living in Canada posed no real threat to Canada's war effort. But after Pearl Harbour, a torrent of speeches, editorials, and resolutions from municipal councils, service clubs, and patriotic organizations in British Columbia and elsewhere poured in to the federal government, demanding that "something be done" about the Japanese in Canada.

The government responded to the pressure. In January, 1942, it ordered that "Japanese male nationals" aged 14 to 45 be relocated away from the coast. On February 25, as Japanese forces overran Southeast Asia, the government ordered the complete expulsion of all Japanese Canadians from the coast. Families were broken up, with some members sent to abandoned mining towns in the Kootenays, others to work camps in B.C., Alberta, and eastern Canada. In 1943, the government confiscated farms, houses, personal goods, and fishing boats, and sold them at public auction. Few of those who lost all their goods received more than a few dollars from auction proceeds. The little money they received had to be used to pay the expenses, such as food and fuel, of living in the camps.

A wartime Order in Council gave the government the authority

A relocation camp for Japanese Canadians in the Interior of B.C. The shacks, suitable enough for a summer holiday, had to shelter families during harsh winters in the Rockies.

to strip Japanese Canadians of their citizenship. Four thousand agreed to go to Japan, a country some of them had never seen. Others were dispersed across Canada. In 1988, after forty years of campaigning by Japanese Canadians and their sympathisers, the federal government apologized for the old injustice and offered $21 000 in compensation for each survivor of internment.

QUESTIONS

1. What prompted Canada's internment of Japanese Canadians?
2. Was it wise for the government to compensate Japanese Canadians for their treatment during the Second World War? Give reasons to support your answer.

A poster urging Canadiennes *to vote against conscription in the federal plebiscite. What arguments were presented? What was the outcome of the vote?*

Plebiscite or Referendum

A plebiscite (from the Latin plebs, *people) or referendum is a chance for all the people to vote on some hotly-debated topic. So far, there have been only two plebiscites run by the federal government: in 1898, on prohibition and in 1942, on conscription. In neither case did the government consider the results binding. Provinces have also used plebiscites. In 1948, two referenda led Newfoundland into Confederation. In 1980, a Québec referendum said "*non*" to the* Parti Québécois' *bid to negotiate sovereignty-association with Canada for the province of Québec.*

QUESTIONS

1. What did King hope would be Canada's chief role in the war?
2. How could a thriving munitions industry satisfy those who demanded that Canada send more troops overseas?
3. What prompted the lend-lease agreement?
4. Why do you think the government ruled that "able-bodied" men could not do certain jobs?
5. What was the purpose of the Wartime Price and Trade Board?

Canada's War: At Sea and in the Air

For Canada's Prime Minister, the best contribution Canada could make to the war effort was Canadian unity. King knew that sending soldiers to the First World War had led to conscription and a divided country. It seemed unlikely to him that a navy or an air force could suffer losses as great as those of an army. Therefore, Canada's war effort would be concentrated in the air and at sea. Moreover, Canadians themselves were more eager to serve in the glamorous, exotic air force and navy than in the army.

Canada's admirals saw their chance to prove what a real navy could do. Canada's four destroyers had raced to Britain during the crisis of

1940. Many of the best officers of the tiny peacetime navy were used to build up the Canadian fleet. However, the situation which had developed in the Atlantic led Canada to build escort ships for the convoys of merchant vessels that supplied Britain.

The reason behind the decision lay in the success of the German navy in the war on the Atlantic. In 1917, during the First World War, a German submarine blockade had brought Britain to the verge of starvation. The same thing was happening between 1940 and 1943. Hitler had failed in 1940 to conquer Britain by *blitzkrieg*; he would try to do so by cutting off its Atlantic lifeline. The U-boat fleet could win Germany's war.

The British had a few advantages. Early in the war, they had broken the German secret naval code with help from a primitive computer called "Ultra". They could intercept orders to U-boats, and direct convoys away from them. In addition, the Royal Navy had worked hard between the wars on ways to find and destroy submarines. With superb training, teamwork, and the best equipment, surface ships had a chance against their stealthy, dangerous underwater enemy. Long training and first-class equipment, however, were luxuries that Canada's wartime navy could not afford. Instead, admirals and politicians agreed that they would provide as many escort vessels as possible to protect convoys from enemy submarines. Canadian shipyards could build "corvettes", as the first small warships were called. Their crews, hurriedly recruited and trained, would learn on the job.

The sailors on the corvettes had a harsh introduction to war. Corvettes "rolled in a heavy dew"; at sea, everything—and everyone—was soaked by the icy Atlantic waves. Their lack of armament ensured that they would be outgunned by most submarines. The British soon modified their own corvettes to make them more seaworthy. They also

A convoy of merchant ships in the North Atlantic, en route for Britain. What German weapon made the convoys necessary? What was Canada's role in the convoy war?

H.M.C.S. Clayoquot *sets out on her shake-down cruise in June, 1943. The corvette lacked sonar and most of the other gear that would have helped it locate submarines. Why did the Canadian government not see the necessity for such expensive equipment.*

installed new submarine detection devices, such as sonar, as soon as they became available. The Canadian government saw such expensive modifications as unnecessary. What was important was to build and man more ships. The new crews were just as inexperienced as the first ones had been. Often the captain—a veteran of the merchant navy or a yacht owner—was the only person who could navigate the ship. The Canadians certainly learned fast on the job, but nothing could make up for the lack of training and equipment. The cruel result was that convoys escorted by Canadian ships suffered heavier losses than those protected by the British.

The situation on the Atlantic became worse after the United States joined the war. Prior to that time, the Americans protected many convoys bound for Britain as far as Iceland. After Pearl Harbor, the American navy was sent to the Pacific. Canadian corvettes were needed to protect American shipping in the Caribbean and off Florida. By the winter of 1942–1943, inexperience and lack of ships were leading to the defeat of the Allies in the Atlantic war. Hundreds of merchant and escort ships and millions of tonnes of cargo went down under the onslaught of the German "wolf packs"—teams of submarines. U-boats even entered the St. Lawrence River. The trail of sinkings which resulted led Ottawa to close the river to shipping for the rest of the war. By this time, too, the German navy had changed its communications code. Britain and its allies could no longer predict when it would be safe to manoeuvre convoys between wolf packs.

Something had to be done. In March, 1943, Canadian, British, and American admirals met in Washington. It was agreed that the British would train and re-equip the Canadian escort groups. Canada would then take over the protection of the entire northwest Atlantic. The United States would supply the long-range aircraft essential for covering the convoys, especially in the "Black Hole" in the mid-Atlantic where the wolf packs got most of their prey. Fortunately, just after this meeting the British once again broke the German naval code and regained their advantage. The tide turned dramatically. Faced with sudden heavy losses, the Germans withdrew their submarines in the summer of 1943. They sent them back later with new equipment, but they had lost their edge. The Canadians, trained and re-equipped by the British, were more than a match for the U-boats.

By this time, too, Canada's admirals had had their wishes answered. New, modern Canadian destroyers battled German surface ships in the waters off Norway and France. Two Canadian-manned aircraft carriers gave Canada experience with the newest kind of naval warfare. By the end of the war, the Canadian navy was the third largest in the world, with 373 warships and over 90 000 men and women.

Thanks to the air training program set up by the RCAF, Canada's pilots were better trained than its sailors. The British Commonwealth Air Training Plan (BCATP) had over 130 000 graduates in all, nearly

FIGURE 4.1 *World War II: Battle of the Atlantic*

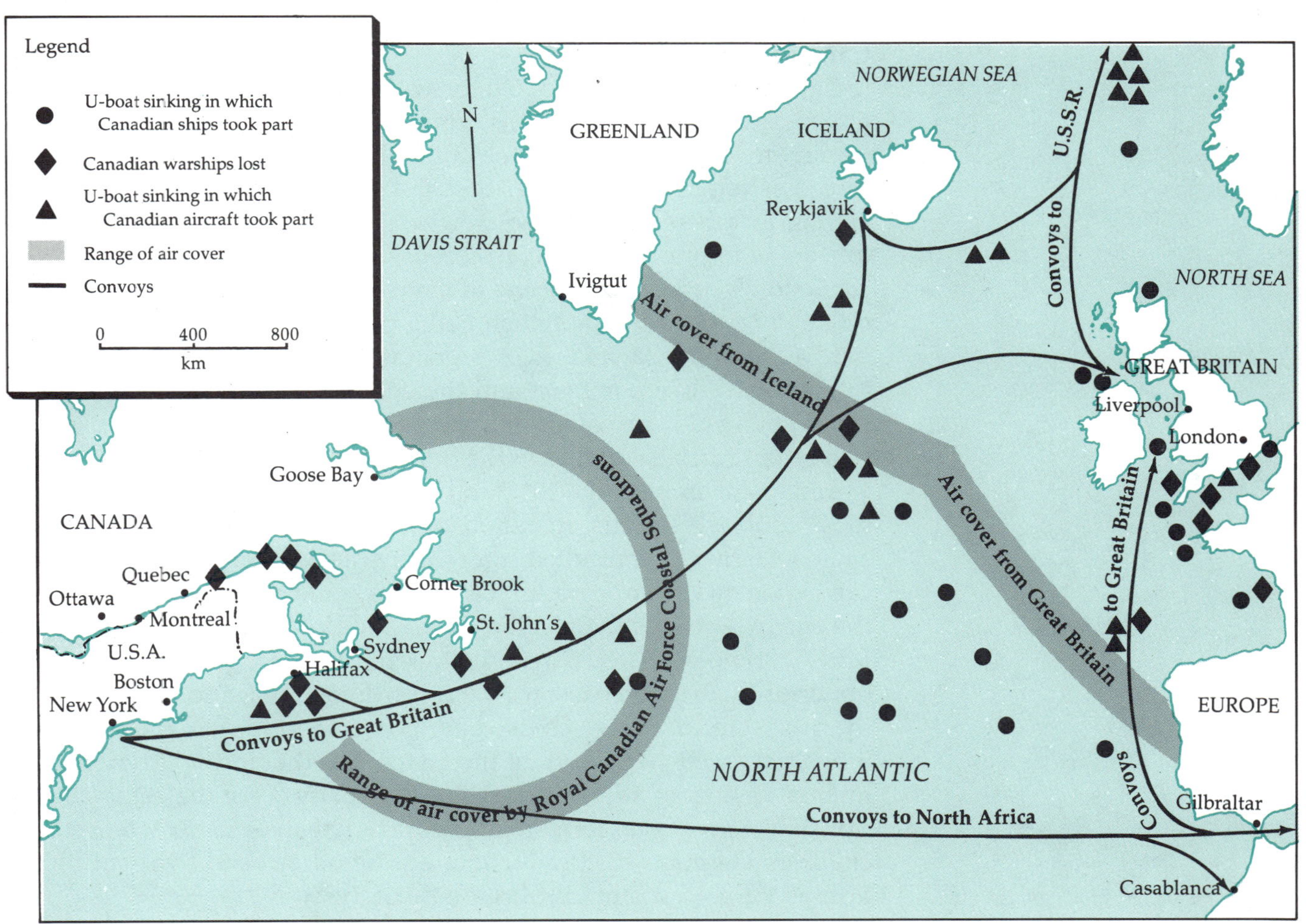

There were women's divisions for each of Canada's armed services. These women, part of the RCAF, are attending Flying Training School at St. Hubert, Québec.

50 000 of them pilots. In addition, since almost all the airplanes used in training were Canadian, the Plan contributed enormously to Canada's aircraft industry. However, most of the nearly 90 000 Canadian graduates of the training program joined the RAF. As part of the agreement between Canada and Britain over the BCATP, the British had agreed to create and fund RCAF squadrons in Britain. But by the end of 1941, only 500 Canadians were serving in the 25 RCAF overseas units. Even by the end of the war, only 40 percent of Canadian air crews served in Canadian squadrons.

Canadian airmen who joined the RAF rubbed shoulders with Poles, Czechs, Norwegians, Belgians, Americans, French, and, of course, Commonwealth flyers. Whether or not they belonged to a Canadian air force mattered less to them than the comradeship which grew up among members of the same crew or squadron. It was senior RCAF officers who pressed for expansion of Canada's own air force. Politicians slowly agreed. By the end of the war, the 25 Canadian squadrons originally created by the British had grown to 48 overseas squadrons, with 40 more in Canada. RCAF squadrons flew fighters, anti-submarine aircraft, dive bombers, and transports. One Canadian squadron fought in the defence of Ceylon (now Sri Lanka) against the Japanese; two others carried supplies in the Burma campaign.

Canadians in both the RAF and the RCAF took part in the largest, most controversial air operation of the war: the bomber offensive against Germany. It resulted from the insistence by British and American exponents of airpower that air forces could win wars by crippling the enemy's production facilities. After the 1940 bombings of London, British Prime Minister Winston Churchill was delighted to have the opportunity to strike back at Hitler. Wartime propaganda insisted that the huge allied raids achieved pinpoint accuracy on military and industrial targets. The truth of the matter was that most of the over 1.2 million victims of the air attacks on Germany were the same as the British victims of the German Luftwaffe—civilians, mainly women and children. German war production, on the other hand, was cut by as little as 1.2 percent until the last phase of the war.

Supporters of the bomber offensive insisted nevertheless that the merciless raids hurt German morale. They also pointed out that, while the attacks did not stop German industry, neither did they allow it to expand to match the growing output of the Allies' factories.

The Germans fought back. Their anti-aircraft guns and swift night fighters found the lumbering allied bombers easy targets. In 1942, bomber crews had less than one chance in three of surviving a 30-mission tour of duty.

In 1943, Canadian bomber squadrons were formed into an all-Canadian formation, 6 Group. As the junior organization in Bomber Command, the Canadians were slow to get the powerful new Lancaster bombers. Their airfields in the north of England were also farthest from Germany and most likely to be fogged in. By June, 6 Group's losses were so high that only one crew in eight could hope to survive its tour of duty. Morale plummeted, but most crews doggedly set out on their missions, knowing that a fiery death was a more likely fate than a German prison camp.

With training, experience, and better aircraft and equipment, 6 Group cut the terrible losses. A new Canadian commander, Air Vice Marshal Mike McEwen, took over in 1944 and insisted on all three. The longer they survived, the better the bomber crews were able to avoid the hazards of their deadly trade. Still, the costs were high. Of 17 701 RCAF members who died in the war, 9880 were killed with Bomber Command. Some of them paid the price for inferior aircraft, inexperience, and a strategy that many then and since considered misguided.

World War II Flying Officer Beurling shakes hands with Prime Minister W.L.M. King. Beurling earned the title of "flying ace" after shooting down 28 enemy aircraft within 4 months.

QUESTIONS

1. What contribution did Canada's navy make to the war in the Atlantic?

2. (a) What, if any, alternatives did the Canadian navy have to adopting a "learn-on-the-job" training program?
(b) What was the price Canada paid for this strategy?

3. What contribution did Canadian pilots make to the war effort?

Winning the War

Although the army began as the least popular of the three Canadian armed forces, by the end of the war 730 625 men and women had joined it. Many were the "NRMA men" who were called up for training under the *National Resources Mobilization Act*. After 1941, they were kept on permanent home defence duty. The rest served overseas.

General A.G.L. McNaughton, commander of the Canadian army in Britain from 1939 to 1943. A former professor of chemical engineering, McNaughton believed that victory would come through better technology, not through sending more and more soldiers into battle.

General A.G.L. McNaughton, who commanded the Canadians in Britain, had pressed for a strong overseas army and insisted that it work together to make a name for Canada, just as the Canadian Corps had done in the First World War. He had won his argument. "This is the kind of army a soldier dreams of commanding," boasted one senior officer, "hard-hitting, beautifully balanced, incredibly powerful." Yet year after year the Canadians waited and trained in England, while the war went on around them.

Most Canadian soldiers adjusted well to garrison life, but the generals and politicians were not content. Prime Minister King was happy to save Canadians' lives, but even he wondered what Canada's voters would think if victory came before the army saw action. That anxiety helped persuade the government to send two battalions to Hong Kong in 1941 and two brigades on the Dieppe raid in August, 1942. Both turned into disasters for the soldiers involved. Both also showed that training was no substitute for battlefield experience. At Dieppe, 907 of the 4963 Canadians who landed died, and 1949 remained as prisoners.

In 1943, General McNaughton agreed that one of his divisions could join the allied armies for the invasion of Sicily. It could then return to England to share its experience with the rest of the Canadian army. The campaign worked out well. By the end of the 38-day struggle, Major-General Guy Simonds and the 1st Division had become experienced fighters with hard-won victories to their credit. In Ottawa, the government enjoyed the favourable publicity. Editors and politicians insisted that more troops be sent. On the basis of the 1st Division's success, King agreed. McNaughton protested, but was ignored. Defence Minister J.L. Ralston, who had never liked McNaughton, removed him from his post on the advice of the British.

In one of his colourful phrases, Winston Churchill had argued for reconquering Europe from its "soft underbelly", the south. It was an error; the mountains and rivers of Italy formed a series of strongholds for skilled German troops. The conditions reminded Canadian generals of Passchendaele in the First World War. It took a month and 1372 dead

Canadian soldiers in the small Italian seaport of Ortona. The Canadian infantry fought German forces here for most of December, 1943, eventually driving them out and capturing the town.

FIGURE 4.2 *The Italian Campaign*

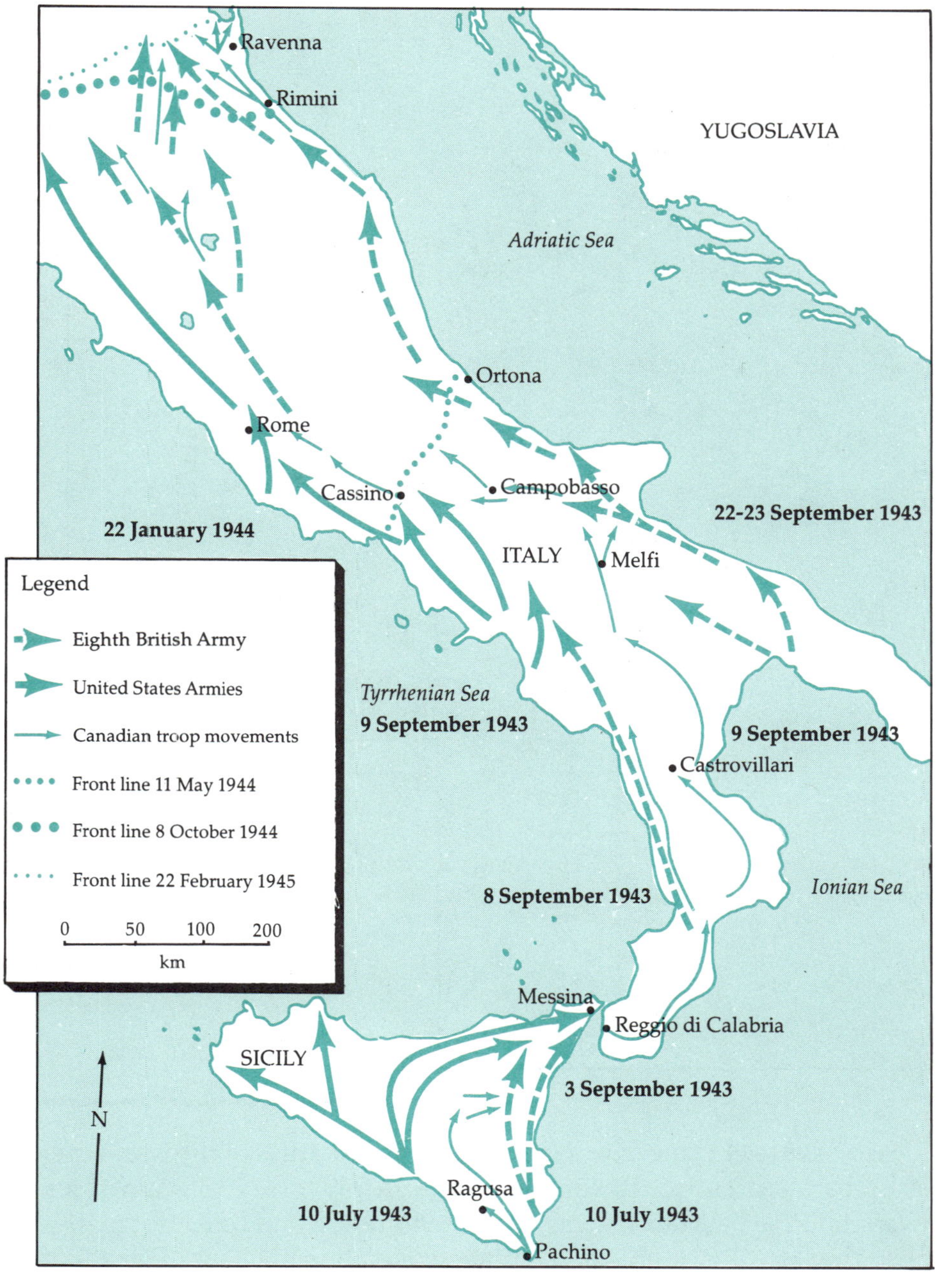

Ravenna
Rimini
YUGOSLAVIA
Adriatic Sea
Ortona
Rome
Cassino
Campobasso
22-23 September 1943
22 January 1944
ITALY
Melfi
Tyrrhenian Sea
9 September 1943
9 September 1943
Castrovillari
8 September 1943
Ionian Sea
Messina
Reggio di Calabria
SICILY
3 September 1943
N
Ragusa
10 July 1943
10 July 1943
Pachino

Legend
Eighth British Army
United States Armies
Canadian troop movements
Front line 11 May 1944
Front line 8 October 1944
Front line 22 February 1945
0 50 100 200
km

Troops of Québec's Royal 22nd Regiment—the Vandoos—en route to Mount Gildone, Campobasso, Italy, 1943. The "soft underbelly" proved to have rugged terrain, which led to bitter fighting.

to capture just one coastal town, Ortona. In the winter of 1943–1944, Canadian troops suffered in mud, rain, and bitter cold, just as their fathers had in the earlier war. In the spring, Canadians helped spearhead the attempt to capture Rome. With heavy losses, they smashed through two German lines, only to find themselves blocked in the narrow Liri Valley. French and American divisions took Rome on June 4, 1944.

FIGURE 4.3 *War in Europe (1944-1945)*

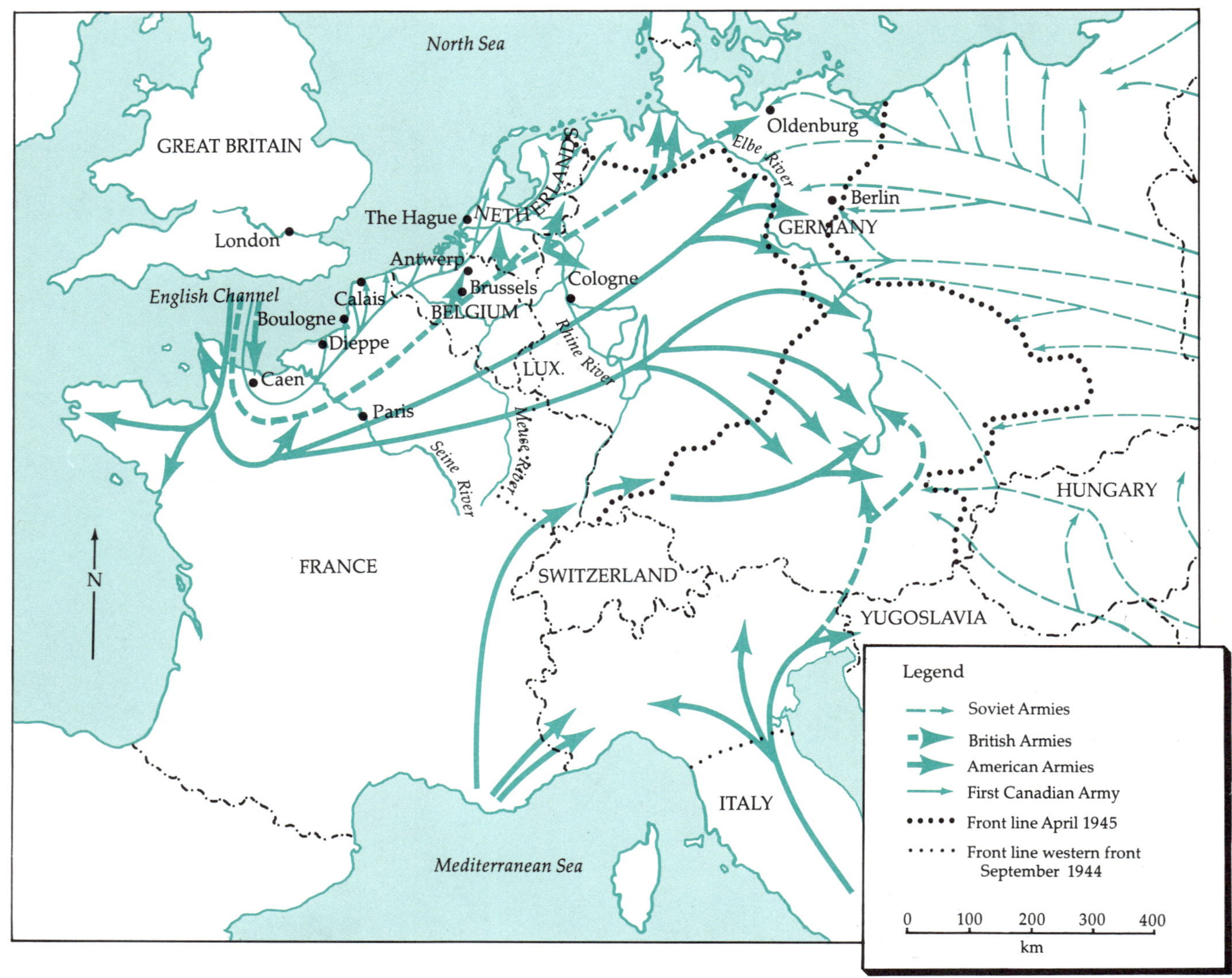

Two days later came one of the most decisive battles of the war. Years of preparation ended on June 6, 1944—D-Day. Five thousand ships swept into the Baie de la Seine; fighters, bombers, and transport planes filled the skies. In the greatest combined operation in history, Canadian sailors, flyers, and soldiers all played a major role. One of the five landing beaches, code-named Juno, had been assigned to the 3rd Canadian Division. A Canadian parachute battalion had dropped down in Normandy the night before. The disaster of Dieppe had shown the need for special training and equipment, and Canadians had learned their lessons well.

Allied planners had expected enormous losses on D-Day and a much easier time once the troops were ashore. They had forgotten that Normandy's thick hedges, stone houses, and narrow lanes made ideal defensive territory for the Germans. Nor had the Canadians expected their tanks and guns to be outmatched by those of the Germans. Nevertheless, the allied strategy worked. The British and three Canadian divisions held the bulk of the German forces on their front and made it easier for the Americans to break out and outflank them. The price of the series of British and Canadian attacks was 18 500 Canadian casualties, one-third of them dead.

The soldiers of the Second World War, whether in Italy or Normandy, shared the fears, misery, and exhaustion of their fathers in the First. It is true that trucks now carried troops on their longer marches, and that obsolete tanks had been adapted as armoured personnel carriers. Nevertheless, Canadian soldiers still marched—each one under a 27 kg burden of a rifle, ammunition, food, water, a shovel, and a shrinking list of items once considered necessities. The earth was their only protection; the first chore when camp was made was to hack a "slit trench" in the dirt. Perhaps Canadian soldiers ate somewhat better than in World War I, but the rations were still monotonous and unsatisfying. War, they quickly found, was run on the army rule of "hurry up and wait"—long stretches of boredom interrupted by periods of sheer terror which grew harder and harder to control.

Canadian soldiers' fears were justified; Canada lost many men on the northern and southern battle fronts. In Normandy, the 3rd Canadian division lost many thousands of men. In Italy, the 2nd Canadian division was ordered to break through the murderous Gothic Line. A month of savage fighting cost 4000 casualties and 1500 cases of battle fatigue. The losses would have to be replaced. Suddenly, the Canadian army faced the crisis which King had tried to avoid: a lack of trained men.

By the summer of 1944, infantry replacement pools were empty. When Major Conn Smythe, owner of the Toronto Maple Leafs, came

A Canadian soldier sits on the edge of a slit trench. These narrow trenches often served as the infantry's only protection from enemy bombs and shells.

Troops of the North Nova Scotian Highlanders and the Highland Light Infantry of Canada landing on the beach at Normandy on D-day, June 6, 1944. Some carry bicycles to get inland more quickly, to where the heaviest fighting awaited.

home to nurse a wound, waiting newspaper reporters learned of the crisis. Untrained men, Smythe claimed, were being drafted to the infantry divisions. Defence Minister Colonel Ralston headed to Europe to see for himself. His conclusion was simple. The NRMA men in Canada were trained soldiers; it was time for them to go overseas. Conscription was necessary. King did not agree. He knew the war was almost won. Surely the army could find the few thousand soldiers it needed from volunteers. Soon the Prime Minister began to suspect a conspiracy: Ralston and the more conservative ministers in his Cabinet were trying to force him out of power. Then he remembered: Ralston had resigned in 1942 over the conscription issue. King still had the letter in his desk. On November 14, 1944, King announced to a shocked Cabinet that Ralston had resigned. General McNaughton, whom Ralston had fired a year earlier, would be the new Minister of National Defence. With dignity, Ralston rose and left.

McNaughton had been certain that his prestige would persuade the NRMA men to volunteer. He was wrong. Threats, promises, and insults had not changed their minds—why should a new minister? In British Columbia, where most of the NRMA men were stationed, the general in command, Major General George Pearkes, reported the futility of the plan to the local press and resigned. Humiliated, McNaughton had to report that his generals could not turn conscripts into volunteers. King was secretly delighted. By describing the generals' advice as a kind of mutiny, he could convince even some of his Québec members into supporting limited conscription. Faced with a decision to sent 15 000 NRMA men overseas, Parliament supported King 143 to 70. Among the opposed were 34 Québec Liberals.

The crisis was not yet over. In Montréal, crowds rioted. At Terrace, B.C., a brigade of NRMA men took over their training camp, pointed guns up and down the railway line, and refused to budge. After a week, senior officers talked them into obeying orders. In the end, about 13 5000 conscripts went overseas. By that time, they were hardly needed. After an October of brutal fighting in northern Europe, the war had moved into a quieter phase for the Canadians. Political pressure to reunite the Canadian army finally brought the two divisions from Italy north to join the main body, which was by now fighting in the Netherlands. In the spring of 1945, Canadians fought long, hard battles in the Netherlands and Germany, but few of the 6000 casualties were conscripts. On May 6, as Canadians completed the liberation of the Netherlands, Germany surrendered. Japan followed suit on August 14. As in 1918, the fortunes of war had made conscription unnecessary—but the crisis had deepened divisions within Canada.

QUESTIONS

1. What was D-Day, and what role did Canada play in this event?
2. Why were Canadian troops concentrated on the European front rather than in the Pacific?
3. How had war changed for infantry soldiers since World War I?
4. How did King's handling of the conscription issue differ from that of Borden during the First World War?

Setting a New Course

After 1942, Canadians and their allies could be confident of victory. That winter, the Soviet army destroyed or captured an entire German army of 550 000 men in the battles of Stalingrad and Leningrad. By the end of the year, the tide turned for the British in the North African campaign. In the Pacific, the Americans began the island-hopping campaign which brought them within bomber range of Japan.

The certainty of victory did not make wartime regulations and shortages easier to bear. Canadians had to get used to ration coupons for gasoline, meat, butter, and sugar. Nylon stockings, a new invention, disappeared. So did bananas and new cars. Canadians had to get by with only a quarter kilogram of sugar a week. Still, by European standards, wartime Canada revelled in luxuries. Visitors to Montréal reported that citizens seemed to ignore the Wartime Prices and Trade Board regulations. Grocers could keep a little extra meat or sugar for long-time customers. An army of officials and an overworked RCMP

A woman shows her new ration book to the photographer. To prevent fraud, numbers became valid when announced by radio and in the newspapers. Canadians found themselves bound by a complicated and growing assortment of government regulations. The benefits of rationing were that, on the whole, people shared fairly in scarce commodities, and there was almost no inflation.

A citizen considers how the war is making shopping difficult. At a time when most people shopped at a neighbourhood grocery store, both buyer and seller had a good idea of the "usual" weekly purchase.

did their best to keep profiteers from using wartime opportunities to make a fast buck, but there were abuses. Nevertheless, most Canadians followed the rules. School children collected cans, bottles, and war savings stamps. High school students drilled in cadet corps or practised first aid. Housewives followed government exhortations to make do, reuse, and do without.

Innovative uses were found for just about everything during the war. Collecting scrap metal, paper, glass, and even bones also gave people a feeling that they were contributing to the war effort. Why was it important to get people involved?

CLOSE-UP

So You Want a War Job

The war touched almost every aspect of Canadians' lives. In 1942, Charles Clay, an editor of the *Winnipeg Free Press*, wrote a series of articles which were republished as a book entitled *So You Want a War Job!* It instructed people about how they could make their greatest contribution to the war effort. Some of his suggestions follow.

1. War costs plenty. Canadians should contribute as much as possible to the war effort, whether they follow the example of some Alberta farmers who pledged a portion of their crops, or an Italian Canadian railway worker, who gave all his wages over $1.30 a day, the amount paid to a private in the army. War-work funds, fund drives, gifts, war savings certificates, and war stamps are also encouraged.

2. Keep the home fires burning. Pay your personal taxes without looking for loopholes, and cut down on personal consumption of such luxuries as clothing.

3. Don't holiday outside Canada; do welcome United States tourists bringing needed American dollars.
4. Don't waste anything. Salvage glass, paper, steel, rags, aluminum foil, fats, bones, and turn them over during salvage campaigns. They are all useful.
5. Guard your good health, and be physically fit.
6. Don't believe Nazi propaganda. Have stout hearts; believe in the allied cause and eventual victory.
7. As much as possible, carry on as in normal times. Hold your usual meetings, do your usual hobbies, take part in sports.
8. Kill rumours. Don't spread war gossip.
9. Keep your mouth shut, please. Don't talk about anything you know about ships, railways, troops, anything even slightly connected to the war.
10. Don't complain, but if you have constructive criticism, voice it.
11. Maintain a sensible attitude; don't hate your neighbours because they come from Europe.

—Adapted from Clay, Charles, *So You Want a War Job!* Toronto: Oxford University Press, 1942.

QUESTIONS

1. Which of the "war jobs" described in the excerpt were concrete contributions to the war effort? Which benefited morale?
2. Are both contributions of equal value to a nation at war? Give reasons for your answer.

Specimen of a Canadian war bond

Most Canadians also made money. The WPTB's regulations kept inflation to only 11.1 percent between December 1941 and December 1945. Pay and prices alike were frozen; wages were steady, and there was plenty of overtime. The government did its best to make sure that the new wealth would not lead to inflation, as it did in the First World War. High taxes and Victory Bond sales drained away thousands of millions of dollars that might have fuelled inflation. Unemployment insurance, which had been rejected as too expensive in the 1920's and 1930's, became law in 1940 largely because the premiums would help use up extra spending power. The government also knew that the huge reserves collected when unemployment rates were close to zero would be needed after the war.

Do you think these war bond advertisements were effective? What sentiments do they evoke?

Despite their wartime prosperity, most Canadians believed that the postwar period would be harsh. Many remembered the unemployment which followed the previous war, and no-one could forget the Depression. Wartime Canada lived with a paradox. People desperately wanted the war to end, but they also feared what would follow.

The adoption of unemployment insurance in 1940 was only the first of many changes in social programs which resulted in large part from the war. Between the wars, most Canadian opinion leaders had opposed government social programs, largely because of the expense. Families were supposed to look after their own problems. When they obviously could not, as during the Depression, politicians and commentators merely deplored the decline of old-fashioned values.

The Second World War reminded Canadians of something they had learned during the First: the government could solve social problems. To encourage Canadians' commitment to "total war", politicians had to promise them a better deal. Arthur Meighen, who had replaced the defeated Robert Manion as Conservative leader, was himself defeated by the CCF in a by-election in 1942. Younger Conservatives now had an argument for pushing more radical ideas: a commitment to full employment, free collective bargaining by unions, and low-cost housing. Manitoba's Premier, John Bracken, one of the few remaining Progressives, agreed to become the new party leader, on the condition that the party be renamed the "Progressive Conservatives". The name was a sign of the times.

The rise of the CCF was another sign of changing social attitudes. In 1940, J.S. Woodsworth's party seemed doomed by its pre-war pacifism. Instead, the war gave the CCF a new lease on life. The first indication came in 1941 in British Columbia, when voters gave the CCF more seats than either the Liberals or the Conservatives. Only a coalition of the two kept the CCF from power. In July, 1943, the CCF in Ontario came from nowhere to miss victory by only four seats. A Gallup poll taken in September, 1943 reported the CCF's national support to be slightly ahead of either the Liberals' or the Conservatives'.

The rise of trade unions was still another symptom of changing times. A shortage of labour and wage controls both gave unions an opportunity to win members. By 1943, workers' militancy surprised even the union leaders. It was the worst year for strikes since 1919, despite the fact that strikes were illegal under wartime regulations. Steelworkers closed the huge mills at Sydney, Nova Scotia and Sault Ste. Marie, Ontario. When the steelworkers got an increase, coal miners in British Columbia and Alberta also walked out. More than wages and hours, the workers' right to bargaining was of concern to union leaders. President Roosevelt's New Deal had given American unions the right to bargain in 1935. Faced with a wartime crisis, Canada followed suit in 1944. The National War Labour Order finally established the legal right of unions to win recognition and to bargain fairly with employers without needing to resort to a strike.

More social reforms followed. In Britain, a commission headed by William Beveridge proposed a far-reaching social program that would protect citizens against the economic hardships of unemployment, sickness, and old age. The report promised a war-weary Britain that the grim past would not return. His ideas also reached Canada, where they triggered a battle between government factions over postwar reconstruction.

Prime Minister King was alarmed by the growing popularity of the CCF and labour unions, and the support for Beveridge-style policies. The idea of family allowances as a way to overcome the poverty of people with large families particularly shocked him. He felt that "handouts" would sap people's sense of responsibility. The popularity of the CCF in the polls gave King second thoughts. So did a reminder from his hardworking secretary, J.W. Pickersgill, that he himself had been raised by a mother on a government war pension. King also came to realize that the ministers who opposed family allowances were the same ones who supported conscription—and so opposed King himself.

When Parliament met on January 24, 1944, little reference was made to the war. Instead, Canadians were promised a postwar future in which the government would be a full partner in their welfare. Family allowances would save large families from poverty. A *National Housing Act* would help the majority of Canadians achieve the dream of becoming home-owners. The most generous veterans' program of any country promised returning service men and women the opportunities for training, education, and financial security which the veterans of 1918 had sought in vain. And that was only the beginning.

As the war ended in Europe, Canadians faced a range of political choices. In June, 1944, the CCF had swept Saskatchewan and its leaders believed they could become a national party. In Alberta, Social

Credit was powerful. Bracken's Progressive Conservatives were confident that they could beat the war-weary Liberals. To rally business backers, they played down their progressive ideas; to gain patriotic support, they promised conscription for the continuing war with Japan. In Québec, a host of independents and candidates from small parties reflected *Canadien* bitterness over wartime grievances and betrayals. King stuck to his social reforms. For the campaign, his advisors devised the slogan "A New Social Order" and set out to recapture votes from the CCF. On June 11, 1945, Canadians made their decision.

The outcome of the election proved that most Canadians wanted social programs without socialism. Though the CCF doubled its support and quadrupled its seats to a total of 28, it fell far short of its expectations. The Progressive Conservatives won only 67 seats. In Alberta, the Social Credit Party, led by Ernest Manning, won 10 seats. Ten of the seats from Québec were held by either independents or small-party candidates; one of the latter was the only Communist M.P. in Canadian history. And King's "New Social Order" won the Liberals a modest majority, with 125 seats.

The end of the war saw national elections in other democracies as well, Britain, the United States, and Australia among them. In Britain and Australia, voters rejected their wartime leaders. By a narrow margin, King and the Liberals survived. They had promised Canada a new social order; now they would have to create it.

QUESTIONS

1. How did Canadians on the home front contribute to the war effort?

2. What measures did the government take to prevent inflation during the war?

3. (a) Why were the war years an opportune time for social reforms?
(b) How did the federal government react to this change in the public mood?

4. (a) What did King's 1945 election slogan "A New Social Order" mean?
(b) Why was it successful in winning votes for the Liberals?

Chapter Summary

The war that began in 1939 changed the world. It involved more countries and killed more people than any previous war, and resulted in a new world map. Although Canada was far from any battlefront, it was deeply affected by the conflict. The need for munitions revived Canada's economy and modernized industrial plants. Second World War veterans would be returning to a more prosperous Canada than the one they had left.

IN REVIEW

1. In what ways did C.D. Howe make patriotism profitable for Canadians?
2. Under conscription, men could be forced into the armed forces. Would you have voted for or against conscription in the April, 1942 referendum? Why?
3. What made the NRMA men unpopular with some Canadians at home and with Canadian soldiers in Europe?
4. In retrospect, how did "the fortunes of war" make forcing the NRMA men overseas an unnecessary move?
5. What made 1944 a good year for unions to add to their membership? Why?

APPLYING YOUR KNOWLEDGE

1. In 1939, Prime Minister King said of the new European war, "This is not our war." If a war broke out in Europe today, do you think the present Prime Minister would say the same thing? Why or why not?
2. **(a)** Why did King turn the conscription issue over to a plebiscite?
   (b) Was Québec right to complain about his doing so?
3. Charles Clay suggested (page 129) that Canadians should not hate their neighbours "because they come from Europe". Which nationalities were most likely to be "hated"? Do you think this was fair?
4. Why was the United States able to conscript men for overseas service during the two World Wars, without the sort of public controversy that took place in Canada?

FURTHER INVESTIGATION

1. The widespread killing of Jews in Nazi Germany is known as the Holocaust. Do research to discover why the Jews became the main targets for the Nazis' plan of annihilation.
2. The allied invasion of continental Europe began on D-Day (June 6, 1944). What sorts of problems faced the men who planned the invasion?
3. Choose a Second World War battle which interests you, and find out as much as you can about it.

C H A P T E R 5

First of the Middle Powers

By early in 1945, most Canadians realized the war in Europe would soon end. It was time to plan for the postwar world. In planning for the future, Canadians were as concerned with the international community as with Canada. It is for this reason that Canada became a founding member of the new forum for peaceful discussion of world conflicts—the United Nations.

At home, Canadians looked forward to returning to normal—working, settling down, and raising families. The late 1940's and the 1950's were years of economic growth and wealth. Government policies once again welcomed immigrants. By the end of the 1950's, Canada experienced a population boom that would influence the nature of Canadian society for decades to come. Other changes, too, occurred on the political front, as the government became ever more involved in Canadians' lives. Even the map of Canada changed when, in 1949, Newfoundland become Canada's tenth province.

As you read this chapter, you will discover some answers to these questions:

- *How did Canada become a "middle power"?*
- *What did this status mean for Canadian involvement in world affairs?*
- *What changes occurred in Canada during the late 1940's and the 1950's?*
- *How and why was the long reign of the Liberal Party in the twentieth century interrupted in 1957?*
- *Why did the widespread affluence and content of the 1950's turn to turmoil and problems by the start of the 1960's?*

Canada's World Role

On January 24, 1944, the day that Prime Minister King presented his postwar social program to Parliament, Lord Halifax, Britain's ambassador to the United States, was speaking before a Toronto audience. In the course of his speech, Lord Halifax asked his audience whether postwar Canada would choose "national isolation" or join in making the British Empire "a beneficent world force". When King heard of it, he was furious at this "conspiracy on the part of the Imperialists". His anger was unnecessary. By 1944, most Canadians wanted Canada to play its own role in the world.

From 1921 to 1945, King controlled every part of Canada's foreign policy. He did so because he believed that issues concerning war and the Empire would easily break Canada's fragile unity. His favourite answer to questions about Canada's future was "Parliament will decide." In reality, however, King was determined that Parliament would have few decisions to make. His handling of the conscription issue showed his approach clearly: delay and compromise.

King's cautious policy led him to avoid consulting with the Allies about strategy during the war. Consultation could lead to commitment. Twice, when Franklin D. Roosevelt and Winston Churchill met in Québec City to plan strategy, King appeared in the official photographs but took no part in the serious business. King felt humiliated that Canadians admired Churchill and Roosevelt as war leaders, but not their own Prime Minister. It was the price he paid for his policy of caution.

In fact, the British and the Americans had little desire to involve Canada in wartime decisions. Those American officials who no longer saw Canada as a British colony now lumped it instead with other minor nations of the western hemisphere such as Costa Rica or Colombia. This attitude of the United States towards Canada was made clear in 1942. Thousands of U.S. army engineers moved into the Yukon and northern Alberta to build the Alaska Highway—without asking or even informing Canadian officials. Thousands more Americans poured into Newfoundland during the course of the war. Though Newfoundland was a British colony, Canada regarded it as a future province. The Canadian garrison of Newfoundland was increased to keep pace with the Americans. Nor had the United States ever officially admitted

Ships such as this docking at Halifax loaded with veterans and refugees were greeted by a Canada changed after six years of war.

Canada's 1881 claim to the Arctic. Therefore, when the Americans built air bases in the eastern Arctic as stopovers on the flight to Europe, Canada made arrangements to buy them. There was no denying that, by the end of the war, the United States had replaced Britain as Canada's closest friend and ally in political, economic, and social matters. Still, King and his government felt that the Americans had an alarming tendency to make themselves at home in Canada.

While King managed to steer clear of strategic issues, his officials in the Department of External Affairs felt that Canada must have a voice in matters of direct concern to the country. For instance, since Canada provided much of the Allies' food, Canadians insisted on being included in the Combined Food Board, the organization which decided on the distribution of food among the Allies. After the hostilities had ended, Canadians believed they had a contribution to make in the areas of atomic energy and disarmament. After all, Canadian scientists and Canadian uranium had played a part in the early development of the atomic bomb. The officials of the Department of External Affairs described this approach to Canada's world role as the "functional principle". In the words of one of them, Hume Wrong, "the influence of the various countries should be greatest in connection with those matters with which they are most directly concerned".

The functional principle fitted in well with most Canadians' view of their country's role in the postwar world. Immediately after the war, Canada was the fourth or fifth most powerful and prosperous country in the world, with its large navy and air force, booming industries, and undamaged economy. Still, few Canadians considered Canada one of the "great powers". The United States led the world in wealth; the Soviet Union, in military might. China, although exhausted by internal war and invasion, had to be considered a great power by virtue of its vast population. Britain and France, also crippled by war, retained their status as world leaders for historic reasons. Canada's place in the world was not among these nations. Rather, in the years following the war, Canada emerged as a leader among the "middle powers". In the postwar world, Canada could be useful, creative, and influential precisely because it was not strong enough to threaten to dominate any nation, but was prosperous enough to be independent.

The Formation of the United Nations

In all, 50 countries met to sign the United Nations charter. The document's main outlines followed a draft worked out by the great powers at Dumbarton Oaks in Washington, D.C., a year earlier. Lester Pearson and other Canadian diplomats tried to persuade the other nations that the middle powers deserved special recognition as the only countries strong enough to share the real costs and burdens of the United Nations. Their attempt failed. The only nations which would have special consideration would be the five great powers, with their veto. All other members would be considered as equals.

The shape of the postwar world became clear when the allied countries and some neutral nations met in San Francisco in June, 1945 to plan the United Nations. The failure of the League of Nations to avert World War II had shown that a new body, with true political power, was needed. This power against aggressors would be exercised through a Security Council consisting of 12 members. The five great powers promptly insisted not only on permanent membership on the Security Council, but also on a right to veto any U.N. action. The other seven seats could be rotated among other nations on a temporary basis. Some smaller powers, notably Australia and New Zealand, raged at the arrogance of the five. They felt certain that the other members of the

The birth of the United Nations at San Francisco on June 26, 1945. How did the U.N. differ from the League of Nations?

United Nations would be powerless in the face of the veto. However, the functional principle dictated that those with power should be concerned with affairs in which power mattered. The five great powers had their way.

Canada, economically strong after war, became part of the United Nations Relief and Rehabilitation Agency. The Canadian role in the creation of the atomic bomb led Canada to join the Atomic Energy Commission—as the only member from outside the Security Council. In matters of world policy, Canada considered itself a disinterested observer which was nevertheless very much interested in preserving peace.

In 1946, Prime Minister King appointed Louis St. Laurent as head of the Department of External Affairs. St. Laurent, who was of Irish and *Canadien* origins, had a keen interest in the world and the role Canada could play in it. His roots helped make St. Laurent sensitive to the claims of small nations, and sympathetic to the leaders of countries that had been ruled by Britain. In 1945, Britain's new Labour Party government carried through a wartime promise to grant independence to the countries of its Indian and southeast Asian Empire. It was Louis St. Laurent who convinced the new Prime Minister of India, Jawaharlal Nehru, to remain in the British Commonwealth after India finally achieved independence in 1947. Nehru's example, in turn, persuaded most of the other former British colonies and possessions to join the increasingly multi-racial Commonwealth.

FIGURE 5.1 *The Commonwealth (1980)*

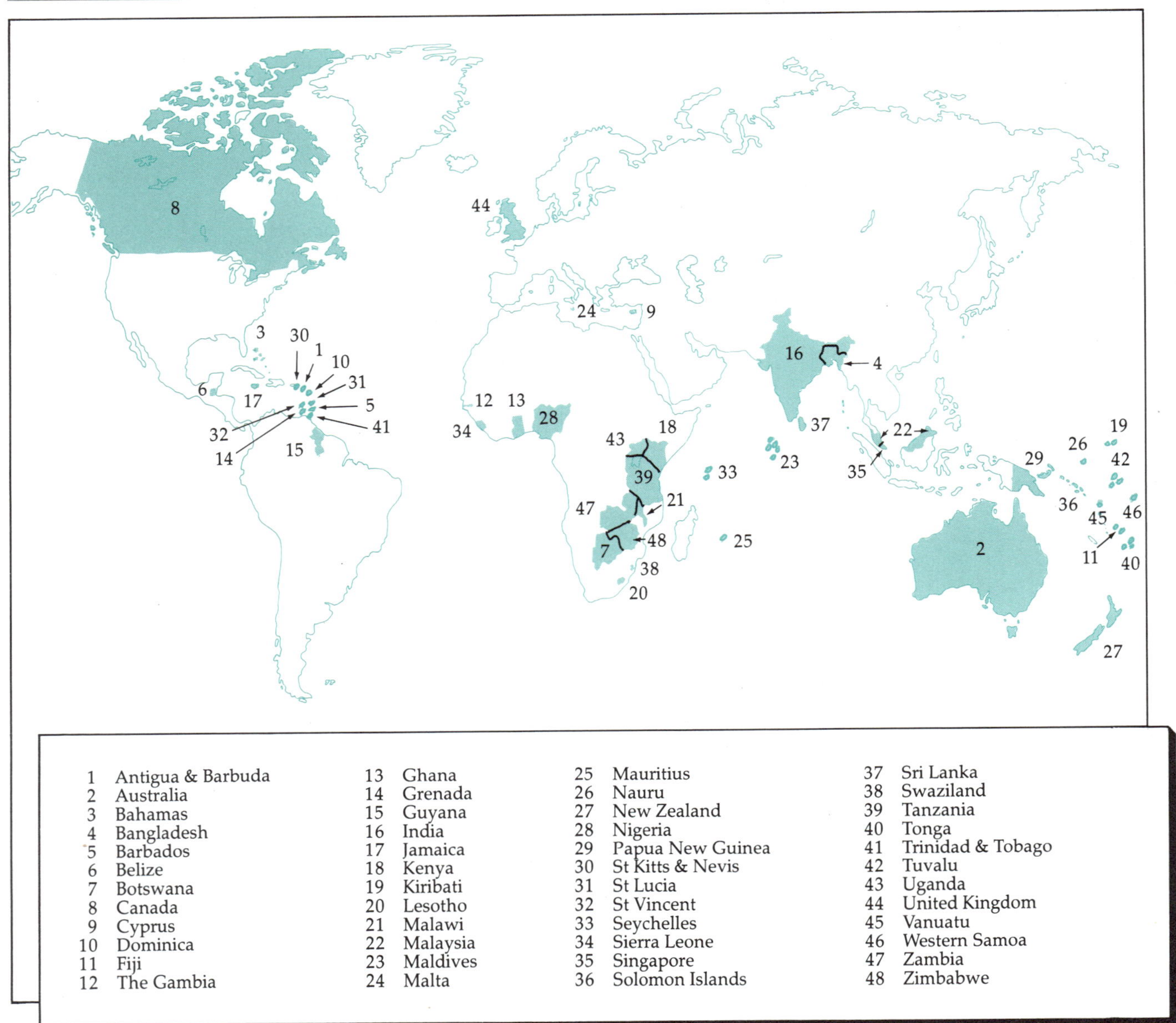

Despite Canada's active membership in the Commonwealth, the fact remained that Canada was increasingly tied to the United States. After the war, Canadians found that the United States remained anxious about the security of the North American continent, particularly the nearly empty Arctic. On February 13, 1947, the two nations came to an agreement about the role of Canada's armed forces in the joint defence of North America. Military bases, facilities, and training would gradually come to be shared between the two countries.

A year later, Canadian economic advisers worked to link the two countries even more closely. They worried about how Canada's economy could prosper otherwise. Together with American officials, they produced a draft scheme for virtual free trade with the United States. Under the agreement, all customs barriers would come down within five years. News of the deal reached Prime Minister King on May 5, 1948, during his preparations for retirement. King reacted with outrage. "I would never cease to be a Liberal or a British citizen," he wrote, "and if I thought there was a danger of Canada being placed at the mercy of powerful financial interests in the United States, and if that was done by my own party, I would get out and oppose them openly."

King could retire in peace. The free trade scheme was shelved. Canada overcame its postwar economic difficulties through strict, though temporary, foreign exchange controls. A Liberal convention chose Louis St. Laurent as the new party leader. Five months later King had retired, and on November 15, 1948, St. Laurent became Prime Minister.

QUESTIONS

1. How did King's policy of delay and compromise influence American attitudes toward Canada?

2. What was the "functional principle"? Give one example of how it was applied to Canada's foreign policy.

3. (a) What advantages might Canada enjoy as a middle power?
(b) What might be some disadvantages of middle power status?

4. (a) What prompted the 1948 free trade initiative?
(b) Why did this attempt to reach a free trade agreement fail?

Canada and the Cold War

In 1939, Prime Minister King had met the outbreak of war with the despairing prophecy that either Hitler or Stalin would win. Like many Canadians, he saw little difference between two grim tyrannies. But when the Soviets joined the Allies, fought valiantly, and suffered terrible losses, opinions softened. So much Canadian equipment was shipped to the U.S.S.R. that Canadian-made radios and weapons bore labels in Russian as well as English. In Canada, the Communist Party profited from wartime respectability to expand its influence in the labour movement. Since communists opposed wartime strikes—because they wanted nothing to hurt support for the Soviet war effort—employers preferred them to CCF sympathizers and those union members who did walk out for better pay or working conditions.

Just days after the war ended on all fronts, something happened to change this attitude. On September 5, 1945, a cypher clerk at the Soviet embassy in Ottawa gathered up secret material and set out to hand it

The Cold War

The term "Cold War" was first used by U.S. presidential adviser Bernard Baruch in 1947. It described the situation that developed between the United States and the Soviet Union and their respective allies in the aftermath of World War II. The Cold War was fought with politics, economics, and propaganda rather than weapons, because both sides feared nuclear war.

Igor Gouzenko caused a furor when he defected, exposing an extensive Soviet spy ring in Canada. In public appearances, he always wore a hood to conceal his identity. He is shown here on a 1966 television program promoting his novel, The Fall of a Titan.

over to Canadian authorities. For two terrifying days, Igor Gouzenko tried to find someone in charge who would take him seriously. When someone finally did, Canada found itself caught in the opening rounds of the Cold War. Gouzenko's material revealed that Canada's Soviet ally had built a spy ring which extended into the Prime Minister's own office. The Soviet Union's primary goal was to steal the secrets of the atomic bomb. Many of the agents unmasked by Gouzenko believed that the North American monopoly on atomic weapons was a threat to the U.S.S.R.

Few Canadians wanted a Cold War to replace the war with Hitler. However, they had little choice. Canada's close relations with the United States made it impossible to remain completely neutral. A series of takeovers of eastern European countries by the Soviet Union, culminating in the overthrow of a social-democratic government in Czechoslovakia in March, 1948, also influenced Canadian opinion. At home, some of the energy of the Labour movement after the war was drained by a struggle between CCF members and communists for control of key unions in British Columbia and Ontario. Maurice Duplessis, having been defeated in the 1939 Québec election, had made a comeback as premier in 1944. Now, the Cold War gave him an excuse for using the notorious Padlock Law against critics of his *Union Nationale* government.

Despite the change in public opinion, and the urging of the Progressive Conservatives, Canada refused to outlaw the Communist Party. Canadians were generally spared the "witch hunts" which took place in the United States. There, the House Un-American Activities Committee under Senator Joseph McCarthy accused thousands of Americans of being communists or sympathizers. Most of the accused lost their liberty, their jobs, their friends, or, through suicide, even their lives. Some Canadian communists, especially in the labour movement, did suffer because of their beliefs and because they used their influence to back Soviet interests. However, the attack on communism in Canada was never so fierce as in the United States. Influential former sympathizers could repent their enthusiasm for communism without being exposed or dismissed.

Canada was also a moderate in the global Cold War. Though its alliance was never in question, geography had placed Canada squarely between the two world superpowers. Americans and many Europeans believed that the worldwide revolution predicted by communists was inevitable. Canada's ambassador to the Soviet Union, Dana Wilgress, said that the U.S.S.R. was anxious to avoid war and rebuild, but was also determined to keep its gains in eastern Europe. After the war, the Soviet Union, unlike other nations, had retained its wartime army. It did so because the troops were needed to occupy its new eastern European acquisitions and because, not having the atomic bomb, it feared attack by the United States. Weakened by the war and unprepared, other nations would be no match for the Soviet steamroller. Nor would the United Nations, frozen by a Soviet veto, be of any help.

The answer to the dilemma, largely formulated by Canadian diplomats, was an alliance of North Atlantic nations. The treaty signed on April 4, 1949, which brought the North Atlantic Treaty Organization (NATO) into being, had many advantages. It would prevent the United States from retreating into isolationism, and lead the Americans to share a commitment to Europe, which they had fulfilled only belatedly in the two World Wars. It would give western Europe the confidence and resources to defend itself. With 12 (presently 16) nations involved, individual countries could spend less on their own defence. In Canada, it would please pacifists that the alliance contained a clause which committed the member nations to trade and cultural exchanges in addition to defence.

The creation of NATO led western nations to believe that the problems of the Cold War were solved. A little over a year later, an event on the opposite side of the world shattered their complacency. Korea, an ancient kingdom which had become a Japanese colony in 1910, had been split in 1945 at the 38th parallel, into a Soviet-dominated North and an American-dominated South. On June 25, 1950, the North Korean army, equipped by the Soviets, crashed across the dividing line of the 38th parallel, determined to unite the country under a communist government.

FIGURE 5.2 *NATO Nations*

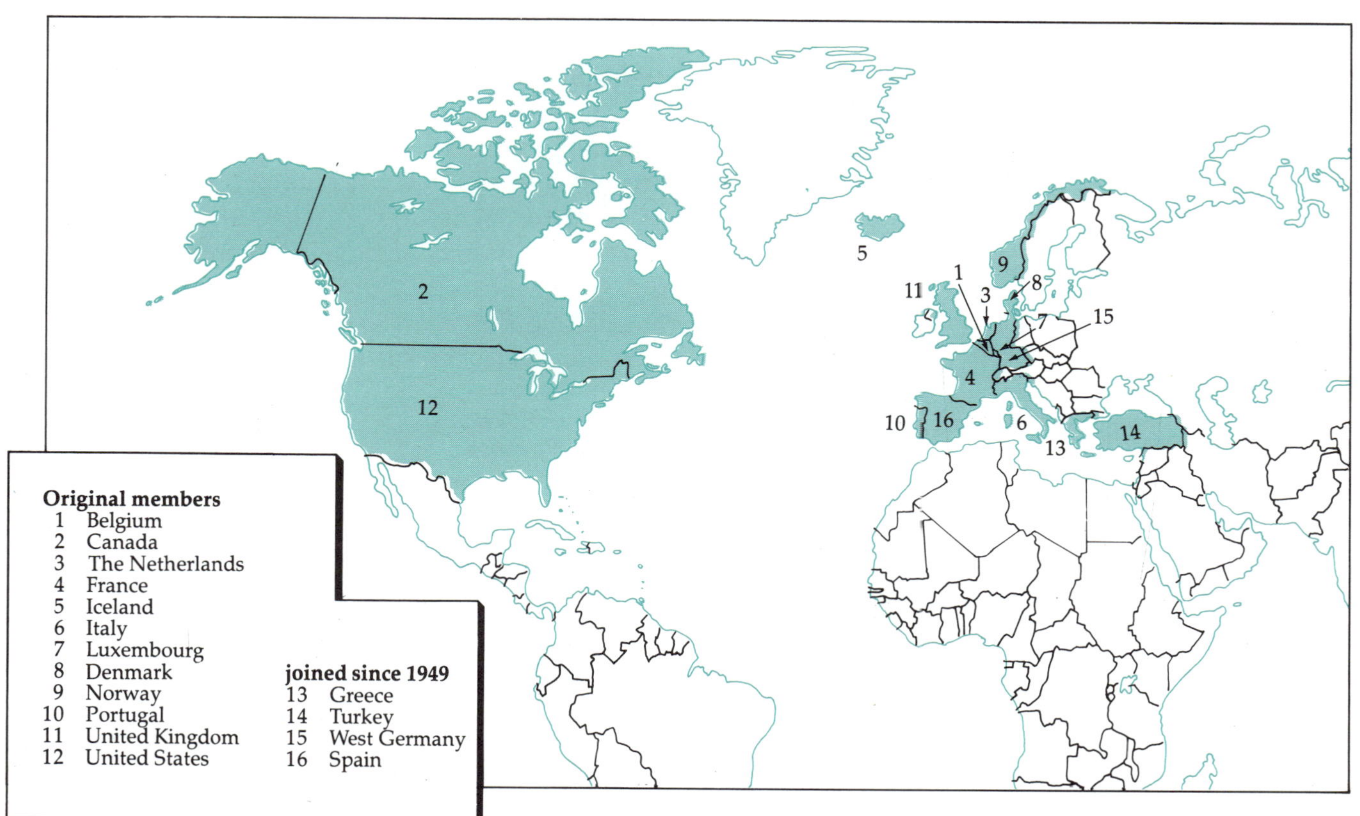

Was this the Soviet agression which would precipitate another world war? The United Nations Security Council was called into session. For once, the U.S.S.R. would not exercise its veto. Its representative's seat was empty, since the U.S.S.R. was boycotting the United Nations because the other members would not recognize the new communist regime in China. The United Nations acted swiftly without the Soviet veto. An American army of occupation stationed in Japan sent troops. Canada ordered destroyers from Esquimalt to join the U.N. effort. In August, 1950, Canada agreed to send soldiers as well. A special Canadian brigade was recruited which would be available for United Nations service. By March, 1951, its first units saw action. In late 1950, Chinese communists joined the North Koreans in their struggle against the South Korean and United Nations forces. The war raged up and down the narrow peninsula, finally settling near the 38th parallel. By the armistice, on June 8, 1953, Canada had sent 21 940 soldiers and 3600 sailors, of whom 312 died in action.

A few months of the Korean War raised a chilling thought in the minds of NATO leaders. Almost the entire American field army was in the Far East; was the Korean War a Soviet plot to divert their forces and leave Europe defenceless? In the autumn of 1950, NATO began seriously to rearm. Canada did its share. In 1949, Canada had spent $361 million—2.2 percent of its gross national product—on defence. By 1953, Canada was committed to spending nearly $2 thousand million, 7.6 percent of its GNP. Surplus weapons, an infantry brigade, and 12 fighter squadrons were sent to Europe. To meet any Soviet submarine threat, the navy was modernized with Canadian-built destroyer escorts. Nine air interceptor squadrons were formed to defend Canada's skies.

Canadians were not unanimous about the issues raised by the Cold War and Canada's active role in NATO. Peace petitioners stood on street corners, canvassing for signatures to take Canada out of the alliance. The editors of some political magazines denounced NATO. Many Conservative politicians—though rarely party leaders—lamented that Canada was becoming an American satellite. In Québec, opinion polls showed only modest enthusiasm for involvement in the

The Canadian ship H.M.C.S. Nootka, *firing at an enemy target in Songjin, South Korea. Other Canadians served with the Commonwealth Division near the 38th parallel. Why did Canadians go to Korea but not to Vietnam?*

Drop in the Bucket
"Doesn't it seem kind of academic to be debating whether WE should have nuclear weapons?"

Korean War and NATO. Premier Duplessis charged that rearmament and the emergency powers associated with the Korean struggle were a ploy to rob Québec of its provincial powers. Yet the Liberals, under their new leader St. Laurent, had held onto power with an overwhelming majority in the 1949 election. They took 193 seats, against the Progressive Conservatives' 41, the CCF's 13, and Social Credit's 10. In 1953, when the war ended, they did nearly as well, winning 171 seats. In both elections, Québec voted overwhelmingly for St. Laurent and his Liberals.

As always, concerns about possible divisions at home affected Canada's overseas commitments. But the most important factor in shaping Canada's world role was its team of talented, moderate diplomats, with their desire to be "helpful fixers" in the cause of preventing war. In 1948, when India and Pakistan went to war over the border state of Kashmir, both its United Nations and its Commonwealth ties prompted Canada to send military officers to be truce observers. Other observers served in Palestine, watching over the fragile peace between the tiny new state of Israel and its angry Arab neighbours. In 1954, Canada joined India and Poland in forming an International Control Commission, to try to bring peace to Cambodia, Laos, and a divided Vietnam. In later conflicts in Indochina and Egypt, too, Canada demonstrated what the "helpful fixers" of a middle power could accomplish.

In 1949 the Soviet Union became a nuclear power. Fearful of the consequences of war between the two Superpowers, ban the bomb marches took place in Canada and throughout the world.

CLOSE-UP

The Suez Canal Crisis

The Suez Canal crisis of 1956 showed Canadians the potential—and the problems—of their status as a middle power.

The French had constructed the Suez Canal between the Mediterranean Sea and the Red Sea in the 1860's. Soon after, the British had bought a majority of shares in the Suez Canal Company, to make the canal part of their route to India. Then they had occupied Egypt. In 1955, with Britain's eastern Empire gone, British Prime Minister Sir Anthony Eden agreed to withdraw the garrison from Egypt.

That was one triumph for Egypt's leader, Colonel Gamal Abdel Nasser. Another would be the completion of the Aswan High Dam across the Nile. In 1956, because of Nasser's dealings with the Soviet Union, Britain and the United States cut off aid for the Aswan project. In return, Nasser seized the Suez Canal Company. He also stepped up guerrilla attacks on Israel, and invited the Soviets to help Egypt finish the dam. Eden was furious. He was sure that the Americans and the Commonwealth shared his viewpoint.

The Commonwealth, with the exception of Australia and New Zealand, did not. Newer members were not sympathetic to what they saw as old-fashioned British imperialism. As for Canada, it had no interest in who owned the canal, but a great deal of interest in the new members of the Commonwealth. Above all, Canada realized what Eden did not: that the Americans might disapprove of Nasser's action, but would not approve of the violent retaliation Eden was planning.

France, on the other hand, sided with Britain. So did Israel. It was planned that Israel would strike first, on November 1, 1956; then the French and British would use the attack as a pretext to step in and guard the vital international waterway. If Nasser's government was toppled by the attack, all three attackers would be pleased.

To Canada, this plan promised disaster. Canada's two parent nations would be set against its powerful neighbour, the United States. The newer Commonwealth nations would be outraged, and the Soviet Union delighted.

On October 29, Israeli paratroops struck. On October 30, Britain and France ordered both Egypt and Israel to stay 16 km away from the canal—preventing any Egyptian attempt to meet the Israeli invasion. Only then were Canada and the other Commonwealth countries informed. Next, the Royal Air Force moved to

Canadian soldiers serving with the United Nations Emergency Force to keep the peace along the Egypt-Israel frontier. Canadian troops would repeat this role in crises such as the Congo (1960), Cyprus (1964), and along the Iran-Iraq border (1988).

bomb Egyptian airfields, and an Anglo-French invasion force was organized to land near the canal.

The Soviet Union issued an ultimatum: Atomic bombs would rain down on London and Paris if the invasion did not end. Far from being toppled, Nasser's government gained popular support. The Americans were furious with the British. Secretary of State John Foster Dulles raged at Lester Pearson, now Canadian Secretary of State for External Affairs: "They've damaged the whole cause of freedom by placing us in an inferior position morally to the Russians." When the U.N. Security Council ordered Israel to withdraw, Britain and France used their vetoes for the first time. Yugoslavia used a ploy which the western allies had used earlier against the Soviet Union: It moved to have the issue taken before the U.N. General Assembly. There, 65 nations supported a resolution denouncing the invasion and ordering a cease-fire. Canada abstained.

Canada was divided over the issue. The Gallup poll showed that a small majority supported the British invasion. Prime Minister St. Laurent and his government certainly did not. He and Pearson had done their best to prevent a breach of international law and to keep NATO allies together. The British and French had not only ignored them but had kept their true plans secret. Then Eden had asked Canada for help in what St. Laurent and Pearson saw as an act of imperialism. The reply was that there would be no help at all. The British had counted on Canada; Pearson's reply caused consternation in London.

Pearson told other delegates at the United Nations that he had abstained from the resolution because it offered no more than a cease-fire. Something more was needed. On November 3, Pearson proposed that an "emergency international United Nations force" be sent in. The proposal was supported by 57 nations, with none opposed. By November 7, Pearson had collected enough offers of troops to make a U.N. Emergency Force possible. The French and British had a pretext to withdraw. Nasser agreed that

Lester Pearson holding the Nobel Peace Prize, given to him for his efforts in resolving the Suez Canal crisis

the force was acceptable, but it must leave when he directed, and there must be no Canadians. They were, he said, "too British".

Nasser's ban on Canadians was a blow to Pearson and the others who had worked hard for a solution to the crisis. The support of the U.N. Secretary General, Dag Hammarskjold, softened Nasser's position. Canada could provide the Emergency Force's supply and support troops, but a battalion of the Queen's Own Rifles, one of Canada's oldest regiments, had to return to Calgary. The name was "too British".

Canadians watched the events with mixed feelings. "Canada Turns Her Back on UK", shouted the Vancouver *Province*. That view was echoed by the Progressive Conservatives and Social Credit. Many Canadians were bewildered that Canada had not supported Britain; few understood what Pearson had done.

The achievement was impressive; Pearson had found the formula which kept Britain and France from utter humiliation at the U.N. NATO and the Commonwealth survived the crisis. Eden's career was over, but his successor, Harold Macmillan, soon rebuilt British prestige and prosperity. In 1957, Pearson was awarded the Nobel Peace Prize for his efforts. It was the climax of Canada's role as the first of the middle powers.

QUESTIONS

1. Outline the events of the Suez Canal crisis.

2. What role did Lester Pearson play in resolving the crisis?

3. How did the Soviet Union react to the invasion of the Canal by Israel, Britain, and France?

QUESTIONS

1. What was the Cold War, and why was it given this name?

2. What was so startling about the information Gouzenko brought to the Canadian government?

3. Why was isolationism an impossible choice for Canada after the Second World War?

4. **(a)** What was the purpose of NATO?
(b) Why did NATO seem "a providential solution" to Canadian diplomats? Was it?

5. How did Canada's involvement in the Korean War affect Canadian attitudes towards NATO?

At Home After the Wars

If Canadians were satisfied with their active world role, with giving foreign aid, and with an unprecedented peacetime defence burden, it was because their postwar prosperity was also unprecedented. Returning veterans had all the benefits for which the veterans of World War I had struggled: free education, cheap land, and low-interest mortgages to buy a home and furnish it. Production remained high after the war. Those Canadians who did lose jobs in the return to peacetime production had the benefit of unemployment insurance. The census showed that fewer Canadians were poor after the war than ever before. Until 1951, the census had regularly found that about two-thirds of Canadians were poor by any reasonable standard. The 1951 census, however, showed that the poor formed only one-third of the population.

Still, their presence proved that not all parts of Canada benefitted from postwar prosperity. Affluence bypassed most rural areas and the Maritime provinces. Newfoundland entered Confederation in 1949 when a narrow margin of Newfoundlanders preferred provincial status to renewed dominion status. Despite the benefits which accompanied Confederation, such as family allowances and unemployment insurance, Newfoundland remained the poorest province. But Ontario, Alberta, and British Columbia boomed as they had in the 1920's, because their resources and manufactured products were in demand. Almost everywhere, cities prospered and grew.

More energy was needed to fuel the boom. The supply of hydroelectricity was increased in the 1950's, as huge projects in British Columbia and Labrador came to completion. Discoveries of vast oil and natural gas reserves in Alberta during the 1940's and 1950's brought Alberta into the postwar boom. They also gave Canada a new energy source, and the possibility of meeting its own energy needs. In 1952, Canadian scientists began to develop an even newer energy source—nuclear power—with the production of the Canadian Deuterium Uranium (CANDU) reactor.

An oil well in Alberta. Why did energy needs increase so dramatically after the war?

Far from hurting prosperity, the Cold War fuelled Canadian growth. American capital poured into Canada to finance the exploration and development of resources demanded by the American military and civilian markets. More capital created branch plants to supply Canadians with cars, refrigerators, radios, and, after 1952, television sets. New industries grew from the new demands. The huge aluminum smelter at Kitimat, B.C., was a typical example.

In every era of prosperity, Canadians had launched bold plans to link the country together. In the 1950's, new railways reached north to Lynn Lake in Manitoba and Pine Point in the Northwest Territories for nickel, to Knob Lake in Labrador for iron, and through the rugged interior of B.C. for timber and a rich variety of minerals. The St.

A Saskatchewan farm family watches its new television set. A postwar boom in Canada contributed to widespread prosperity, which made possible such luxuries as television.

Lawrence Seaway was finally launched, because a booming nation could no longer do without it. A system of canals and locks was completed in 1959 at a cost of $460 million, $130 million of it invested by Americans. The Seaway allowed ocean-going vessels to move between the Atlantic Ocean and Thunder Bay, on the western shore of Lake Superior. Ottawa also decided that the time had come for a Trans-Canada Highway, and offered to share the costs (projected to be $150 million) with the provinces. Begun in 1948, the roadway was completed 17 years later, at six times the estimated cost.

The guiding spirit of the postwar economy was C.D. Howe, now Minister of Trade and Commerce. Howe disagreed with what he termed the "Security Brigade", those government officials who wanted more social programs to prevent the possibility of renewed depression. Howe believed that prosperity would come if business thrived. He believed in free enterprise, but his actual program was somewhat different. Howe saw the economy as a partnership between government and business, with the government providing loans, credits, and tax devices. As during the war, Howe was also swift to move if investors would not. He continued to found Crown corporations, while those he had created in wartime prospered. The postwar boom continued strong until 1949. Then, when it showed signs of flagging, the Korean War and rearmament added another spurt.

Prosperity encouraged a development which Howe did not welcome, however. In 1946, employers and unions squared off in the worst year for strikes since 1919. The walkouts began in the forestry camps of

British Columbia and moved east. By the time they were all settled, both the unions and prosperity had survived. Many unions had won the Rand formula, a unique Canadian approach to union security. It obliged all workers, even those who refused to join a union, to pay for union representation. It was only in Québec and in the dying coal industry of the Maritimes that unions suffered defeat.

The postwar boom encouraged political stability. Louis St. Laurent won huge majorities in both 1949 and 1953. His victories were made easy by prosperity and Newfoundland's entry into Confederation. The provinces, too, enjoyed stability. Duplessis remained premier of Québec from 1944 until his death in 1959. In Saskatchewan, Tommy Douglas, leader of Canada's only CCF government, kept his party in power for 20 years. Alberta's Social Credit premier, Ernest Manning, retained his position for a quarter-century. Ontario elected a Conservative government in 1943 which remained in power for the next 42 years. In British Columbia, a disenchanted Member of the Legislative Assembly, W.A.C. Bennett, left the Liberal-Conservative coalition to form his own Social Credit Party. By championing free enterprise, encouraging prosperity, and building public works, Bennett stayed in power for 20 years after his 1952 victory. Every government found the money to build schools, dams, and roads, and to pay off debts going back to the Depression.

The ice breaker Ernest Lapointe, *the first ship ever to use the newly completed St. Lawrence Seaway, enters the locks at Saint-Lambert, Québec on April 16, 1959.*

Growth and prosperity were blessings that no-one who could recall the Depression would question. Still, it troubled some Canadians that much of the investment which fuelled growth came from the United States. Critics also noted that many of the new development schemes seemed to serve American as well as Canadian interests. Railways, highways, and pipelines might open up Canada's North, but they often ended in the United States. As in the 1920's, nationalists and imperialists alike worried that Canada's economy was falling under American control. Neither Ottawa nor the provinces shared their concern. Even Duplessis' alliance of conservative *Canadien* nationalists was comfortable with foreign investment.

Political controversies disturbed few Canadians. Many of them were affluent for the first time. Families with a steady income could afford what had previously been luxuries: a car, a television, and a small home in the new suburbs. The *National Housing Act* made it easier to save for the down-payment. Union contracts won benefits for members and non-members alike. The work week slipped down to 40 hours per week, with bonus pay for overtime. Two weeks' holiday with pay became an expectation, not a privilege. So did a series of insurance benefits which gradually crept into work contracts until they became part of legislation for all Canadians. Government-run hospital insurance, begun by the CCF in Saskatchewan in 1947, became federal law in 1958.

Prosperity brought population increase. The size of human families has fallen steadily throughout history. By the 1920's, the average

Canadian family had just two or three children. In the late 1980's, the average was under two children per family. But during the two decades following World War Two, the Canadian birth rate suddenly increased, so that the average family had four children. This postwar "baby boom" occurred in several other countries, including the United States, Britain, and Australia. However, nowhere did the boom last as long or cause the population to increase by so great a percentage as in Canada.

Canada's population also grew rapidly after the war because of the largest flood of immigration since the Sifton years. Between 1945 and 1957, 1.5 million people came to Canada. They brought the industrial skills and professional expertise which the expanding, industrializing nation needed. Most of them went to the cities; Canada was no longer a rural country. By 1956, half of British Columbia's people lived in Victoria or Vancouver, and one-third of Québec's population clustered in Montréal or its suburbs. Half the immigrants were from Britain or the United States; most of the other half came from all the nations of Europe. Toronto, once an English Protestant bastion, replaced Montréal as Canada's largest city, taking in waves of Italians, Greeks, and others. Prosperity eased their acceptance by established Canadians. Their arrival changed Canada as much as Canada changed them. Restrictive laws on drinking, Sunday entertainment, and censorship began to crack under the resentment of both immigrants and the Canadian-born. At the same time, Canadian social practices strained some immigrants' ideas about parental authority and the role of women.

Although change was eased by prosperity, it still met resistance. Protestant churches defended the Sunday laws and felt threatened by the number of Catholics among the immigrants. In their turn, Catholics fought to keep birth control a criminal offence and deplored the soaring

The Tommy Hunter Show *(left) and* Cross Canada Hit Parade *(right) were two early Canadian shows on the CBC television network. Why was so much of the network's programming purchased from the United States? Do you think this was a sufficiently good reason?*

The Stratford Festival Theatre, while under construction in 1953. What economic and social factors led to increased public support for the arts at this time?

divorce rate. As in previous decades, Canadians blamed the United States for its immoral example. Now television joined the ranks of American influences on Canadian society. By 1952, the CBC had started programming for television as well as radio, but the high cost of production forced it to buy most of its programs from American networks. The CBC did, however, spend huge sums on building a national network which could link Canadians for such occasions as *Hockey Night in Canada*.

In one area, Canada had ended the war in bankruptcy. Never had Canadian arts and culture been more impoverished. Vancouver's symphony orchestra performed in an arena. A Royal Commission on the Arts and Letters in Canada reported in 1951 that the government would have to pay if the country were to have universities worth attending and artists, musicians, and writers worthy of Canada's new world status. The report went unheeded. Prime Minister St. Laurent would not risk offending the provincial premiers. Nor, he assumed, would taxpayers want their money spent on poets or ballet dancers.

Many Canadians did not agree. Prosperity, immigration, and increasing levels of education combined to place pressure on politicians. In 1953, the Ontario town of Stratford started its famous Shakespearean Festival—in a tent. Tens of thousands attended. The *Théâtre du Nouveau Monde* opened in Montréal. Cities across Canada began building theatres and cultural centres as a matter of civic pride. The deaths of two multi-millionaires gave Ottawa such a windfall of inheritance taxes that it launched the Canada Council in 1957 with an endowment fund of $100 million. Deserving writers, artists, and performers could finally obtain the financial assistance they required.

QUESTIONS

1. **(a)** Which regions in Canada benefitted most from the economic boom of the 1950's?
   (b) Give reasons why these regions benefitted, while other regions did not.
2. Why did Canada invest in new transportation systems during the 1950's?
3. Explain C.D. Howe's role in guiding the Canadian economy.
4. Why did economic prosperity encourage political stability?
5. Why were some Canadians anti-American in the 1950's?

The Limits of Affluence

The immigrants who poured into Canada after the war believed that they were coming to a uniquely prosperous, stable, and favoured land. Canadians enjoyed the second-highest standard of living in the world. They had little reason to envy their American neighbour which had the highest living standard, but also had all the pressures and costs of being a great power.

Nevertheless, there were critics. As fast as new highways, hospitals, and schools appeared, there was a clamour for more. Conservatives (and Québec's Premier Duplessis) denounced spending on foreign aid. The pacifist wing of the CCF condemned NATO and rearmament. Nationalists and imperialists alike worried about the growth of American economic and cultural influence.

It was anti-Americanism which fuelled the main political furor of the mid-1950's, but the government's overconfidence created the bonfire. In 1956, C.D. Howe put together a Canadian-American consortium (group of companies) to build a natural gas pipeline from Alberta to Ontario and Québec. Construction depended on fast approval by Parliament. Howe did not even wait for discussion to begin before he moved to limit debate. The result was a furious, time-consuming uproar, as the Conservatives and the CCF defended Parliament from what they saw as government arrogance. The large Liberal majority carried the day. The pipeline was constructed, and served a necessary purpose, but the debate over it raised the question of whether the Liberals had held power for too long.

The next year, Canadians had an opportunity to answer that question. The Progressive Conservatives had a new leader. The Conservative candidate, John Diefenbaker, had long held the sole seat for his party in Saskatchewan, a region dominated by the CCF and the Liberals. He had won it with strong oratory and a well-publicized hatred of injustice. In the eyes of some Conservatives, Diefenbaker's chief flaw was his lack of connections with the Toronto and Montréal

A Labour-Progressive Party demonstration over the pipeline controversy. The protest concerned a loan of 80 million dollars by the federal government to Trans-Canada Pipelines, an American company.

financiers whose money backed the party. Other saw this as a benefit, a chance for the party to take new directions. Diefenbaker found plenty of issues on which to base his campaign. Prairie farmers grumbled about unsold wheat; old-age pensioners protested a mere $6 monthly increase at a time when the government boasted a budget surplus. Still, most Canadians expected that St. Laurent would return to power.

CLOSE-UP

How Would You Have Voted?

In June, 1957, *Maclean's Magazine* asked Joan and David Watts, a young Canadian couple voting for the first time in a federal election, to write to the leader of each political party and ask him why they should vote for his party. Below are excerpts from the replies they received.

From Louis St. Laurent, Prime Minister and Leader of the Liberal Party:

> I agree with you that Canadian democracy is in a healthy state... I cannot agree, however, that the Canadian people have somehow failed our democracy by keeping Liberal Governments in power "too long". I suggest a party has not been too long in office until, in

Louis St. Laurent was Secretary of State for External Affairs from 1946 to 1948. Until his time, it was the Prime Minister who handled Canada's external policies. St. Laurent became Prime Minister after King's retirement in 1948.

the opinion of the electors, it is no longer capable of giving better government than one of the opposition parties.

We are, first of all, frankly fearful of too much government. We want nothing done federally that can be done better at the provincial or local level—or that, best of all, can be left to the individual to work out for himself.... Liberalism centres on the citizen: to keep him free from oppression.

Today more Canadians are at work than ever before—producing more, earning more, saving more than ever before; the future has never been brighter. I don't suggest, of course, that Liberal policies create prosperity—but they do encourage the sort of conditions that give prosperity its best chance... We believe there must be some redistribution, through government, of our national income in order to help those who are too young, too sick or too old to help themselves, and to help those who are temporarily out of work.

More convincing than words are the one million or more postwar houses built, and the one and one half million new Canadians who, by coming here, have shown how much they like the way things are going in Canada.

From John Diefenbaker, Leader of the Progressive Conservative Party:

We of the PC party regard the Supremacy of Parliament as one of our basic tenets. We consider our system of government in jeopardy... The proof lie(s) in incontrovertible facts—the concentration of too much power in the small group of men who are the federal government, the insistence upon the retention of extraordinary warborn powers, the multitude of crown corporations established and placed beyond the scrutiny and control of parliament.

The Conservative party is the party of the moderate right in Canada... (It) is opposed to unnecessary excursions into the nation's business and industrial life. Such excursions only superimpose bureaucracy upon bureaucracy... (and) result in a concentration of authority in ministerial hands in Ottawa to the detriment of parliament.... We Conservatives believe this dependency on the U.S. has gone too far, that Canadian well-being, the Canadian economy, are far too vulnerable to American whims and American reversals.

All Canadians should share in the nation's general economic advance. There should be no permanent "haves" and "have nots" in Canada... Hence our conviction that the fiscal arrangements with the provinces should provide adequately for the province's needs... The Conservative Party, and I as Leader, are dedicated to the ideal of One Canada, governed by national and not divisive policies; a Canada that is a truly free and vigorous democracy, a grand partnership of ten provinces.

From M.J. Coldwell, Leader of the CCF:

> We in the CCF realize... that the gains from the present economic expansion are not being fairly shared. We know that, for instance, farm income has declined sharply in the last five years. We know that the income of wage-earners has lagged behind the increase in national production. We know that many old-age pensioners today are eking out only a miserable existence in the last years of their lives... We know of the tragic waste of human resources that has resulted from periodic large-scale unemployment.
>
> The CCF believes we should plan as effectively to win the peace as we did to win the war... today an economic crisis of a different kind is confronting Canada... To counter inflation, we require a wide measure of democratic social planning... In such an economy there would be an important role for public, private and co-operative enterprise working together in the people's interest.
>
> The CCF believes that our society must have a moral purpose that transcends the drive for private gain and special privilege. We believe that a new relationship of mutual respect and understanding and human brotherhood must be built among people in a world of peace. We believe that poverty and hardship in the midst of plenty must be abolished. We believe that there must be equality of opportunity so that the talent of all may be developed to the full.

From Solon Low, Leader of the Social Credit Party:

> (We believe) government should keep out of business—let private enterprise, not social enterprise, prevail. Every person shall be free to manage his life; free to speak, free to assemble, to work, to worship, to choose, to live, provided only that he or she allow all others that same privilege.
>
> Every Canadian shall be afforded the opportunity to obtain a fair and just share of Canada's national production. Government by the people themselves at the "grass roots" level shall be made more and more possible, and actual, by decentralizing administration and spreading the truth about things as they actually are.
>
> Canada's natural resources shall be developed in Canada for Canadians of today; and shall be husbanded and preserved for Canadians of tomorrow... What is physically possible and desirable shall be made financially possible.

QUESTIONS

1. List the arguments you found most persuasive, giving your reasons.

2. Which party would you have supported? Explain your choice.

The 1960 passage of the Canadian Bill of Rights was one of Prime Minister John Diefenbaker's proudest moments. The principle of legislating a guarantee of basic freedoms for all Canadians was controversial at that time; a controversy that resurfaced during the constitutional conferences of the 1980s.

Instead, one-quarter of those who had backed the Liberals in 1953 switched their votes. On June 10, 1957, the Conservatives won 112 seats, the Liberals 105, the CCF 25, and Social Credit 19. Though they had a minority government, the Conservatives had displaced the Liberals after 22 years.

St. Laurent, now 76 years old, left politics. The Liberals chose Lester Pearson as his successor. Pearson had made a name as a skilled diplomat, but had much to learn about domestic politics. In his first parliamentary speech as opposition leader, he offered to take back the government for the Liberals. Diefenbaker, who was aware of the popularity of his government, responded by calling an election for March 31, 1958. The Conservative leader was an excellent campaigner who invited Canadians to "catch the vision" of a new North in his powerful speeches. The contrast between the energetic Diefenbaker and the low-key Pearson gave the Conservatives the largest sweep in Canadian history until that time: 208 seats to the Liberals' 49. The CCF held on to only 8 seats, while Social Credit won none. Even Québec, traditionally Liberal, gave the Conservatives 50 of its 75 seats. Diefenbaker had a majority in every province except Newfoundland, which remained Liberal.

Ontario Premier Leslie Frost and Québec's Duplessis were particularly pleased at the outcome of the election. They had supported the Conservatives, because St. Laurent had refused to give their provinces larger transfer payments. If the provinces wanted more money, he had said, they should raise taxes. Diefenbaker repaid Québec and Ontario for their support by increasing the provinces' share of income taxes from 10 percent to 16 percent.

Yet it was the West, not Ontario and Québec, which gained most from Diefenbaker's election. The Prairies had long been dominated by the Liberals and the CCF. In the 1953 election, the Conservatives had won only 9 of the 65 western seats. In 1958, the Conservatives got 60 of them; the rest went to the CCF. Diefenbaker wished to confirm and reinforce the conversion. His efforts earned him a reputation as a "prairie populist". First, he raised old-age pensions, a measure popular in the West. While in opposition, the Conservatives had denounced Liberal interference with free markets. Once in power, however,

Diefenbaker adopted costly support payments to protect 24 farm products from price drops. He retained the Wheat Board, but also passed a revolutionary *Agricultural Rehabilitation and Development Act*. The *Act* gave farmers access to loans and encouraged the mechanization and growth of farms. In opposition, Diefenbaker had been a fervent anti-communist. But when China wanted to buy wheat in 1960, Diefenbaker forgot about ideology for the sake of selling the West's enormous grain surplus. Western farm incomes increased, as did shipping in Vancouver harbour. When lower-priced oil from Arab countries threatened Alberta's budding energy industry, the new National Energy Board readily convinced Diefenbaker that it had to be protected. Canada, as far east as the Ottawa River, was obliged to buy Alberta oil.

Diefenbaker's most cherished project was the passage of a Canadian *Bill of Rights*, to ensure equal rights to all Canadians. Memories of the discrimination he had suffered because of his own name fed his determination. The *Bill of Rights* became law in 1960. However, as a federal statute, it could be changed at will by Ottawa or ignored by the provinces, so it was not an airtight statement of the rights of Canadians. Canadians had to wait over two more decades for their rights to become part of the Constitution. In addition, the *Bill of Rights* ignored the issues of culture and language rights which troubled *Canadiens*. For Diefenbaker, it was enough that Ottawa now issued bilingual cheques. Any more concessions to bilingualism would threaten his belief in what he called "unhyphenated Canadianism".

Neither his tax concessions nor the *Bill of Rights* won Diefenbaker complete harmony between the federal government and the provinces. The two levels of government were unable to reach an agreement about how to amend Canada's Constitution, the last step in gaining full autonomy from Britain. A new amending formula was scuttled in 1960, when Québec demanded fresh powers from Ottawa.

There were other sources of conflict. Premier W.A.C. Bennett of British Columbia refused to accept an agreement between Canada and the United States to develop power on the Columbia River. He also demanded control over B.C.'s offshore resources. At the other end of the country, Newfoundland Premier Joey Smallwood was angry as well. Ottawa insisted on meeting the 1949 terms of Confederation to the letter; Smallwood had an interpretation which would be more generous to Newfoundland. Smallwood was also furious when Diefenbaker refused to send the RCMP to crush a loggers' strike in 1959.

Despite postwar prosperity, Canada's economy was vulnerable to international changes. After the war, the world had needed almost everything Canada could grow, mine, or manufacture. Primary resources—lumber, minerals, and wheat—remained in high demand. Slowly, however, Europe's industries returned to production. Canada experienced mild recessions in 1949 and 1953. Their effects were masked by unemployment insurance and pre-election spending. Another recession was in progress when Diefenbaker won in 1957. Once in power, the Conservatives blamed it on the Liberals.

Diefenbaker's government did what it could to overcome the 1957 recession. More Progressive than Conservative, it raised federal spending by 32 percent between 1957 and 1961. Grants to universities doubled. Vocational training programs taught skills to hundreds of thousands of young Canadians and kept them out of the overcrowded job market. Far from dismantling protection for unions, the government considered extending such rights to civil servants. A winter works program not only provided work in a slack season but also showed the construction industry that it could build year-round.

But many Canadians blamed the government for the problems and gave it little credit for what went right. What they saw was a government in turmoil. Every year, Finance Minister Donald Fleming promised a surplus—and produced another deficit. A public row led to the removal of James Coyne, governor of the Bank of Canada. Coyne's policy of high interest rates pleased bankers and investors, but it also hurt most businesses, added to unemployment, and made the government look bad. Even when economists denounced his policies, Coyne would not budge. Finally the government forced his removal. Few Canadians really understood the issues; what they did understand was that such things had not happened when the Liberals were in power.

QUESTIONS

1. "Diefenbaker's government was more Progressive than Conservative." What does "Progressive" mean? "Conservative"? Do you agree or disagree with this assessment of Diefenbaker's regime?
2. Why was Diefenbaker's election victory of 1958 called a "sweep"?
3. How did Diefenbaker try to protect the rights of all Canadians?
4. How would you describe the relationship between Diefenbaker's government and the provincial governments?
5. What effects did changes in the world economy have on Canada?

National and Nuclear Choices

Diefenbaker's government did better in most domestic policies than Canadians realized. It was weak, however, in the areas of diplomacy and defence. In external affairs, Diefenbaker had to live up to the reputation of Lester Pearson, who had won the Nobel Peace Prize. After winning his huge majority in 1958, Diefenbaker toured the world, seeking to inherit St. Laurent's and Pearson's prestige among

Testing the atomic bomb in the Nevada desert. Soldiers who participated in the test would later report a high incidence of cancer. Why did Canada have such a profound interest in U.S. defence plans?

newer Commonwealth members. Diefenbaker attempted to imitate Pearson's achievement by bringing Canada into the U.N.'s peacekeeping operation in the Congo in 1960. Unfortunately, the chaos which ensued in central Africa allowed no-one much credit. A year later, however, Diefenbaker upheld Canada's reputation in the Third World by helping to drive South Africa from the Commonwealth because of its policy of apartheid. This was not the sort of policy some Tories expected from their government, but John Diefenbaker had more surprises in store.

Throughout the 1950's, advances in nuclear and other weaponry—the "arms race"—brought Canada closer to the United States. Early in the decade, both the Americans and the Soviets had perfected the hydrogen bomb, which was far more powerful than the devices which had obliterated Hiroshima and Nagasaki. In 1952, General Dwight Eisenhower, who had been the allied commander in Europe during World War II, became president. His Republican administration hoped to cut defence costs and conscription, both unpopular, by delivering "a bigger bang for a buck". Eisenhower set out to develop a fleet of strategic bombers able to drop nuclear weapons on the Soviet Union.

The Avro Arrow flies over Niagara Falls, Ontario. Diefenbaker cancelled construction of the Canadian-designed and -built fighters in 1959. Why did he make this decision?

The defence of North America became the top priority of American military planners. Situated on the flight path between the two opposing superpowers, Canada became closely involved in American defence planning. By the middle of the decade, it had nine squadrons flying Canadian-built CF-100 aircraft. However, the CF-100's were slow and outdated; they had to be replaced by modern supersonic aircraft. At Malton, outside Toronto, 13 000 of Canada's top engineers and aircraft workers hurried to develop the CF-105, or Avro Arrow. The project was exciting, but so expensive that even C.D. Howe was alarmed. If the Liberals had been re-elected in 1957, they would likely have scrapped it. Instead, they left the Conservatives to make two defence decisions: whether to continue with the Avro Arrow, and whether to join the proposed Canada-U.S. North American Air Defence Command (NORAD).

Diefenbaker moved boldly. Before External Affairs officials could explain that NORAD was the type of American-dominated arrangement which the Liberals had tried to avoid, he signed the agreement. As for the Avro Arrow, a year's study showed that its costs were soaring, parts were no longer available from the United States, and no other country wanted to buy the aircraft. On February 20, 1959, Diefenbaker scrapped the project. Avro, the contractor, fired its workers in a day.

Diefenbaker justified his decision by saying that the missile age had arrived; fighters and bombers were obsolete. Then Canada bought Bomarc-B missiles and F-101 Voodoo fighters from the United States. Both were designed to fight bombers; both would be effective only with nuclear warheads. The Americans offered the warheads, too, but strictly under their own control. For the first time since it had developed its own navy, air force, and army, Canada was dependent on foreign military technology.

Diefenbaker's decisions over NORAD and the Avro Arrow coincided with the spread from Britain to Canada of a powerful crusade against nuclear weapons. Women's groups, intellectuals, the CCF, and the Liberals declared that Canada must remain free from any nuclear weapons. The anti-nuclear cause was probably aided by a government campaign to persuade Canadians to build fall-out shelters. The campaign made the full horror of nuclear attack clear to Canadians. The anti-nuclear movement also had a strong supporter in Howard Green, the British Columbia politician whom Diefenbaker had appointed as Secretary of State for External Affairs. Green, a veteran of World War I, had a horror of war and no faith in the Americans.

Diefenbaker was now torn between his friend Green, who was backed by key officials in External Affairs, and a defence department whose equipment depended upon nuclear warheads. In the end, he insisted that Canada had made no commitment to acquire nuclear weapons, and that the new missiles and fighters would function without them. Diefenbaker's statements shocked colleagues and journalists, and the about-face undermined Canada's relations with the United States. Under Eisenhower, relations between the two countries had been smooth. In 1960, however, a new president took over. John F. Kennedy and Diefenbaker took an instant dislike to each other. The personalities and styles of the two men were in direct contrast. Diefenbaker particularly resented the admiration that Canadians felt for the handsome, articulate American president.

How did the political styles of John F. Kennedy and John Diefenbaker differ? Why did many Canadians prefer Kennedy?

A victorious T.C. (Tommy) Douglas (left) is carried to the convention platform after having been named leader of the New Democratic Party in August, 1961. Why did the CCF want to change its image? Réal Caouette's Créditistes (right) appealed to old-fashioned concerns in rural small-town Québec. His style of nationalism brought a foretaste of political issues of the 1960's, except Caouette was also a strong federalist.

By 1962, Canadians looking for political alternatives had them. Ambitious younger politicians had rebuilt the Liberal Party. Business leaders who were dismayed by Diefenbaker and remembered the Liberals' C.D. Howe gave money to support the Liberals. New Canadians were angry at Conservative restrictions on immigration during the recession and vowed to vote Liberal.

The CCF, too, was revitalized. It had approached the Canadian Labour Congress and the "liberally minded", and, in August, 1961, assembled 2000 delegates in Ottawa. The delegates launched the New Democratic Party (NDP) and chose Premier Tommy Douglas of Saskatchewan as their leader. The new party hoped that union backing and a policy of social-democratic reform would bring it to power.

Québec was the most vulnerable element in Diefenbaker's support. The Liberals had regained their strength there. In addition, a spellbinding orator named Réal Caouette had created a mass movement of people in the rural areas of the province, under the banner of Social Credit. Caouette's *Ralliément des créditistes* drew support from former Liberals and Conservatives alike.

Other great changes were afoot in Québec. Despite Premier Duplessis' powerful and conservative government, enormous changes in Québec society had been wrought by affluence and education. Well-educated *Canadiens* were frustrated that the best jobs were held by an anglophone minority. The leaders of the influential Roman Catholic Church shared the stirrings of reform. They were angry and humiliated that Duplessis provided funds for their schools and hospitals only as a reward for the Church's dutiful cooperation. Duplessis' stand against Ottawa on behalf of Québec had helped keep him in power. By his support of Diefenbaker in 1958, Duplessis lost influence in his own province. When he died in 1959, his successors struggled to formulate reforms which might safeguard their power. Change now favoured the Liberals.

The Québec Liberal leader, Jean Lesage, attacked Ottawa as Duplessis had once done. He also promised the new generation of educated, affluent Québec voters a chance to be "*maîtres chez nous*", "masters in our own house". Lesage's victory in 1960, under the slogan "*Il faut que ça change*" ("It's time for a change"), brought in a new political era in Québec.

In the general election campaign of 1962, Diefenbaker's government had to contend with these political changes. Many predicted that the Conservatives would lose their majority; some even said that the Liberals would win. The devaluation of the Canadian dollar during the campaign, though it helped the economy, upset voters and delighted the Liberals. Nevertheless, Diefenbaker was a powerful campaigner, while Pearson was not. The Conservatives got a minority government, with 116 seats to the Liberals' 99, the NDP's 19, the Social Credit Party's 30, and 1 other. All but four of the Social Credit seats came from Québec. Western Canada remained true to the "prairie populist".

As leader of a minority government, Diefenbaker was indecisive. The government seemed to be out of ideas. Canada's missiles and jet fighters remained unarmed. In October, 1962, the Cuban missile crisis broke the peace. For a few tense days, President John Kennedy challenged the Soviet Union's decision to provide nuclear weapons to its Cuban ally. NORAD's American forces were put on full alert; its Canadian components, which covered New York and Pittsburgh as well as Montréal and Toronto, were not.

Most Canadians were shocked by Diefenbaker's failure to respect the NORAD agreement. Opinion polls showed a dramatic swing in favour of acquiring nuclear weaponry and playing a full, if subordinate, role in NORAD. In January, 1963, Pearson switched the Liberals' stand on the issue. If elected, he would meet Canada's nuclear commitments, then negotiate a way out of them. A retiring NATO commander who visited Ottawa bluntly told a press conference that Canada had failed to live up to its promises. When Diefenbaker gave Parliament a confusing and largely misleading account of Canada's defence commitments, the American State Department revealed the facts. Canada, it claimed, had proposed no arrangement "sufficiently practical to contribute effectively to North American defence".

Headed by the Minister of National Defence, some prominent Conservative Cabinet members resigned. The government was in peril of defeat. A polite approach to Caouette's *Créditistes* might have saved it, but Diefenbaker did not make the effort. On February 5, 1963, the government was defeated in the House of Commons. Diefenbaker promised a full statement on the defence issue, but never delivered it. Instead he claimed that the United States had engineered his downfall. Even the newspapers which traditionally backed the Conservatives abandoned him. Deserted by voters in the cities and Québec, Diefenbaker turned to his traditional supporters—the rural areas and the West.

In the election on April 8, Pearson led the Liberals to a minority victory, winning 129 seats, all but 30 from Ontario and Québec. Diefenbaker won 95 seats, including 43 of the 48 prairie ridings. The Social Credit Party won 24 seats, and the NDP 17. The astonishing national support which Diefenbaker had enjoyed in 1958 had vanished in just five years. A minority government would once again face a divided country.

QUESTIONS

1. Why was Canada inevitably involved in American plans to defend itself against the Soviet Union?
2. Why was the Avro Arrow scrapped?
3. Were Canada's Bomarc missiles largely useless?
4. What issue appears to have contributed most to the defeat of the minority Diefenbaker government in 1963?

Chapter Summary

Canada entered a new era after the war, in a world where power was divided between communist and western democratic nations. In this world, Canada defined a new place for itself, as a middle power, affluent and involved in international politics.

At home, Canadians enjoyed a time of unprecedented prosperity. Industry boomed. Trade with the United States became a vital part of Canada's economy, as American influence in all areas of Canadian life became ever more pervasive. By the early 1960's, however, the difficulty of maintaining the postwar momentum had brought changes in federal politics. In the provinces, especially Québec, momentous changes were stirring that would bring sharp confrontations between the federal and provincial governments in the next decade.

IN REVIEW

1. What was the basis of the Cold War? What did each side seek?
2. What makes a country a "middle power"?
3. Why might some nations which joined the United Nations have been sceptical about the organization's ability to maintain peace?
4. **(a)** What contributions did Diefenbaker make to Canada during his years as Prime Minister?
   (b) What brought about his defeat?

APPLYING YOUR KNOWLEDGE

1. Why do some voters feel that it is not good for Canada if the same provincial or federal party remains in power for a long time?
2. Were Canadians' concerns about American influence on Canadian culture justified?
3. **(a)** What economic policies could Canada have adopted to maintain its strong position at the end of the Second World War?
   (b) Are your suggestions politically realistic?

FURTHER INVESTIGATION

1. The five "great powers" chosen to hold permanent seats and veto power on the U.N. Security Council were the United States, the U.S.S.R., France, Britain, and China. If the permanent members were chosen today, which of these nation(s) do you think would not be included? Which one(s) would be added as replacements? Give reasons for your answers.
2. Why did former British colonies join the Commonwealth when they became independent, rather than break off all partnership with Britain and other former colonies?
3. If you had a chance to ask today's leaders of the federal political parties three questions, what would you ask? How would the answers to your questions influence your vote?
4. Identify five areas of Canadian life in which there is a strong American influence.

CHAPTER 6

A Nation in Conflict

The minority Liberal victory of 1963 reflected the divisions within Canadian society. Of Ontario's 85 seats, 52 went to the Liberals. In Québec, Canadiens, *who believed that John Diefenbaker had never understood their concerns and never would, gave 47 seats to the Liberals, 20 to the* Créditistes, *and only 8 to the Conservatives. Westerners, on the other hand, stayed faithful to "The Chief" and his party; they were mindful of the wheat sales to China and the Soviet Union which Diefenbaker had arranged.*

At the time, working people remembered the recession of the late 1950's and early 1960's under Diefenbaker, and the worst unemployment in Canada since the Depression. The wealthy blamed Diefenbaker for his concern for the elderly and the poor, and for bad management of his government. New Canadians recalled that immigration had been sharply cut back during the recession. These factors, among others, gave Lester Pearson and his Liberals their victory—but also allowed the Conservatives to retain their foothold.

The divisions among Canadians emerged more clearly as the decade continued. In fact, the 1960's became a time of rapid change in Canadian society which occurred at least partly in response to these divisions. The issues associated with the independence movement in Québec, bilingualism, and the trend toward the "liberation" of society all contributed to shaping Canada into the country it is today. As you read about these issues in this chapter, keep the following questions in mind:

- *How did Pearson try to redefine "Canadian" in the 1960's?*
- *How did Québec's fight for "*la survivance*" affect Canadians both within and outside of Québec?*
- *What are biculturalism and multiculturalism? How have they affected Canada?*
- *Why are the 1960's called the "liberation era"?*
- *Which international developments most influenced Canada's relations with the world?*

Prosperity and Problems

The 1960's began with a recession and ended in prosperity. The wheat sales engineered by John Diefenbaker helped not only western Canada, but every region of the country. So did the recovery of the American economy. By 1963, Canada was booming. Between 1961 and 1965, Canada's gross national product increased by as much as it had through the entire 1950's. Unemployment hit a low of 3.6 percent in 1965. Everywhere in Canada, getting money for new developments and government programs posed no problem. In British Columbia, a government surplus and a demand for electric power on both sides of the Canada-U.S. border fostered Premier W.A.C. Bennett's plan to develop both the Columbia and the Peace Rivers for hydroelectricity. People wanted and got new multi-lane highways, hospitals, universities, theatres, and art galleries. They also enjoyed a host of new social programs. The most important of them, universal medical care insurance, was joined by the Canada (and Québec) Pension Plan, student loans, a Canada Assistance Plan for the poor, and other plans to cut poverty.

None of these programs seemed to increase the popularity of Pearson's Liberal government. A poorly written first budget, the quarrels over a new design for the Canadian flag, and a series of minor scandals involving government ministers all conveyed an image of Liberal confusion. They also allowed Diefenbaker, now in opposition, to show an effectiveness he had lacked when in power. The Liberals naturally blamed their problems on the existence of a minority government. Thinking that the prosperity Canadians enjoyed by 1965 would win them a majority, the Liberals called an election in November. Their optimism was misplaced: the Liberals won just one more seat than they had before the election. Only the NDP made real gains.

The design for the new Canadian flag was not popular with all Canadians. Some nicknamed it "Pearson's pennant", after the Prime Minister who staked his career to give the country a distinctive flag. Why was there so much resistance to the change?

Still, Pearson was pleased by at least one change in his party: the election of the "Three Wise Men" from Québec, Jean Marchand, Gérard Pelletier, and Pierre Elliott Trudeau. Pearson felt Marchand, a former Québec labour leader, might make a good French Canadian lieutenant. Pelletier, editor of French Canada's biggest newspaper, *La Presse*, could be the voice of Québec intellectuals in the Liberal Party. Pearson was less sure about what Trudeau might contribute. He would soon find out.

Both prosperity and problems continued uninterrupted by the election. In 1966, a wave of strikes swept the country. Young workers wanted an even larger share of the new prosperity. Moreover, Ottawa and the provincial governments had given civil servants the right to strike. Government employees felt that it was time for their wages to catch up with those of other Canadians. Postal workers, hospital employees, and teachers walked out almost for the first time in Canadian history. At first, the public was sympathetic to workers' demands. However, settlements such as the 30 percent increase granted by federal negotiators to St. Lawrence Seaway workers prompted an outcry from the public.

Worse was still to come. A political problem which had smouldered since the battle on the Plains of Abraham now threatened to explode. Québec's Quiet Revolution, begun in 1960 by Jean Lesage, had gained momentum throughout the 1960's. Lesage had demanded "special status" for Québec. By 1967, that was not enough; some of Quebec's leaders wanted absolute equality with the rest of Canada. If it was not granted, Québec would separate from Canada. Such was the threat of the new independence movement created in 1967 by a former Liberal and member of Lesage's Cabinet, René Lévesque. Many Canadians began to fear for Confederation. (These developments in Québec are discussed more fully in the following section.)

Once a popular television broadcaster and Liberal politician, Lévesque became a leader capable of uniting quarrelsome factions into a strong movement. Lévesque's dependence on cigarettes was a characteristic often portrayed in cartoons and caricatures.

In the midst of this crisis, Pearson found Pierre Trudeau more useful than either Marchand or Pelletier. Unlike other *Canadiens*, the Montréal law professor was not a Québec nationalist. Unlike other Québec intellectuals, Trudeau rejected special status—or any status which would turn Québec back into the closed, isolated society it had been before the Quiet Revolution. Instead, he supported bilingualism throughout Canada as one of the best ways of making all Canadians, francophone and anglophone, feel at home in a unified Canada. In 1968, when Pearson summoned provincial premiers to a constitutional conference, Québec Premier Daniel Johnson demanded a status equal to the rest of Canada. Trudeau stood up to him boldly, arguing against special status and for a strong Canada. Television viewers were impressed. Pearson's retirement had already been announced. Suddenly, Trudeau seemed the obvious successor.

In April, 1968, Liberal delegates bypassed more experienced party campaigners to make Trudeau the leader of the federal party. Most Canadians approved. In the election campaign that followed, Trudeau

Trudeaumania! After taking over the government from a retiring Lester B. Pearson, Pierre Elliott Trudeau led the Liberals to a decisive victory in the 1968 election.

swept many Canadians off their feet into a state some people called "Trudeaumania". But Trudeau hid none of his message from the voters. Even in the interior of British Columbia, he warned audiences—in both French and English—that Canada's future depended on bilingualism and equal opportunities for people who spoke both languages. He also warned voters that the extensive government spending of the middle years of the decade was over: "No more free stuff." The new Conservative leader, Robert Stanfield, a former premier of Nova Scotia, was still wearied from the leadership struggle with Diefenbaker. He was no match for Trudeau. Nor was the NDP's Tommy Douglas. On June 25, 1968, Trudeau won the majority Pearson had been denied: 155 seats to 72 for the Tories, 22 for the NDP, and 14 for the *Créditistes.* A new era had begun.

QUESTIONS

1. In what way was the minority Liberal victory of 1963 a token of the divisions within Canadian society?

2. How did Trudeau's views of Québec's relations with Canada differ from those of most *Canadien* intellectuals?

3. How did government involvement in the lives of Canadians increase during the 1960's?

The Matter of Québec

The fact that both Québec Premier Lesage (right) and Prime Minister Pearson (left) were members of the Liberal party did not prevent conflict over the issue of federal and provincial rights.

Throughout the 1960's, many Canadians were puzzled by the crisis which threatened their country. The problem was that the answer to "What does Québec want?" was either too obvious or too complicated. In simplest terms, what *Canadiens* wanted was *"la survivance"*—survival as a distinct nationality with its own language and culture. However, what was involved in achieving *la survivance* was too complex and uncertain for easy explanations. The survival strategy of Québec in the two centuries since the conquest had been to turn inward. Religious, intellectual, and political leaders alike had insisted that Québec could survive only by maintaining a strong Roman Catholic faith, a highly rural population, and an unquestioning obedience to the leadership.

By the 1950's, this strategy had become unacceptable to many *Canadiens*. The '50's in Québec were marked by bitter strikes, as working people struggled to get their share of the rich new North American lifestyle. The Union Nationale government under Maurice Duplessis, which remained in power for over two decades, sided with employers and old ways. In 1959, Duplessis died.

The new decade brought Québec a new government: Jean Lesage and his Liberals. The Lesage government immediately launched a program of reforms to modernize politics, industry, education, and social services in Québec. These reforms became known as the "Quiet Revolution". The key institution of *la survivance* became the government. In token of its new significance, the provincial legislature was renamed the National Assembly. Other changes soon followed. The Liberal government attacked Duplessis' habit of giving government positions and money to party supporters only, and created a professional civil service. It also limited the amount that could be spent on election campaigns.

In 1962, the Liberals went to the people, asking for a strong majority in a new election, so that *Canadiens* could call themselves *"maîtres chez nous"*. A major goal of the campaign was the nationalization of the hydro power industry. Controlling the sources of hydroelectricity would allow the government to influence industry. It would also replace the anglophone corporations that controlled Québec's electricity industry by expanding the publicly owned and francophone Hydro-Québec. The force behind this part of the campaign was the chain-smoking star of Lesage's Cabinet, René Lévesque. Lesage got his majority and, by 1967, engineers had completed a huge new power plant at Manicouagan and were planning massive developments on the rivers leading into James Bay.

The Quiet Revolution fostered social change as well. Lesage introduced a medicare plan and other assistance programs. Perhaps most important, the government took control of Québec's educational system. Until that point, French-language education in Québec had been

The Manicouagan hydroelectric plant in Québec. Why was the project so important to the nationalist aims of Lesage's government?

run by the Roman Catholic Church. Only a small percentage of students went past elementary school; those who did received a classical education which emphasized Latin and Greek. Few *Canadiens* studied science and engineering. Lesage wanted Québec students to be able to participate fully in an increasingly industrial, technological world. He wanted *Canadiens* to be able to run the province's industrial and financial institutions, as well as its political and educational systems. To this end, new secondary schools, colleges, and technical schools were built. The subjects taught at the universities were modernized. By the end of the decade, the school system had expanded by half a million students, and over 40 000 went on to college or university.

Québec also fought for and won the right to withdraw from federal social programs and to obtain funds to establish its own. The test case was the Canada Pension Plan (CPP), established under Lester Pearson. Lesage wanted a provincial plan so that the province could collect higher premiums and use the fund for provincial purposes until it was needed for pensions. Provincial premiers supported Lesage, and Ottawa gave in. Although the other premiers ultimately agreed to a nation-wide CPP, Québec had its QPP. It provided a huge revenue from contributors, to be invested in businesses which *Canadiens* would run.

By the middle of the decade, Québec had taken giant strides into the modern world. However, many of its people were still dissatisfied. Some felt that Québec could never attain its full potential as long as it was a province with the same powers as all the others. They—and the Lesage government with them—wanted special status within Confederation which would bring almost total independence for Québec, with merely economic links to Canada. These people rejected the term "*Canadiens*"; they were, they insisted, "*Québécois*", citizens of Québec first. Others, whose spokesmen were Daniel Johnson and the *Union Nationale* Party, wanted "equality or independence" from Canada. Still others were simply angered by the higher taxes necessitated by the reforms. In 1966, these forces combined to reject Lesage and make Daniel Johnson premier.

CLOSE-UP

Two Visions of Québec

At one point, René Lévesque and Pierre Trudeau were colleagues. But each man had a very different vision of the future of Québec. The excerpts below present some of the arguments each made for his vision. The first is taken from Lévesque's book *An Option for Québec*; the second, from Trudeau's *Federalism and the French Canadians*.

> We are Québécois. What that means first and foremost... is that we are attached to this one corner of the earth where we can be completely ourselves; this Québec, the only place where we have the unmistakable feeling that "here we can really be at home".
>
> Being ourselves is essentially a matter of keeping and developing a personality that has survived for three and a half centuries. At the core of this personality is the fact that we speak French. Everything else depends on this one essential element... To be unable to live as ourselves, as we should live, in our own language and according to our own ways, would be like living without an arm or a leg—or perhaps a heart.
>
> We are a nation within a country where there are two nations... This means that in fact there are two majorities, two complete societies... The present regime also prevents the English-speaking majority from simplifying, rationalizing and centralizing as it would like to do... This is an ordeal which English Canada is finding more and more exhausting, and for which it blames the exaggerated anxieties and incorrigible intransigence of Québec. It is clear, we believe, that this frustration may easily become intolerable.
>
> For our own good, we must dare to seize for ourselves complete liberty in Québec, the right to all the essential components of independence, i.e., the complete mastery of every last area of collective decision-making. This means that Québec must become sovereign as soon as possible... It... also is the one and only common goal inspiring enough to bring us together with the kind of strength and unity we shall need... This new relationship of two nations, one with its homeland in Québec, the other free to rearrange the rest of the country at will, would be freely associated in a new adaptation of the current "common market" formula, making up... a Canadian Union.
>
> —from René Lévesque, *An Option for Québec*, Toronto: McClelland and Stewart, 1968.

The Québec Legislature has no authority to speak on behalf of "French Canada". French Canada includes 850 000 Canadians whose mother tongue is French, who live outside Québec... On the other hand, Québec includes a million people whose mother tongue is not French.

People speak of the principle of nationalities, affirm the right of these nationalities to govern their own destiny, and conclude that for reasons of dignity and pride French Canadians (Quebeckers) must have their own national state... I recognize the right of nations to self-determination. But to claim this right without taking into account the price that will have to be paid, and without clearly demonstrating that it is to the advantage of the whole nation is nothing short of a reckless gamble. Men do not exist for states; states are created to make it easier for men to attain some of their common objectives.

What emerges from all this promoting independence as an end good in itself, a matter of dignity for all self-respecting peoples, amounts to embroiling the world in a pretty pickle indeed... Every Québec separatist should advocate... independence for twenty-five million Bengalis included in the state of India. Should the separatists... say they would indeed like to see this independence for Bengal, I would ask why they would stop there in the good work; in Bengal ninety different languages are spoken; and then there are still more Bengalis in Pakistan—what a lovely lot of separations that would be!

—from Pierre Trudeau, *Federalism and the French Canadians*, Toronto: The Macmillan Company, 1968.

QUESTIONS

1. **(a)** Cite three of the reasons given for Québec independence in the excerpts from *An Option for Québec*, and three of the reasons against independence in *Federalism and the French Canadians*.
   (b) With which viewpoint do you agree?

Johnson's message was that Québec must obtain absolute equality with the rest of Canada—a 50-50 sharing of power—or the separatists would win their goal. The actions of René Lévesque in late 1967 and early 1968 made the threat more real. In September, 1967, Lévesque split the Québec Liberals with his call for a "Québec option". By December he had launched the Sovereignty-Association Movement. Lévesque succeeded in uniting the socialist and conservative supporters of the independence cause into the *Parti Québécois*. Intellectuals, media leaders, and the trade unions heeded his call. Such was the situation in Québec when Pierre Trudeau came to power in 1968.

Trudeau was living proof that not all *Canadiens* wanted separatism. He attacked Lévesque's vision of the future of Québec, calling it a return to the "ancestral wigwam", the oppressed, conformist society he detested. Trudeau's favoured solutions to the problems of francophones in Canada were bilingualism and equal opportunities for *Canadiens* in Ottawa and across Canada.

QUESTIONS

1. What is *"la survivance"*?
2. Summarize the positions on the "matter of Québec" of Lesage, Johnson, Lévesque, and Trudeau.
3. Why was the nationalizing of the hydroelectricity industry so important to Québec in the 1960's?

Bilingualism—Cure, Compromise, or Calamity?

The roots of the concept of bilingualism go back to the turn of the century, when Henri Bourassa pleaded for a bilingual, bicultural country. His arguments went unheeded at the time, and during the following six decades. Was Canada ready for bilingualism now? Even in the 1960's, few Canadians outside Québec understood what was happening there. The idea of two "founding nations" offended people who were of neither British nor French origin. Furthermore, they saw no reason to be bilingual. In western Canada, particularly, people had long believed that what John Diefenbaker called "unhyphenated Canadianism" was the only way people of many heritages could live together peacefully.

Yet the conflict between Canada and Québec had to be solved. Lester Pearson accepted the challenge, for he believed that Canada could not survive the loss of Québec. Also, his sense of justice made him sympathetic to the frustrations of *Canadiens*. His solution to the problem was the same as Bourassa's. To achieve his ends, Pearson appointed a Royal Commission on Bilingualism and Biculturalism in July, 1963. Its ten fluently bilingual members, headed by André Laurendeau and Davidson Donton, a former head of the CBC, travelled across the country, listening to people in all regions. Alberta Premier Ernest Manning warned that the commission would do more harm than good; René Lévesque insisted that there was no such thing as bilingualism and never could be.

Bilingualism, even trilingualism, was a fact of life for most Canadiens, *as this English, Italian, and French sign in a Montréal shop window in 1962 demonstrates. But the federal government was yet to convince the rest of Canada of the importance of a bilingual policy.*

After nearly four years, the commission made its recommendations. The federal Parliament and the government of Canada should be officially bilingual, as should New Brunswick, Ontario, and "bilingual districts" where at least ten percent of the people spoke the other official language. The proposed solution prompted fresh outcries. Westerners claimed that bilingualism would lock them out of government jobs. Lévesque warned that it would lull Québec into a false sense of security. Despite the uproar, Canada changed because, in general, people were more willing to accept the concept of bilingualism than at any time previously. In 1969, all parties voted for an *Official Languages Act*, designed to make Parliament and the federal government bilingual slowly but systematically. The provinces gradually improved educational and other services for francophones. Ontario had a French-language education system from kindergarten to university in place as early as 1967. In 1970, Manitoba restored the French schools banned in 1916. British Columbia's Premier W.A.C. Bennett announced that French language instruction would be made available in B.C. schools.

In Québec, however, people still feared for the survival of French culture. The Québec birthrate had dropped from the highest to the lowest in Canada. In addition, thousands of immigrants from non-French and non-English backgrounds who came to Montréal preferred to educate their children in English, seeing it as the dominant language of North America. Already a minority in Canada, *Canadiens* feared that they might become a minority in their own province. Until the late 1960's, Québec had treated its anglophone residents with tolerance.

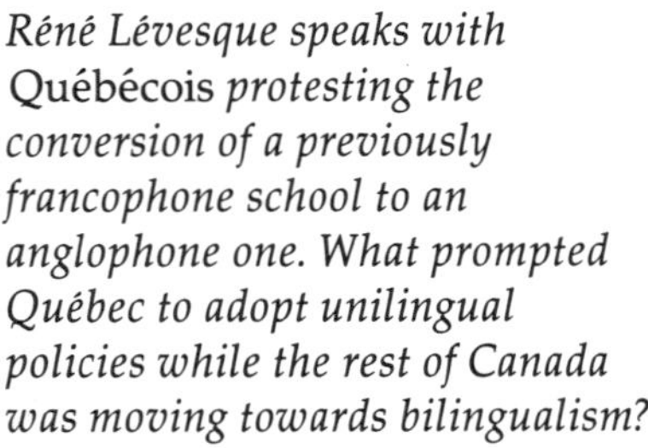

Réné Lévesque speaks with Québécois *protesting the conversion of a previously francophone school to an anglophone one. What prompted Québec to adopt unilingual policies while the rest of Canada was moving towards bilingualism?*

Now, that attitude changed. Demonstrators demanded that immigrants be obliged to sent their children to French schools, and that McGill University convert entirely to francophone instruction. At the end of the decade, as the rest of Canada adjusted to bilingualism, *Québécois* nationalists set out to make Québec unilingual.

QUESTIONS

1. **(a)** What courses of action did the Royal Commission on Bilingualism and Biculturalism recommend?
   (b) What changes in federal government language policy occurred as the result of the commission's report?
2. What two things were happening to the population of Québec that caused *Québécois* to fear for the survival of French culture?

The Liberation Decade

Even today, the 1960's still convey powerful images to people's minds: "women's lib", "civil rights", "free love", "peace", "doing your own thing". The attitudes expressed by these catch phrases helped to shape our society and still continue to have a deep impact. What factors combined to bring about such a concentration of social changes within a single decade?

Between 1945 and 1965, an unprecedented number of children were born in Canada (and elsewhere in the world). This population bulge became known as the "baby boom". Born after World War II, Canadian baby boomers grew up in unbroken peace and prosperity, unlike their parents, who had experienced the Depression and one or more wars. The parents worried about security in the form of a job and a home. The children, who took these things for granted, worried about personal freedom—liberation.

In the early and mid-'60's, the desire for freedom was expressed in long hair, casual dress, and loud music. As the decade progressed, liberation grew to encompass protest marches on behalf of peace and the rights of various groups, including Blacks (especially in the United States), women, gays, and students. The new mood set individuals above the authority of groups and what were considered to be outdated moral standards. Conformity was despised. Business and government were thought to defend conformity. In particular, corporations were seen as impersonal organizations which robbed their customers and polluted the environment in order to make profits. Ralph Nader, a hero of the age, proved that General Motors made unsafe cars. A drug company sold thalidomide as a painkiller without testing it; it left thousands of babies worldwide with stunted limbs and other defects. Government was seen as the accomplice of business, instead of the protector of citizens and the environment.

The emotions behind the protests were powerful and could not be ignored. Environmental activists succeeded, at least partly, in making business more accountable, though the effort continues. Governments granted funds to environmental groups and started to pass laws controlling pollution and protecting consumers. However, as if to retaliate, business co-opted the "youth culture" as a market for blue jeans, fast food, records, and stereo equipment. To harness the energy of the youth movement, the federal government funded the Company of Young Canadians (CYC). Started under the Pearson government in 1964, the CYC sent young Canadians across the country to help local groups with social work and public works programs. When members turned radical, however, funds were cut off. Similar projects followed in the 1970's: Opportunities for Youth, the Local Initiatives Program, and Katimavik.

Governments answered the call for liberation in other areas as well. Student protests and a prevailing attitude that people shouldn't have to learn what they didn't want to learn brought sweeping changes in education. From primary school to university, requirements were made more flexible, sometimes to the point of disappearing. One casualty was French; in a country which was trying to become bilingual, many universities dropped French as an entrance requirement.

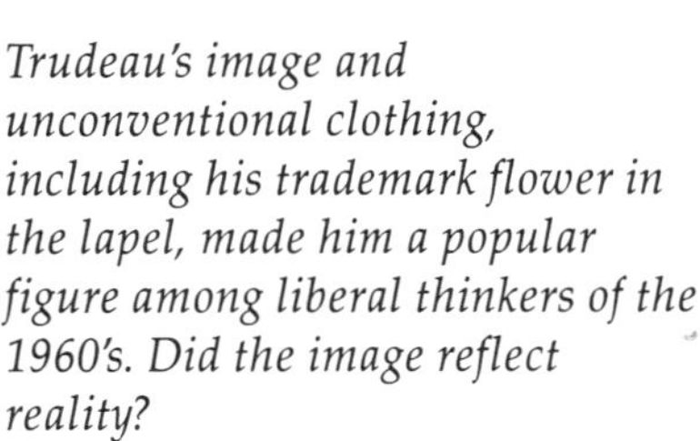

Trudeau's image and unconventional clothing, including his trademark flower in the lapel, made him a popular figure among liberal thinkers of the 1960's. Did the image reflect reality?

Like students, women were ready for liberation. A dependable birth control pill, introduced in the early 1960's, made it possible for women to delay or avoid having children. Many women who had previously left the work force upon marriage, or never worked at all, started to look upon wage-earning as a lifetime prospect. Women's groups banded together to campaign for equal rights, equal opportunities in the job market, and an end to discrimination based on sex. In response, the Pearson government set up a Royal Commission on the Status of Women in Canada under Florence Bird. It was the first federal commission ever to be chaired by a woman. After three years of study and hearings across Canada, the commission made 167 recommendations that would lead to equality of opportunity for men and women. Suggested reforms covered equal pay for work of equal value, maternity leave, day care, birth control, family law, education, the workplace, and the *Indian Act*. Like the recommendations of the Royal Commission on Bilingualism and Biculturalism, these changes were not implemented immediately. Society was not yet ready. It took a number of landmark court decisions concerning the division of property upon divorce, as well as two more decades, before Canadians accepted the majority of the suggested changes.

If there was one political figure who symbolized the liberation era, it was the Prime Minister Canadians elected in 1968. Pierre Elliott Trudeau's unconventional clothing, casual language, and defiance of decorum symbolized liberation. Opinion leaders approved. Trudeau believed that the individual mattered more than the group. As Minister of Justice, he had declared that "the state has no business in the bedrooms of the nation". What better slogan for the new individualism? Trudeau acted on what he had said: He pushed through laws to make divorce easier and to end criminal prosecution for homosexual acts between consenting adults. Trudeau's determination to liberate the individual explains why he opposed a return to the pre-1960's, conformist Québec society. In a later decade, it would also explain why he considered the patriation of the Constitution, with its *Charter of Rights and Freedoms*, as his greatest achievement.

Trudeau's belief in the individual made enemies. Even those who opposed separatism in Québec were furious at his denial of a need for special status to protect *la survivance*. Then, in 1969, Trudeau's individualistic attitudes brought him his first political crisis when he proposed to abolish *The Indian Act*. Native leaders had denounced the *Act* as unfair and restrictive, so the decision seemed reasonable. Trudeau promised that without the *Act*, Native people would enjoy "full, free and non-discriminatory participation in Canadian society". He was shocked when Native leaders accused him of planning "extermination through assimilation". In response to Trudeau's proposal, the leaders formed new organizations to protect and increase the special status of Native people.

Nor were the Native leaders the only Canadians to turn away from individual "liberation". Most Canadians, especially those of older generations, continued to live much as they had. "Liberation" was always more evident in the cities than in rural areas. When leaders of the major churches adjusted some of their teachings and form of worship to reflect the changing world, some members stopped going entirely, or switched to denominations which kept traditions intact.

Even Canadians who approved of the positive changes in society

Prime Minister Trudeau thought his efforts to abolish the Indian Act *would be popular among Native people. But Native leaders actively opposed the proposed abolition.*

recognized that there were costs as well. Easier divorce and sexual freedom led to the breakup of many families. The virtual abolition of censorship opened the door to brutal forms of pornography. Increased use of alcohol and drugs by the young ruined thousands of lives. Suicide became a major killer of young people. None of these problems was wholly new, but the changes brought by liberation made many of them worse.

QUESTIONS

1. What did "liberation" mean in the context of the 1960's?

2. **(a)** What were the qualities and attitudes of the "youth culture" of the 1960's?
(b) How did youth culture compare with Canadian culture in general?

3. Name four leading social causes of the 1960's.

4. What Canadian politician could be said to have symbolized the liberation era? Why?

5. How did Trudeau's view of the role of Native people in Canada clash with the views of Native leaders?

6. What were three negative effects of the liberation era?

Montréal mayor Jean Drapeau stands beside French President Charles de Gaulle. De Gaulle's cry of "Vive le Québec libre" *delighted* Québécois *separatists, outraged the rest of Canada, and cast a pall on relations between France and Canada for years. Did Canadians over-react?*

Canada and the World

In 1967, Canada was 100 years old—and Canadians were proud. For years before the event, people schemed, invented, and plotted innovative ways to make the Centennial a year to remember.

The largest project by far was dreamed up by Montréal's Mayor Jean Drapeau: Expo '67, a world's fair to be hosted by his city. Drapeau begged and bullied Québec City and Ottawa into financing his vision. Many Canadians were sour about the prospect; it would be expensive and, besides, Montréal needed a new sewer system more than a world's fair. Then, to everyone's delight, Expo '67 turned out to be wonderful fun. It defied its critics, opened on time, and proved to be a triumph of style and excitement. Many Canadians drawn to Expo '67 made their first trip to the province of Québec. If only for a short while, most Canadians felt part of a united country.

But the Centennial did not spread universal good will, despite Expo '67. Québec nationalists attached labels to their licence plates which said *"cent ans d'injustice"* ("one hundred years of injustice"). The event also caused one of the decade's major crises in foreign affairs. To help Québec celebrate the Centennial, Premier Daniel Johnson invited France's President Charles de Gaulle to Expo '67. President de Gaulle was delighted to accept the invitation and encourage Québec's autonomy. In previous years, the French government had made life miserable for Canada's ambassador. It had refused to receive Governor General Georges Vanier and had treated Québec's representative in Paris almost as the voice of an independent country. France had also persuaded Gabon, a former French African colony, to invite Québec, not Canada, to an international conference. Perhaps, de Gaulle reasoned, he could pull off an even greater coup against Canada at Expo '67.

To most Canadians, the French President's visit was just one more celebration amidst the centennial euphoria. To Johnson and Québec nationalists, however, de Gaulle was a powerful symbol of defiance. On July 24, 1967, before a vast throng of Montréalers, the old French general raised his arms skyward and intoned: *"Vive Montréal! Vive le Québec! Vive le Québec libre!"*

Outside Québec, Canadians were furious that de Gaulle had repeated the separatist slogan. "Canadians do not need to be liberated," declared Pearson, who cancelled de Gaulle's visit to Ottawa. In turn, most *Québécois* condemned the condemnation. Daniel Johnson and those who wanted independence for Québec were delighted. Whether prompted by vanity, a desire to make mischief, or pre-arrangement, de Gaulle had advanced the separatist cause.

As Québec looked across the ocean to links with France, the rest of Canada looked across the border, to the United States. In the early part of the decade, most Canadians felt close to the U.S. They envied the dynamic atmosphere of President John F. Kennedy's Washington. They were excited by Kennedy's youth, his support of civil rights for America's Blacks, and his seeming concern to defend democracy in the world. Canadians also admired the struggle of the Reverend Martin Luther King to win equal rights for his fellow Blacks. A few young Canadians joined the anti-racist Freedom Riders in the southern United States. Later in the decade, Canadians admired the "War on Poverty" launched by Kennedy's successor, Lyndon B. Johnson.

Canadians, of course, could not escape a special relationship with the huge country with which they shared the continent. One reason for the Liberal victory in 1963 was fear that John Diefenbaker had gone too far in trying to make Canada independent of U.S. strategy. At one time, Britain had been the main power in Canada's economy; after 1945, the United States far outweighed all other countries as Canada's supplier, customer, and investor. These influences were subtly reinforced by the mass media. Television, radio, film, and books and magazines poured American content into Canada. Only local newspapers proved immune to U.S. control. Nevertheless, most of what Canadians saw, heard, and read came from south of the border.

Yet, for all Canada's ties to the United States, relations soured by the end of the decade. The centennial celebrations of 1967 gave Canadians pride in themselves and their creativity. The idealism of the Kennedy

If the woodpecker is General de Gaulle, what do you think the tree represents?

Canadian peace demonstrators registering their dissent. Their banners read, "Stop the War in Vietnam. End Canadian Complicity." How might Canadian foreign policy have been interpreted as supporting American involvement in Vietnam?

years faded in violence. President Kennedy himself was assassinated in 1963. His brother Robert and civil rights leader Martin Luther King were murdered in 1968. Race riots in the "long, hot summers" of the 1960's filled the streets of great American cities with flames, looting, and the soldiers of the National Guard. Television brought the news to every Canadian home. Canadians could also see the brutality of the war in Vietnam, in which journalists cast the U.S. as a callous invader. While Americans wrestled with their dilemmas, Canadians could feel superior.

When Trudeau came to power in 1968, Canadians were probably more critical of the United States than they had ever been. With little of Lester Pearson's deep sympathy and knowledge of Canada's neighbour, Trudeau echoed the feeling, though he scorned nationalism in any form. In the 1970's, he would try to expand Canada's trade frontiers away from the United States, to include the nations of Europe, Africa, and the Pacific. At the same time, he would cut Canada's defences and its commitment to NATO. Yet politics would not change history, geography, or economics. Canada and the United States were inextricably linked.

QUESTIONS

1. Why was Canada's first world's fair held in 1967?

2. Why were Pearson and other Canadians so angered when de Gaulle shouted "*Vive le Québec libre!*"?

Chapter Summary

The 1950's were relatively quiet times for Canada. The 1960's were not. Minority governments, Québec separatism, protest movements, all marked the decade. So did changing personal and social values.

During the 1960's, Canadians were asked to reconsider what it meant to be a Canadian. Ties with Britain continued to be cut, as Canada adopted a new flag and made O Canada *its national anthem. Canadians celebrated their Centennial in the midst of struggles to keep the country together in the face of Québec nationalism's challenge to the old terms of Confederation. The federal government responded to Québec's challenge, and two new words were introduced to help define Canada: bilingual and bicultural.*

IN REVIEW

1. During the Quiet Revolution, the government took control of Québec's educational system. Why do governments, especially those which are trying to bring about change, feel the need to control education?
2. What do you think Diefenbaker meant by "unhyphenated Canadianism"?
3. What prompted some *Québécois* to attach signs saying *"cent ans d'injustice"* to their licence plates in 1967?

APPLYING YOUR KNOWLEDGE

1. Explain the concept of biculturalism. Is biculturalism discriminatory? Which Canadians may have felt left out by the adoption of the concept of biculturalism?
2. Why did some *Québécois* want full independence from Canada?
3. Why would a Canadian Prime Minister object strongly if a provincial government invited another country's President or Prime Minister to visit without involving the federal government?

FURTHER INVESTIGATION

1. Do research to discover more about why *Québécois* felt dissatisfied with Confederation in the 1960's.
2. Find out what services in your community are available in both French and English. Do you feel your community needs to offer bilingual services? Give reasons for your answer.
3. From relatives, friends, books, and back issues of newspapers and magazines, find out about how life in Canada changed between 1960 and 1970.

CHAPTER 7

The End of "Liberation"

Canada in the 1970's was forced to concentrate on two issues: Québec and the economy. As the decade opened, Québec's "Quiet Revolution" made front page headlines. By the end of the decade, Canadians anxiously awaited the results of a referendum that would decide whether Québec would remain within or withdraw from Confederation.

The economic issues of inflation and unemployment also preoccupied Canada throughout the 1970's. High inflation reduced Canadians' spending power, and high unemployment created anger and despair among Canadian workers.

As Prime Minister throughout most of the 1970's Trudeau was the driving political force of the decade. The Trudeau of the '70's was, however, different from the Trudeau who symbolized liberation in the '60's. Rather than unifying the country, his belief in a strong federal government brought about divisions between Ottawa and the provinces. The feeling of alienation was especially strong in western Canada.

In international affairs, Trudeau increased Canadian awareness of the Third World. New foreign aid programs were introduced to build stronger ties with the Third World. New foreign policy brought full recognition of China, and a bid for better trade relations beyond the American and European markets.

As you read this chapter, you will find answers to the following questions:

- *Why did the October Crisis result in a decade-long focus on Québec?*
- *How did the* Parti Québécois *propose to resolve Québec's dissatisfaction with Confederation?*
- *Why were Québec's language laws controversial?*
- *How did inflation and unemployment affect life in Canada?*
- *What policies did the Trudeau government introduce to attempt to solve Canada's economic problems?*
- *How did the Trudeau government's policies lead to tensions in federal/provincial relations?*
- *Why did Canada develop stronger ties with Third World nations during the 1970's?*

The FLQ Crisis

The optimism of the 1960's did not last long into the next decade. On October 5, 1970, Prime Minister Trudeau faced an almost unprecedented challenge to the power of the government. A handful of young Québec nationalists calling themselves the *Front de Libération du Québec* (FLQ) kidnapped the British Trade Commissioner, James Cross. The FLQ had already claimed responsibility for over 200 bombings, mainly of mailboxes and other government symbols. Their newest enterprise was more deadly. Five days after the Cross kidnapping, the FLQ seized Pierre Laporte, a Québec Cabinet minister. The FLQ demanded that members who had been imprisoned for the bombings be released, and that the FLQ **manifesto** be read over the radio.

Manifesto

A manifesto is a public declaration or statement of policy, opinions, intentions, or motives. Probably the best known is The Communist Manifesto, ***written by Karl Marx and Friedrich Engels.***

Radical nationalists, some public figures and labour leaders, and thousands of students applauded the FLQ's actions. René Lévesque joined leading *Québécois* in urging the new premier, Robert Bourassa, to negotiate with the kidnappers. Some even suggested that Bourassa give way to a government of nationalist intellectuals. Bourassa agreed that the manifesto would be read, and offered safe passage abroad for the kidnappers in exchange for the hostages. However, he refused to negotiate the freeing of convicted terrorists.

Bourassa also turned to Trudeau for help. He asked for federal troops to help his overworked police, and for additional search and arrest powers for the Québec police in order to make the search for the hostages easier. In response, Trudeau invoked the *War Measures Act* to deal with what he saw as an "apprehended insurrection". In other words, the government behaved as though the FLQ and their supporters were on the verge of turning their mass meetings into a revolution against the government. The *Act* gave the government powers which had previously been reserved for times of war. It granted the police

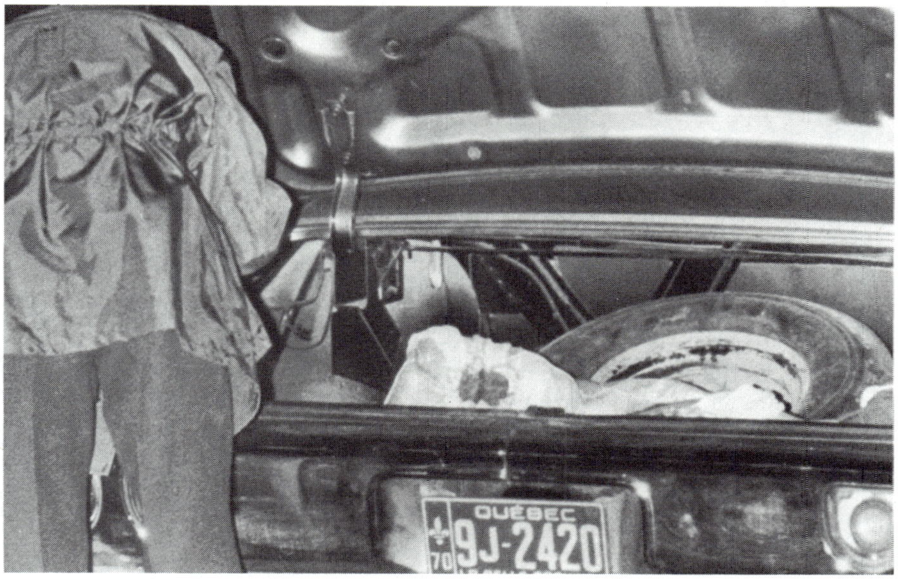

The body of Pierre Laporte was found in the trunk of this car on the day after Trudeau invoked the War Measures Act. *What impact did this discovery have on the Canadian public?*

almost unlimited authority to investigate and make arrests. Ten thousand troops swept into Montréal, Québec City, and Ottawa to back the police. Nearly 470 people were arrested—some of them for no other reason than their public support of the FLQ.

The *Act* came into effect on October 16. The next day, Pierre Laporte's corpse was found in the trunk of a car. Applause for the FLQ came to an abrupt halt. Early in December, the RCMP and Québec police discovered that James Cross was still alive. The government negotiated his release in return for safe passage to Cuba for his kidnappers. A month later, the kidnappers of Pierre Laporte were found; they were tried, convicted, and sentenced to prison.

CLOSE-UP

The *War Measures Act*—Pro and Con

Although 88 percent of Canadians (and 86 percent of Québec residents) approved of the declaration of the *War Measures Act*, those who disagreed put forward some strong arguments against it. For months after the October Crisis, newspapers and magazines carried opinions, both pro and con. Below, Gérard Pelletier, a Liberal minister who agreed to the proclamation of the *Act*, explains why he voted in favour. Tommy Douglas, leader of the NDP and one of 16 members, all of them from the NDP, who voted against the proclamation, gives his reasons for dissenting.

> I have stated publicly that I was sick at heart when I voted for the proclamation of the *War Measures Act*... I voted... for the special measures because I believed (and I still believe) that in the circumstances it was the *least bad* solution—since it would be hard to speak of a "good" solution that involves the proclamation of the *War Measures Act* in a country like Canada.
>
> The decision was all the more critical because of the time factor. Urgency limits the possibilities for reflection, consultation and... studies, and forces those involved to take more or less calculated risks. This, of course, is exactly the effect sought by those who create a state of emergency by resorting to violence.
>
> Resort to a law that is as grim as its title as it is wide in its powers... was a move that, even if justified by the gravity of the situation, was still very difficult politically. In fact, the proclamation of this law extended the Québec crisis to the country as a whole. Is it conceivable that we would have alarmed Vancouver voters for a problem 3,000 miles [4800 km] distant without good reason? International repercussions could not be overlooked either, since the proclamation of such a law might jeopardize Canada's reputation for internal political stability....

Children watch armed soldiers on duty in Montréal during the October Crisis.

The *War Measures Act* was proclaimed, therefore, to nip any new plan of violence in the bud and to enable police action to be more efficient and more rapid... Generally speaking, the various police forces were neither prepared nor equipped to cope with criminal activities like those of October, 1970. Is this something to be deplored? Do we know what the existence and omnipresence of special anti-subversive police would mean?

—from Gérard Pelletier, *The October Crisis*, Toronto: McClelland and Stewart, 1971.

This is the first time to my knowledge that the *War Measures Act* has been invoked in peacetime... We (the NDP) have been prepared and are prepared to support enlarging the police powers if the government thinks it necessary to give the police greater authority in the matter of searching for dynamite and offensive weapons... We are prepared to support the government in taking whatever measures are necessary to safeguard life and to maintain law and order in this country. But... we are not prepared to use the preservation of law and order as a smokescreen to destroy the liberties and freedom of the people of Canada.

This is overkill on a gargantuan scale... Right now, there is no constitution in this country, no Bill of Rights, no provincial constitutions. This government now has the power... to do anything it wants—to intern any citizen, to deport any citizen, to arrest any person or to declare any organization subversive or illegal....

The action of the government constitutes a victory for the FLQ. This is exactly what they wanted. They want a confrontation between themselves and the government of Canada. They want to be recognized as a revolutionary force with whom the government of Canada must deal, and because of whom the the government of Canada must mobilize all its resources to declare war... we cannot protect democratic freedom by restricting, limiting and destroying democratic freedom.

—from *Til Power is Brought to Pooling: Tommy Douglas Speaks*, L.D. Lovick, ed., Lantzville, B.C.: Oolichan Books, 1979.

QUESTIONS

1. **(a)** How does Pelletier justify the imposition of the *Act*?
   (b) What reasons does Douglas give against imposing the *Act*?
2. Write a dissenting argument which responds to either Pelletier's or Douglas' position on the Trudeau government's declaration of the *War Measures Act*.

The October Crisis ended the decade of hopeful protest and liberation. Trudeau's role as symbol of liberation ended along with it. Some of his admirers were dismayed by his use of force. Others warned that he had created martyrs to the cause of Québec separatism. Nevertheless, most Canadians approved of his actions. How did Trudeau himself reconcile invoking the *War Measures Act* with believing in the rights of the individual? To Trudeau, there was no contradiction. Freedom meant self-discipline. Freedom was possible only in an organized society strong enough to defend its principles. Most important, Trudeau insisted, law mattered more than freedom, because only the rule of law made freedom possible. Thus, it was not the terrorists themselves, but the people who cheered them on and who wanted to undermine the authority of an elected government, who had led Trudeau to the *War Measures Act*. How far would he go, asked a reporter at the start of the crisis. "Watch me," said Trudeau.

QUESTIONS

1. **(a)** What caused the October Crisis?
   (b) What did the FLQ hope to achieve through their actions? Were they successful?
2. **(a)** How did the Québec government respond to the crisis?
   (b) What was the response of the federal government?
3. Why was the proclamation of the *War Measures Act* a surprising move?
4. Do you agree or disagree with Trudeau's view that law matters more than freedom?

Québec: Moving Towards Independence

The FLQ crisis certainly did not improve relations between Québec and the rest of Canada. The language issue which had arisen in the 1960's continued to smoulder. In 1970, it contributed to the downfall of the *Union Nationale* government. The new premier was Robert Bourassa, a Liberal who had been chosen as provincial Liberal leader with Trudeau's support. The Prime Minister's support helped Bourassa win his position, but it did not help him keep it. For a few years, Bourassa's government delayed making any decision about the language issue. The pressure on the Liberals grew. More and more *Québécois* turned away from the concept of bilingualism towards francophone unilingualism. Finally, in 1974, the Liberals introduced Bill 22, which made French the official language of Québec. One of its main effects was to take from parents the right to choose the language of education for their children. But even Bill 22 was not enough for many *Québécois*.

Throughout the early 1970's, the fortunes of René Lévesque's *Parti Québécois* improved. In 1970, they won one-fifth of the votes; in 1973, almost one-third. The Liberal government increasingly seemed to ignore the wishes of the people of Québec. In addition, the Québec economy was faltering, and the media were hostile to the Liberals. In the campaign of 1976, Lévesque offered the voters something entirely new. If the *Parti Québécois* was elected, he promised, there would be a referendum to determine whether the people of Québec wanted to stay within Confederation or separate from Canada. Levésque also promised economic and other reforms, honest government, and defence of the French language.

A seemingly unrelated issue helped the *Parti Québécois* make gains. Ottawa had declared that both French and English could be used in Québec's air space. When anglophone pilots and air traffic controllers protested that air safety would be affected, the federal government backed down. A year later, when their fears had been proved false, bilingualism was restored. By this time, the rest of Canada was scarcely interested in the issue. But *Québécois* remembered. In November, 1976, 46 percent of voters gave the *Parti Québécois* an impressive victory.

One early result was Bill 101, passed in 1977. In a series of sweeping measures, English was virtually driven out of public sight. By law, French would be the only language of government, business, education, and communications. Signs, both public and private, had to be in French. Even bilingual menus might be illegal.

Bill 101 demonstrated how far Québec would go to protect its language. Thousands of anglophone residents of Québec responded by leaving the province. Others stayed and learned French. Most Canadians believed that this was the first victory: separation and independence would follow with the referendum that Levesque had promised. Others realized that *Québécois* had achieved one of their main goals: to keep their language—and therefore their culture—safe. Would this be enough to keep the province within Confederation? The answer would not come until the start of the next decade.

QUESTIONS

1. **(a)** What was the purpose of Bill 22?
   (b) What was the purpose of Bill 101?
   (c) What difference was there between the two laws?
2. How did Bills 22 and 101 affect life in Québec?
3. How did Canadian airline pilots and air traffic controllers become involved in the *Québécois'* struggle to maintain their language?
4. Why did the *Parti Québécois* think language laws were necessary?
5. **(a)** Review the *Parti Québécois'* language policy, then write two arguments for and two arguments against it.
   (b) Which set of arguments do you think is stronger? Why?

Inflation and Unemployment: Battling the Two-Headed Monster

Although few Canadians would have believed it at the time, the 1970's saw a continuation of the dramatic growth of the Canadian economy which began in the '60's. Between 1959 and 1969, Canada's GNP had risen by $34.3 thousand million in actual value; between 1969 and 1979, it rose by another $43.6 thousand million.

On a more personal level, too, there was economic improvement. The average family income rose 15 percent faster than inflation during the 1970's. The Maritimes, assisted by federal transfer payments, came close to the national average income for the first time since the Laurier era. Saskatchewan, Alberta, and British Columbia grew the fastest; B.C. ended the decade with the highest average family income in Canada. Living standards across the country continued to improve.

Newly-adult baby boomers needed housing. Massive apartment blocks changed city skylines, and housing developments expanded into what had been farmland. Most Canadians had more to spend on leisure and entertainment. New cable systems delivered television programs on scores of channels to city-dwellers. Promoters in Toronto and Montréal bought major league baseball franchises, while Vancouver, Calgary, Edmonton, and Winnipeg purchased franchises in the National Hockey League, once dominated by six eastern teams. Across the country, people took to the ski slopes, jogging tracks, and tennis and squash courts, as a trend to fitness boomed. A mid-winter holiday in some sunny resort seemed normal, not a rare privilege, for many working Canadians.

Prosperity was fuelled by the development of vast energy projects. In Alberta, government and private interests combined to finance Syncrude tar sands production. In Québec, one of the world's largest hydroelectric projects took shape on the rivers around James Bay, producing power for Québec and for export to the United States.

Yet not all the economic signs were positive. More and more baby boomers entered the job market, and ever-greater numbers of women began to work outside the home. Simultaneously there was a technological revolution which seemed to shrink the number of available job opportunities. Industrial automation stopped the growth in well-paid blue-collar jobs. Because of mechanization, fewer people were needed in the resource industries to fell trees, dig mines, or harvest crops. The explosion in the use of computers meant that people increasingly found employment in information industries. As a result of all these factors, and others, unemployment increased steadily.

What Canadians, worried by technological change and a shifting economy, did not realize at the time was that the unemployment rate could have been much worse. Throughout the 1970's, jobs were being created by government and business at a rate unprecedented even in wartime. But job creation could not keep up with all the trends. Because profits were high and labour was plentiful, industries had more reason to hire office staff and consultants, and less reason to buy labour-saving machinery. As a result, industrial efficiency and productivity decreased, further hurting the economy.

Unemployment was one of the two major economic problems of the 1970's. The other was inflation. The price of goods and services had been edging upwards since the low point of the Depression. Suddenly two events occurred which caused inflation to explode. The first was the devaluation of the American dollar. Devaluation struck President Richard Nixon and his advisers as an easy way to slash the debts built

Who comprises the tag team opposing inflation and unemployment? Do you feel the optimism is warranted?

up during the Vietnam War. Since 1944, the American dollar had been the standard to which most other currencies were compared. Thirty-five American dollars would buy an ounce (28.35 g) of gold, no matter what the British pound, Japanese yen, or Canadian dollar were worth. In 1971, the U.S. dollar was allowed to "float" to its actual value compared with other currencies. As a result, gold prices soared. So did inflation.

The second event which contributed to inflation followed in 1973. The Organization of Petroleum Exporting Countries (OPEC) quadrupled the price of oil. OPEC had realized that its product was so vital to modern countries that it could set almost any price it wanted. In addition, Arab members of OPEC wanted to punish western countries for supporting Israel. Other members wanted to speed up their own development.

At first, Canadians were not concerned. They could meet their needs from the oil fields of Alberta. The Trudeau government decided to freeze the price of Alberta oil. It put an export tax on oil shipped to the United States. The proceeds of the tax were used to subsidize the cost of oil imported from OPEC and used in eastern Canada. Albertans were angry: Ottawa had invaded a hard-won provincial jurisdiction over natural resources. Alberta wanted to use the profits from higher oil prices to create a Heritage Fund for hard times and to finance the hunt for new oil and gas reserves. The struggle between Alberta and the federal government made Trudeau and the Liberals unpopular in western Canada. It also fuelled western separatism, to the point where some people began to fear that the West would leave Confederation before Québec.

The first radical OPEC price hike, and another in 1979, were only part of the explanation for Canada's worst experience with inflation since the First World War. During the 1970's, prices for most goods and services doubled; some prices went much higher. Inflation worried everyone, but it was worst for those living on a fixed income, such as pensioners. A couple who retired on $6000 per year in 1967 were well off; by 1979, they were in deep poverty.

There were many popular scapegoats for inflation, from landlords to labour unions. In his first term, Prime Minister Trudeau had promised to wrestle inflation to the ground. Later, he confessed that it was a world problem, beyond the control of a single country. But Canadian voters wanted their problems solved—and they were not certain the Liberals could do so. In 1972, Canadians elected the most evenly split Parliament ever: 109 Liberals to 107 Conservatives. The NDP, with 31 seats, held the balance of power. The price freeze on both Alberta oil and OPEC oil which followed the 1973 energy crisis was intended to please the majority of voters, though it certainly angered Alberta. At the urging of the NDP, Trudeau brought in other ways of shielding Canadians from inflation. Pensions and family allowances were linked to the cost of living index. Liberal Finance Minister John Turner also kept a Conservative promise to make sure that taxes did not rise with income levels. This solution, known as **indexation**, meant that government spending would rise with inflation, but its income would not. The only possible result would be a budget deficit... a problem for the future. Such policies helped the Liberals win a new majority in the 1974 election.

During the campaign, Trudeau had mocked a Conservative promise to fight inflation through wage and price controls. But by 1975, the dollar was losing a penny a month in buying power, for an annual inflation rate of over 12 percent. In October, 1975, Trudeau reversed his stand and announced the creation of an Anti-Inflation Board (AIB) to enforce wage and price controls. Union leaders who had backed Trudeau in 1974 felt betrayed; they felt that wage increases were necessary to match inflation and protect workers. Some workers had won good contracts; others, thanks to controls, would never catch up. On the first anniversary of the AIB, October 14, 1976, a million union workers went on a one-day strike in protest. However, many Canadians seemed to welcome a policy which promised to hold down inflation.

Inflation was also one of the issues which helped decide the fate of Robert Bourassa and the Liberals in Québec. Civil servants, hospital workers, and teachers—all paid by the government—struck for higher

Labour representatives protest against the wage and price controls enacted by the federal government to fight inflation. Why did governments and business blame unions for inflation?

wages. That angered the voters. When the strikers were forced back to work, they were angry too. In addition, the James Bay hydroelectric development was costing far more than predicted. The 1976 Montréal Olympics left behind a mountain of debt. All these factors, combined with the referendum issue, helped bring the *Parti Québécois* to power: René Lévesque had promised Québec sound financial management.

The year 1978 brought a new inflation-fighting strategy. Trudeau joined the leaders of six other industrialized nations in Bonn, Germany, to find an end to worldwide inflation. He returned with policies that went back to the time of the Depression. Wage and price controls were scrapped. Government spending would be slashed, to control the growing deficit. The indexation of pensions and taxes had brought about a deficit of $12 thousand million... and growing. Decreasing government spending was easier said than done, however. No politician could hope to be re-elected after reducing the money paid to pensioners, families, and the unemployed. Cutting provincial transfer payments would bring howls of protest from the provinces. If grants to business and industry were cut, who would create new jobs?

Neither Trudeau nor Joe Clark, the new leader of the Conservatives, could come up with a program to accomplish the major cutbacks. In his campaign, Clark spoke earnestly about the deficit, but his own program included still more promises of spending and tax cuts. Given the choice between Trudeau and Clark in 1979, the voters were uncertain. In the end, they preferred a change. The Conservatives won 136 seats, against the Liberals' 114 and NDP's 26. Clark formed a government, but the Liberals and NDP could combine forces to defeat him.

Canadians waited in vain for the Conservatives to act. By September, the Liberals had risen sharply in the opinion polls. In November, Trudeau announced his retirement, with a leadership convention to be held in March, 1980. Conservatives took heart: John Crosbie, the

What idea is the cartoonist attempting to portray?

"Would you mind giving this to Joe?"

Conservative Finance Minister, could at last bring in his budget without opposition. The budget was a tough one which raised taxes and cut government spending in many areas. Despite the Conservatives' hopes, the NDP and the Liberals looked at the polls, and joined forces to defeat the budget. After the non-confidence vote on December 13, the Conservatives had to call another election. Canadians had not liked the Crosbie budget, and nothing that Clark did during his campaign changed their minds. Nor had Clark expected Trudeau to return as leader of the Liberals. On February 18, 1980, Ontario, Québec, and Maritime voters gave the Liberals a majority: 147 seats to 103 for the Conservatives and 32 for the NDP, with their new leader Ed Broadbent. In all of Québec, the Conservatives had one seat; so did the Liberals in the West. A decade which had begun in the excitement of liberation ended with Canada more bitter and divided than ever before.

QUESTIONS

1. Which province had the highest average family income at the end of the 1970's?
2. How did the baby boomers contribute to Canada's prosperity (and inflation) during the 1970's?
3. What two factors account for growing unemployment between 1966 and 1982?
4. How did OPEC promote inflation?
5. What fuelled the new concept of western separatism?
6. How did indexation guarantee that a federal budget deficit would occur?
7. Why did workers oppose the Anti-Inflation Board?
8. Why were the Conservatives forced to call a general election for February, 1980?

A Community of Communities

World events deeply affected Canada in the 1970's. During the energy crisis, Canadians had tried and failed to shelter themselves from a world which had changed drastically since the 1950's. The hostility between the two superpowers and their allies remained, backed by growing stocks of increasingly powerful nuclear weapons and the missiles to deliver them. But the rivalry affected a world whose political map was almost entirely new. Scores of nations came into being after World War II, as European countries retreated from their colonies. By the end of the decade, the newly independent nations of the

Caribbean, Africa, and the Pacific swelled the ranks of the United Nations to more than twice the original number.

Like Canada and the rest of the world, these countries experienced a population explosion in the postwar years. What many of them did not have was the wealth and prosperity of Canada. Exploitation during the colonial era, lack of resources, population growth, and other factors helped create desperate problems of poverty for many new nations. Even those with the richest prospects, such as Nigeria, Uganda, and Jamaica, suffered. They were often torn by internal political strife as rival factions struggled for power in the aftermath of colonial rule.

Yet not all Third World countries were poor or politically troubled. The "oil weapon" had made the nations of the Persian Gulf enormously rich. Productivity and ingenuity had spurred Japan to a leading place in the industrial world, so that by the 1970's it was considered a First World power. Economic rivals such as South Korea, Taiwan, and Singapore followed in Japan's wake.

Canadians liked to believe that they had a special relationship with Third World countries. Like them, Canada had been a colony, and most of its trade was still in natural resources. Starting in the 1950's, thousands of idealistic young Canadians travelled overseas to help with development activities. They came home advocating aid and understanding for the problems of underdevelopment. Organizations such as Canadian University Services Overseas (CUSO) and World University Services of Canada (WUSC) provided money and grassroots aid to many less developed countries.

In 1968, the federal government formed the Canadian International Development Agency (CIDA). Foreign aid given through CIDA soon outstripped the Canadian contributions to United Nations assistance and other multi-nation programs. Most of this aid was in the form of food and money. In the latter case, however, the receiving nations had to spend the funds on purchasing Canadian-made products. Before CIDA, Canada's aid to Africa had gone mainly to former English colonies. In the 1970's, much was also given to former French colonies. In this way, the Trudeau government emphasized Canada's commitment to being a bilingual, bicultural nation. Under Trudeau, Canada's foreign role served Canada's domestic interests as well.

Another change during the Trudeau years which affected Canada's relationship with the Third World was in the area of immigration policy. Canada had for many years had a policy which made it difficult for people from developing countries to immigrate, unless they were rich or had jobs already waiting for them. Preference had been given to would-be immigrants from Europe. In 1966, 75 percent of immigrants to Canada came from Europe. The new policy, combined with Europe's new prosperity, meant that just one decade later half of all newcomers were from Asia, Africa, and Latin America. Their presence was another link between Canada and the Third World.

Yet, to most people in the Third World, Canada was a rich, white country, linked to the United States and Europe. In the 1940's, the Soviet foreign minister had called Canada a "squeaky second fiddle" to the United States. The insult bothered Canadians, probably because it so often seemed to be true. After the Second World War, Canada's economic and political life was increasingly tied to the U.S.A. In 1963, Britain had emphasized its new role as part of Europe by applying to join the European Economic Community (EEC), though the hostility of French President Charles de Gaulle kept it out until 1973. As Britain shifted its trade alliances, Canada grew even more dependent on trade with the United States. The rest of Europe, too, was more interested in developing European trade than in dealing with Canada. Japan bought raw materials from Canada, notably lumber and coal from British Columbia, but had no need for Canadian manufactured products. China continued to buy wheat, but, like Japan and other Asian countries, bought few goods. At the same time, Canada increasingly bought manufactured products from Asia. Nevertheless, the United States remained by far Canada's most important trade partner.

In 1971, the costs of the war in Vietnam forced President Nixon to devalue the American dollar, as you read earlier. He also threw up tariff barriers against all foreign imports and restricted the amount of American funds which could be invested in other countries. With two-thirds of Canadian exports heading south of the border, and branch plants being closed, Canada pleaded for an exemption. Washington agreed—at a price. Henceforth, Nixon and his officials said Canada would have to serve U.S. policy goals or fend for herself. The age of "exemptions" was over. The United States could no longer afford them.

Although Canada was the largest trading partner of the United States, Americans continued to take their northern neighbour for granted. Tankers were the cheapest way to bring oil from Alaska to the

A Chinese food store in Toronto. Canada's relations with Third World countries were strengthened as a result of the Trudeau government's policies.

lower 48 states; few Americans were concerned that an oil spill could devastate the British Columbia coast. After the American ship *Manhattan* pioneered a tanker route to the Arctic Ocean, the U.S. decided that the Northwest Passage was an international waterway, whatever Ottawa or the Inuit might say. Canada thereupon extended its claim to its adjoining seas to 200 miles (320 km) offshore.

During the 1970's, Canada made an effort to wrest its economy back from American influence. In 1973, the Trudeau government created the Foreign Investment Review Agency (FIRA) to make sure that foreign investment served Canadian interests. Next came the Canada Development Corporation (CDC) and Petro-Canada, which were intended to buy out foreign-owned companies in Canada. The National Energy Program (NEP), created in 1980, gave special benefits to Canadian-owned and -controlled oil and gas firms. Although most other countries had far stricter limits on foreign ownership, each Canadian program to limit foreign control brought protests from the United States.

Trudeau's efforts to increase Canada's control over its economy once again showed his belief that Canadian foreign policy must serve Canada's interests first. Like Prime Minister William Lyon Mackenzie King, Trudeau distrusted foreign commitments that might drag Canada into other nations' quarrels. His first major foreign policy decision was therefore to cut the armed forces from 100 000 to 80 000 men. The next was to bring half of Canada's NATO forces back from Europe. He might have brought them all home, but he realized that European nations would likely retaliate by cutting their imports from Canada. In fact, Trudeau's NATO cut was one of the reasons why the European

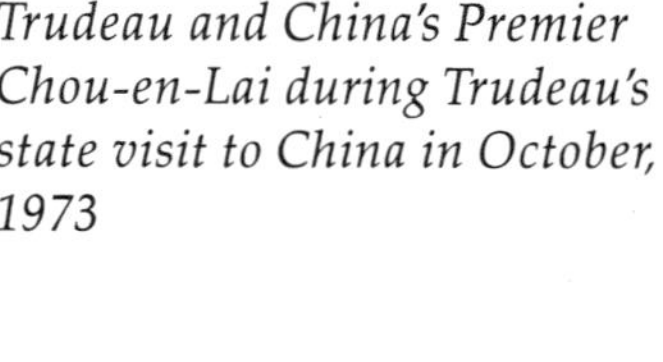

Trudeau and China's Premier Chou-en-Lai during Trudeau's state visit to China in October, 1973

Joe Clark and his wife Maureen McTeer during the 1979 election campaign. Why might Canadians have been willing to support the Conservatives in 1979?

Economic Community continued to limit its trade with Canada. Another policy decision, made in 1970 over U.S. protests, was to recognize the People's Republic of China. Trudeau made the move partly because it made sense to acknowledge a government that had been in power for over 20 years and partly in recognition of past wheat deals and in the hope of future trade. The United States soon followed suit, limiting Canada's brief advantage.

By the late 1970's, experiences such as his misjudgement about the withdrawal of NATO forces from Europe had taught Trudeau that a high world profile was good for national unity—and for his own political fortunes. Trudeau also knew that Canada wanted to play a world role, and realized that it would be possible only if both trade alliances and world connections were strengthened and diversified. At the economic summit in Germany in 1978, and at subsequent gatherings, Trudeau made himself the spokesman for the less developed countries. He also urged the exchange of views between wealthy and poorer countries. During the election campaign of 1979, Trudeau's strategists hoped that his world reputation would reduce his unpopularity over domestic economic issues. As you saw earlier, the strategy did not bring the hoped-for result.

During the same campaign, Conservative leader Joe Clark urged Canadians to think of themselves as a "community of communities". This was a shape the world had already taken. The polarization of the 1950's, with the two superpowers and their allies dominating the world, had evolved into a collection of economic and political communities, sometimes cooperating, sometimes in conflict. It remained up to Canadians to decide the fate of their own community—how it would fit into the world of other communities.

QUESTIONS

1. Why did such countries as Nigeria, Uganda, and Jamaica suffer after independence in spite of having "the richest prospects"?
2. What similarities between Canada and some emerging nations led to a special relationship with the Third World?
3. What is the purpose of CIDA?
4. What change in government policy resulted in an increase in the number of immigrants to Canada from the Third World?
5. Why did President Nixon devalue the U.S. dollar and raise import barriers in 1971?
6. Why did Canada ask for exemption from Nixon's high tariffs?
7. Name four organizations established by the Trudeau government to limit foreign (especially American) influence on Canadian business.

Chapter Summary

The 1970's forced Canadians to re-examine the relationship between the federal and provincial governments. This occurred partly as a result of the election of the Parti Québécois *in Québec, and partly as a result of Trudeau's policies to control inflation and reduce unemployment.*

The Trudeau government's struggle to gain control over inflation and unemployment emphasized the impact of global economic forces on the Canadian economy. In particular, Canada became concerned about its economic dependency on the United States. The government therefore sought to create new markets for Canadian goods outside the United States, in Europe and the Third World. It also established FIRA and other organizations, to regulate and reduce the amount of foreign investment in Canada.

Despite domestic problems, Canadians became more aware of the problems of Third World nations during the 1970's. New foreign aid agencies such as CUSO and CIDA were introduced to increase Canada's role in Third World development.

IN REVIEW

1. If you had been polled the day after the *War Measures Act* was invoked, would you have voted for or against the *Act's* proclamation? Give reasons for your answer.
2. Do you think that the passing into law of Bills 22 and 101 weakened or strengthened support for independence among *Québécois*? Explain your reasoning.
3. Why did Trudeau's role as a "symbol of liberation" end with the October Crisis?

4. What election promises helped Lévesque and the *Parti Québécois* get elected in 1976?

5. **(a)** What steps did the Trudeau government take in 1978 to try to end inflation?
   (b) What was the political result of the strategy?

6. **(a)** Why did Canada cut its armed forces in Europe?
   (b) What was the effect of the decision on the Canadian economy?

APPLYING YOUR KNOWLEDGE

1. How did the October Crisis affect many Canadians' attitudes towards Québec?

2. During times of high unemployment, governments may create jobs within government services. What are the benefits of such a policy? The hazards?

3. During the 1970's, the federal government wanted to keep the price of oil the same across Canada. The government froze the price of Alberta oil, thereby preventing it from rising to world prices, and subsidized the cost of more expensive (world price) oil for eastern Canada.
   (a) Do you think this policy was a sound one? Why or why not?
   (b) What would an Albertan's attitude to the policy have been? A Nova Scotian's? Why?

4. After the 1980 election, the Conservatives had only one MP from Québec; the Liberals had only one MP from west of Winnipeg. Why did some Canadians worry about this situation?

5. **(a)** What developments caused Canadian trade with Europe to decline?
   (b) How did Canada try to protect itself from the impact of these developments?

FURTHER INVESTIGATION

1. **(a)** Some people have suggested that Canada will eventually join the United States. Do you agree?
   (b) Would you favour such a union with the U.S.? Why or why not?

2. Do research to discover the cause of internal strife (at present or in the recent past) in one of these recently established Third World countries: Nigeria, Uganda, Jamaica, Zaïre (formerly Belgian Congo), Zimbabwe (formerly Rhodesia), Mozambique, Sudan, Pakistan (now divided into Pakistan and Bangladesh), Sri Lanka (formerly Ceylon).

CHAPTER 8

A Canadian Society

The twentieth century has brought phenomenal changes to the way Canadians live. The progress and prosperity of Canada as it approaches the end of the twentieth century would surprise even Sir Wilfrid Laurier, the Prime Minister who predicted a great century for Canada. It is unlikely that he could have foreseen that Canada would be a multicultural country, and one where the concerns of the Native peoples were becoming increasingly important. Yet many of the issues that face Canada in the late 1980's would seem familiar to Laurier. As they did in 1900, Canadians continue to puzzle over French-English relations, the role of the federal and provincial governments, the nature of immigration, and Canada's relations with the rest of the world. In this chapter, you will consider the following questions:

- *How was constitutional reform accomplished during the 1980's?*
- *As of the late 1980's, what are the relations between Québec, the other provinces, and the federal government?*
- *What is the current position of Canada's Native people within Canada?*
- *What are Canada's current immigration policies, and how are they affecting Canadian society?*
- *What does it mean to be a Canadian citizen?*
- *To what extent has Canada become a multicultural country?*
- *How does Canada interact with other nations?*

Unfinished Business

Pierre Elliott Trudeau promised Canadians that his sixth election, in 1980, would be his last. Before he retired from politics, however, he had some unfinished business to take care of. First, he wanted to defeat Québec separatists and keep Québec within Canada. He also wanted to bring about constitutional reform in Canada. Finally, he wished to make a contribution to world peace by promoting the cause of the Third World and by trying to warm up the intensified Cold War between the United States and the Soviet Union.

The most important item on the agenda was the first. In the provincial election of 1976, René Lévesque had promised his voters a referendum on independence if his party was brought to power. During the next four years, the victorious *Parti Québécois* considered possible referendum questions until they found one that *Québécois* seemed almost certain to accept: Would they authorize the Québec government to negotiate the terms of sovereignty-association with the government of Canada? If so, there would be another referendum to judge the results of the negotiations.

Sovereignty-association would bring Québec political independence from Canada, but with a common monetary system, a customs union, free trade, and free movement of people across the borders. Québec and the rest of Canada would be equals. Trudeau, backed by his Québec lieutenant, Jean Chrétien, vehemently opposed any such deal. Instead, they promised that a *"non"* vote would lead to constitutional reform. On May 20, 1980, nine out of ten eligible voters cast their ballots. Nearly 60 percent voted *"non"*. The reasons were complex. Perhaps Lévesque's complicated question made people suspicious. Bill 101 had reassured *Québécois* that their language and culture were safe. With *la survivance* a certainty, why abandon Canada?

Most of Québec had agreed with Trudeau that the province belonged within Confederation. Now Trudeau had to deliver on his promise of constitutional reform. Since 1931, when Québec and Ontario had insisted that power to amend the *British North America Act* remain with Britain, efforts to bring home or patriate the Constitution had always ended in failure. The provinces could never agree either among themselves, or with the federal government, as to how constitutional change should be effected. In 1971, Trudeau had come closer to a solution than anyone before him. At Victoria, B.C., every premier had agreed to a complex formula that added to provincial powers and gave Ontario and Québec the right to veto future amendments. But Québec Premier Robert Bourassa changed his mind on the way home. He knew that nationalists would never forgive him for losing Québec's chance to win more concessions from Ottawa.

Most provincial premiers had agreed before the Québec referendum that they would try again. Saskatchewan Attorney-General Roy Romanow joined Jean Chrétien in devising a package of constitutional reforms. Yet by September, 1980, when the premiers met in Ottawa, it was clear that the *"non"* vote had relieved the pressure for agreement. Now each premier felt free to bargain for whatever his province wanted. For instance, the energy crisis had persuaded Alberta's Peter Lougheed that Alberta, too, deserved a veto. British Columbia Premier Bill Bennett insisted on Senate reform. Newfoundland worried about fishing rights. Canadians soon realized that the promise to Québec would be broken.

Trudeau refused to let that happen. On October 6, 1980, he announced to Parliament that unanimous provincial agreement had never been essential for constitutional change. The federal government would proceed on its own with an amending formula, a Charter of Rights, and patriation. Only two provinces, Ontario and New Brunswick, approved; the other eight, and the Conservative opposition, most definitely did not. The Conservatives stalled progress throughout the winter of 1981. Meanwhile, judges heard arguments from both sides on whether Trudeau's proposal was legal, and delivered widely differing opinions and decisions. When its turn came, the Supreme Court, too, gave a divided decision. However, the majority declared that the government was within the law, under the terms of the 1949 amendments to the *B.N.A. Act*. The Supreme Court also stated that more provinces would have to lend their support if conventional practice was to be followed. Nonetheless, since **convention** is not binding, the federal government could, in fact, proceed.

Convention

A convention is a constitutional practice or custom which becomes one of the rules of our democratic system. An example is the duty of a government to resign if defeated on a major matter in the House of Commons or in the legislature.

Trudeau arranged another meeting, under the threat that the federal government would act on its own if the provinces refused to agree. The provinces had already met to work out a meagre constitutional package which allowed no province a veto and which no-one thought would be approved. On November 5, 1981, in the absence of Québec Premier Lévesque, Chrétien, Romanow, and nine premiers reworked this package and found a compromise. Lévesque cried betrayal, but the agreement had been made. Women, Native people, and other groups later won special recognition. Québec, for whose sake constitutional reform had been pledged, did not. On April 17, 1982, Queen Elizabeth II proclaimed Canada's new *Constitution Act* from the steps of the Parliament Buildings. Québec was not represented.

Trudeau had achieved two of his three objectives: He had thwarted

The Queen signs Canada's new Constitution on April 17, 1982. One province was not represented at the ceremony. Why not?

the separatist movement and brought about constitutional reform. Now he moved on to his third aim. He promoted a dialogue between the "have" and "have-not" nations of the world. In 1983-84, he also visited the leaders of communist and western countries, trying to persuade them to reduce nuclear armaments and back off from a renewed Cold War. For his efforts, Trudeau was awarded the Albert Einstein Peace Prize.

Though Canadians applauded his international efforts, many also resented Trudeau's seeming lack of concern for Canadian problems. The sincerity of his peace mission was tarnished by a suspicion that the Prime Minister was trying to restore his own and his party's popularity. It may have been a cynical view, but there was no denying that the situation in Canada needed immediate attention. The new monetary policies Trudeau brought back from Germany in 1978 had indeed reduced inflation, but they had also increased unemployment. By 1982, Canada faced its worst recession since the 1930's. Over one and a half million people were looking for work, and as many more had given up the search as hopeless. After their unemployment insurance ran out, many people relied on welfare, food banks, and soup kitchens. Another feature of the new economic policy was that the interest rates had deliberately been increased to the highest level in modern history. As a result, loan and mortgage payments became so large that many businesses, farmers, and homeowners went bankrupt.

Les Ames, graphic designer, hand lettering the text of the Constitution

Worst hit were the provinces which had done best in the 1970's: Alberta and British Columbia. The worldwide recession made oil prices plummet, and Alberta's oil industry crumbled. Workers were laid off and pulp mills, logging operations, and mines in B.C. closed down as world markets shrank. As if history were intent on repeating the Great Depression, a devastating drought left Saskatchewan and southern Alberta with sharply reduced harvests. Falling world wheat prices did little for those farmers who did bring in crops.

In 1984, Trudeau, having accomplished his goals, decided to leave politics. His successor was John Turner. As Trudeau's Finance Minister, Turner had helped win the 1974 election with his scheme for indexing taxes as well as government spending. Turner had left the Cabinet in 1975. The Liberals trusted that, nearly a decade later, no-one would associate him with a scheme which had caused a deficit of $30 thousand million by 1984. They also hoped that his corporate and political connections would lead him to a victory over Brian Mulroney, the newly chosen Conservative leader. Mulroney had not held a seat in the House of Commons until 1983, after he became leader. But the pitiless eye of television showed Mulroney in a better light than Turner. Mulroney's complete bilingualism was another asset. Moreover, during the election campaign, Mulroney made the promise which mattered most: He would bring Canadians together. After 17 years of conflict and uncertainty, this was the assurance Canadians wanted. On September 4, 1984, one-half of voters chose the Conservatives. The landslide gave Mulroney a majority of the seats and votes in every province—even Québec. With 211 Conservative seats to only 40 for the Liberals and 30 for Ed Broadbent's NDP, it appeared that Canadians had, for once, come together.

QUESTIONS

1. What were Pierre Trudeau's three pieces of "unfinished business" after the 1980 election?
2. In what ways was sovereignty-association not quite independence?
3. What did Trudeau and his political colleagues promise the people of Québec if they voted *"non"* in the referendum?
4. Why was Trudeau awarded the Albert Einstein Peace Prize?
5. What caused many Canadians to declare bankruptcy in 1982-83?

Our Home and Native Land

For many Canadians, the patriation of the Constitution and the passage of the *Charter of Rights and Freedoms* were the greatest success story of the 1980's. For some groups of Canadians, however, the drafting of the Constitution and the Charter seemed just one more chapter in a continuing story of neglect.

When the Prime Minister and the premiers agreed on a constitutional package in November, 1981, they left out all references to Native rights or women's rights. Native people and their supporters protested furiously, as did women's groups. There followed weeks of argument and negotiation between Native groups and the politicians on the one hand, and women's groups and the politicians on the other. Finally, the various negotiators reached suitable compromises. For the first time in Canadian history, the rights of both Native people and women would be entrenched in Canada's Constitution.

For Native groups especially, it had been a long, bitter struggle. During the European conquest of what is now Canada, settlers took over much of the useful land. Yet the land was at the core of what Native people felt it meant to be Indian, or Inuit, or Métis. Native groups always felt that they had been despoiled by the European takeover.

Since the beginning of European settlement, Canada's original citizens had little place in the mainstream of Canadian life. Even during this century, Native people did not share in Canada's growing prosperity. Most continued to live in rural areas; over 60 percent were

Blackfoot Indian children in their home on a reserve

employed in such occupations as trapping, fishing, logging, and unskilled labour, which traditionally were seasonal and paid lower wages than the urban jobs held by most Canadians. Native people also had limited access to education to improve their chance of getting better-paying jobs. When formal education was available, it often seemed of little use to people coming from a tradition where learning through participation and from oral teaching was highly valued. Worst of all, those who ran the schools frequently used education to undermine Native traditions. The superiority of every aspect of "white" society was emphasized. For example, Native children were often forbidden to speak their own language among themselves at school, and, if caught, were punished for doing so. Native groups saw education as being imposed from outside; they felt they had little control over the curriculum or teaching methods. As a result, few of the children who did attend school went past the elementary level.

About half of Canada's Native bands had concluded formal treaties with the British or Canadian government at some time before this century. Under these agreements, they gave up their rights to land or to traditional activities, in return for monetary payments, title to reserves, or certain privileges. In most of British Columbia, northern Québec, and the Northwest Territories, however, there had been no treaties and no land surrendered.

As a tiny minority, Native people knew they could never hope to regain their rights and their control over their affairs by force or through political power. Thus, they turned to Canada's justice system.

Canada's Native People

While Canada's population more than doubled between 1901 and 1941, the number of Indians and Inuit actually fell. After World War II, the number of Native Canadians began to rise again. By the 1980's, close to half a million Canadians claimed aboriginal connections.

About 300 000 of all Native people are status Indians, *registered as members of one of the 565 bands on 2274 reserves across the country. Status Indians may also be registered and live off the reserve. As long as status Indians live on a reserve, they are exempt from paying income tax and most other taxes. They can claim health care and education but, in the past, other normal rights have been regulated by the government under the provisions of the* Indian Act.

There are about 75 000 non-status Indians *in Canada. Non-status Indians are those who have an Indian heritage, but who for some reason do not have full status as Indians. One reason might be that they gave up their status; another is that they lost it through marriage outside the Native community.*

Over 25 000 Inuit live in northern Canada, three-quarters of them in the Northwest Territories, the rest in Northern Québec and Labrador.

Canada's 100 000 Métis are descended from both Native and non-Native roots. The majority of them live in the prairie provinces.

A Native woman performs a traditional dance during a protest for Native rights. What have been the two main areas of concern for Native rights activists?

From the turn of the century on, Native groups put forward claims to their ancestral lands. The battle intensified during the 1920's, and again in the late 1960's. It focused on two main concerns: land claims and self-government.

Nowhere in Canada did Native groups organize earlier or more efficiently than in British Columbia. It is true that the first governor of British Columbia, Sir James Douglas, had paid for the land needed by the Hudson's Bay Company. However, when a Crown colony was created, the government refused to continue the payments. By the 1890's, the Nishga Land Committee was at work, seeking title to land in the northern part of the province. In the 11 years after 1915, the Allied Tribes of British Columbia raised and spent $100 000 to present their case. A joint committee of Parliament rejected their claim, then amended the *Indian Act* to make it an offence to raise money to pursue further claims.

Most subsequent claims made to the Canadian Parliament met a similar fate. Native groups appealed to the British Parliament, under the terms of the Proclamation of 1763, in which King George III had reserved the lands beyond the limits of English settlement for his "loyal native subjects". The British government refused to meddle in what it considered a Canadian affair.

Then, in 1969, came Trudeau's proposal to abolish the *Indian Act*. It was his view that, without the *Act*, Native people would become equal participants in Canadian society. Native groups strongly disagreed with the idea. Indian leader Harold Cardinal accused Ottawa of wanting "cultural genocide". Only if Native people remained a group, Cardinal asserted, could Native cultures and rights survive. Jolted into action, Native people determined not to rest until they had obtained their full aboriginal rights.

Again, it was the Nishga of B.C. who set the pace, with a carefully argued claim to 15 000 km^2 of the Nass Valley. When the case reached the Supreme Court of Canada, the judges' decision was four to three. The deciding judge ruled on a technicality—that the Nishga had not launched their action properly. The Nishga believed that, in defeat, they had won. The close decision showed Native people how to make their case stronger in law. In August, 1973, the Minister of Indian and Northern Affairs finally announced that the Canadian government would negotiate land title with Native groups. The negotiations could cover specific complaints about the way in which treaties had been managed. They could also deal with "comprehensive grievances", thus allowing land claims to be made on the basis of traditional use and occupancy.

Actions followed words. The Québec government decided to settle with the Cree Indians and the Inuit of northern Québec before proceeding with the James Bay hydroelectric project. The Cree and Inuit gave up their claim to 60 percent of Québec, based on their traditional occupancy, in return for 13 844 km^2 of land which they would control completely, and 155 737 km^2 in which they would have the exclusive right to hunt, fish, and trap.

Although other Native groups condemned the Cree and the Inuit for abandoning their original claim, they knew an important precedent had been set. For the first time, the principle of aboriginal rights had been strong enough to bring a government to the bargaining table. The federal government and those provinces where treaties had never been signed, or where previous claims could be challenged, now faced serious Native claims. In the western Arctic, 2500 Inuit sought 181 300 km^2 but settled for about half that area, $45 million, and other benefits in compensation. Other, much larger, claims in northern Canada followed. The 12 500 members of the Inuit Tapirisat claimed the Nunavut area of the Northwest Territories. The Council for Yukon Indians in 1974 claimed 70 percent of the Yukon Territory and $670 million in compensation. The Métis, for their part, claimed much of the land on which Winnipeg now stands.

Native people had succeeded in negotiating with the government about one of their two main concerns: land claims. Now it was time to address the second concern: self-government. For over a century, the government of Canada had had the right to direct the lives of Canada's Native people. Natives wished to regain control over their own destinies. Many Native leaders insisted that the best means of doing so would be a new *Indian Act*, devised by Native people themselves. During the 1970's, attempts were made to redraft the *Indian Act*, but it became harder, not easier, to take all points of view into account. Others thought that the best solution would be to entrench Native rights in the Constitution.

Native leaders confer about a government proposal to include aboriginal rights in the Constitution. What would such an inclusion mean for other Canadians?

As part of the compromise reached with Native people over their inclusion in the Constitution, the Prime Minister and the premiers agreed to a conference to work out precisely what the "aboriginal and treaty rights" guaranteed in the Constitution were. The conference was held in 1983, but no decisions were reached—except that the first constitutional amendment promised a series of conferences on the matter. Neither the Liberals, nor, after 1984, the Conservatives under Mulroney, could make much progress against the determination of the provincial premiers to define exactly what aboriginal rights were before signing anything. Thus, although a section guaranteeing aboriginal rights was included in the *Charter of Rights and Freedoms*, the struggle of Native people for their rights was far from won.

Native leaders and the government tried another approach. In 1985, changes were made to the *Indian Act*. One of the most important was the redefinition of who is or is not a status Indian, as you will see in the Close-up which follows. Like its predecessors, this *Indian Act* failed to satisfy all Native groups.

Native groups agree that self-government must be guaranteed, but not about the details. Should it be equivalent to a municipal or a provincial government? Or should it be equal in power to the federal government? Who should control the natural resources within Native lands—Native people or the federal government? Some Native leaders have dealt with the issue of self-government by drawing up a *Charter of Rights for Aboriginal Peoples*. Through it they claim special representation in Parliament and the provincial legislatures, a share in Canada's international affairs, guarantees for Native languages and culture, a veto over constitutional amendments affecting Native people, and guarantees of the right to hunt, fish, and trap. At present, no final decision on the issue of self-government has been made.

Canadian Native groups are increasingly making common cause with other aboriginal peoples of the world. They sometimes refer to themselves as the "Fourth World", nations still struggling to free themselves from colonialism. At the same time, Native people in Canada recognize the divisions in their own ranks, among chiefs and band councils, among status and non-status Indians, among Indians, Inuit, and Métis, and among leaders with widely differing solutions to the problem of making Canada truly their native land.

CLOSE-UP

When Rights Clash

In 1970, Jeanette Courbière, an Ojibwa from the Wikwemikong reserve in Ontario, married a non-Indian, David Lavell. A year later, the couple had a son. Then Jeanette Lavell received a letter from the Department of Indian and Northern Affairs reminding her that, under Section 12 of the *Indian Act*, she had lost her Indian status by marrying a non-Indian. So had her son.

The rules of the *Act* were different for men: A male Indian who married a non-Indian would still be a status Indian, as would any child of the marriage. Moreover, the *Canadian Bill of Rights*, passed in 1960, stated that no person would suffer discrimination "by reason of race, national origin, colour, religion or sex". There was no doubt that the *Indian Act* discriminated against women; even the Royal Commission on the Status of Women said so in its 1969 report. Many Indian women supported Lavell; during the 1960's, over 4500 of them had run into the same problem as hers. Lavell had powerful arguments and many backers when she took her case to the Supreme Court of Canada.

Indian leaders saw the *Lavell* case very differently. Some insisted that, since Indian custom made a man responsible for his wife and children, they should share his status. Others were afraid that band members would be squeezed out if women brought non-Indian husbands to the reserves. Even those who agreed that the *Indian Act* was unjust felt it was up to Native people themselves, not to the Canadian courts, to make any changes. Harold Cardinal, the young Indian leader who led the fight to save the *Indian Act* in 1969, suspected that the government was trying to use the *Bill of Rights* to undermine the *Indian Act*, since they no longer dared to do so openly. Cardinal and others feared that, if Lavell was successful, she would be followed by other Natives challenging the restrictions on the right to hold private property on a reserve. If Native lands were broken into private holdings, Native people would lose their most important heritage—the land. Many Indians felt that Lavell had known the rules: Community survival was more important than her status.

In 1973, the Supreme Court made its decision. It ruled that "equality before the law"—the wording of the *Bill of Rights*—meant equal treatment before the law. Since Lavell was treated in the same way as all other Indian women, she had not been denied "equality before the law". The decision was close—five to four. "It was too close for comfort," said one Indian leader. The government—and the Native organizations—had won. But women's organizations vowed to change the law, and civil rights groups agreed. To people on both sides of the issue, the *Lavell* case represented another powerful argument for the need to entrench rights in the Constitution.

In 1985, the issue was resolved in favour of women's groups. As a result of the *Charter of Rights and Freedoms*, changes were made to the *Indian Act* which made it possible for both women marrying non-Indians and their children to retain their status. Many Indian women who lost their status under the old law are now applying to regain it. The decision, like many made when rights clash, did not please everyone. Had white courts done justice, or had they interfered once again in Native concerns?

Jeanette Lavell, the first woman to challenge the status laws for Canada's Native people. Why did some Native people feel threatened by Lavell's campaign to retain her status after her marriage to a non-Native?

QUESTIONS

1. How did Jeanette Lavell lose her status?
2. Under the *Indian Act* as it stood at the time, did a Native male lose his status by marrying a non-Native?
3. Why did some Indians oppose Jeanette Lavell's action?
4. What basic issue was at the heart of the argument in the *Lavell* case?
5. If the *Charter of Rights and Freedoms* had been in place at the time, would the outcome of the *Lavell* case have differed? Why?

QUESTIONS

1. "Even during this century, Native people did not share in Canada's growing prosperity." Support this statement with three examples.
2. On what grounds did Native groups appeal to the British Parliament concerning land claims?
3. Why did the Québec government give the Cree Indians and Inuit complete control over 13 844 km^2 of Québec?

Who Should Come to Canada?

At the turn of the century, in the Laurier era, one of the government's primary concerns was finding more people to fill the wide spaces of the West. Even in those early days, immigration policy led to arguments. Working people feared that immigrants would lower wage levels and cause unemployment. Protestants were concerned about the number of immigrating Catholics. Francophones worried that the tide of anglophones would swamp them. People of British origin feared that Canada would become less British. Business wanted workers and consumers, but not troublemakers or people who might be a burden on taxpayers.

Two main questions governed immigration policy until well into the century: What sort of people did the Canadian economy need, and whom did Canadian society want? Canadians often wanted immigrants who would be willing to do unpopular jobs—but they also wanted people who were as much like themselves as possible. This was hard to manage. Immigrants all too often were judged in terms of racial and cultural stereotypes. Certain groups were more discriminated against than others. The *Asian Exclusion Act* of the early part of the century illustrated this attitude. So did the refusal of Canada to admit Jewish refugees fleeing from Nazi genocide during the 1930's and 1940's.

The modernization of Canadian immigration policy really began after World War II. In 1947, Prime Minister William Lyon Mackenzie King reminded Canadians that his government had agreed to let Chinese and East Indian families be reunited after the war. However, he also said that Canada still had a right to choose "desirable future citizens", and that no "fundamental alteration in the character of our population" would be made. Only 6000 Chinese immigrants were allowed in under the new regulations.

Nevertheless, the world—and Canada—had changed. Canada's

Hungarian refugees arrive in Montréal. What political event in their homeland during 1956 prompted them to emigrate to Canada?

membership in the newly formed, multiracial United Nations and the multiracial Commonwealth of Nations made it difficult to maintain racist attitudes and policies. The horrors of Hitler's death camps had clearly demonstrated the outcome of racism. Racist stereotypes and assumptions began fading from both polite conversation and government policy. Moreover, Canada's new prosperity cried out for more consumers and more workers. By 1955, one and a half million immigrants had arrived, only one-third of them from Britain. Many were displaced by the war or fleeing from the Soviet conquest of eastern Europe. In 1956, the Hungarian Revolution swept more political refugees to Canada. Among them was the entire forestry faculty of one university, all of whom were promptly hired by the University of British Columbia. Canadians increasingly felt that restrictive immigration policies were unacceptable. In 1962, the last remnants of explicit discrimination were purged from the *Immigration Act*.

The middle of the 1960's brought a new sense of priorities to immigration policy. Under former Québec union leader Jean Marchand, the Department of Immigration got a new name—Manpower and Immigration—to reflect its new goals. Marchand believed that Canada's manpower needs should form the basis of immigration policy. These needs would best be met by attracting the best people from throughout the world. Henceforth, would-be immigrants were assessed according to a point system in which only education, training, experience, and personal suitability mattered.

Other Canadian needs also mattered to Marchand. One was that people should choose to identify with Québec's francophone culture.

Most immigrants learned English and entered the English-speaking community. Another old problem was that most newcomers settled in urban areas. Marchand and his successors tried to encourage people to settle outside major communities. Finally, Marchand was concerned about the "potential for explosive growth", as Canada increasingly drew immigrants from cultures that favoured large families. Unlike European countries, which admitted "guest workers" but not their families, Canada did not wish to separate immigrants from their dependants. But Marchand feared that the result would be the admission of many unskilled newcomers who would not be able to adapt.

Marchand had to fit these policies into an *Immigration Act* which dated back to the 1950's. In 1973, officials and researchers set out to draft an entirely new law. Their work, sometimes punctuated with angry public hearings, ended in 1978. The new *Immigration Act* reflected both idealism and experience. Immigration would promote the "domestic and international interests of Canada", but it would also maintain a humanitarian tradition with respect to "the displaced and the persecuted". The *Act* forbade discrimination "on grounds of race, national or ethnic origin, colour, religion or sex". It also limited admission for the sake of uniting families to "close relatives from abroad". Although section 95 of the *B.N.A. Act* had given the provinces some control over immigration, Québec for the first time established its right through the new *Act* to refuse immigrants who might have chosen to settle there. The new *Immigration Act* also declared that would-be immigrants must apply for visas from outside Canada, to keep them from "jumping the queue".

The new *Act* recognized three classes of immigrants. In the **Family Class** were included spouses, unmarried children under 21, parents, or grandparents of people who were already citizens or permanent residents of Canada.

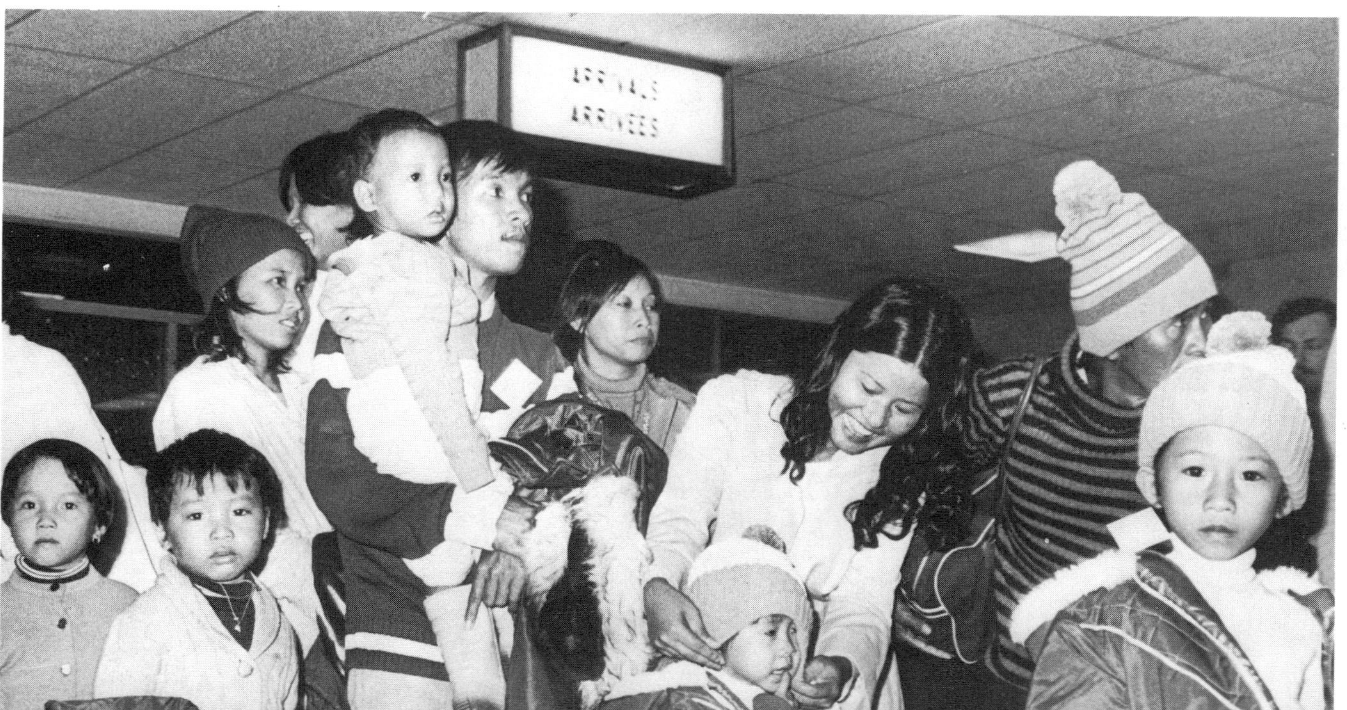

Vietnamese "Boat People" arrive in Canada in 1979. Many Canadian church groups and individuals volunteered to sponsor these homeless refugees, helping them to start a new life in Canada.

CLOSE-UP

A Refugee Crisis

The new category of immigrant created a problem for Canadian immigration officials: how to tell real refugees from those would-be immigrants who claimed refugee status in order to get quick admission to Canada. All those claiming to be refugees had to endure a long process to determine whether their claim was valid. As more and more refugee claimants arrived, the system became clogged; it often took up to several years to evaluate a claim. By that time, bogus refugees had had the opportunity to get a job, earn money, learn the language, and thereby improve their chances of qualifying as immigrants. Meanwhile, would-be immigrants who played by the rules were still waiting their turn in their home countries.

By 1986, the number of bogus refugees brought angry argument over immigration policy. In 1987, the government introduced a new policy which cracked down on fake refugees—but could also keep out genuine refugees. *Maclean's Magazine* commented on the changes:

> The new regulations... will affect thousands... (The) announcement was immediately condemned by refugee-aid groups and both federal opposition parties. Liberal MP Sergio Marchi said that the Conservative government had "turned back the clock on what has been a proud and humanitarian refugee tradition." Added Montréal immigration lawyer Joyce Yedid: "There is an abundance of double-talk about how Canada will continue to accept "real refugees", but that is just a guise to keep people away. The real message, is 'Die at home'."
>
> Bouchard (Immigration Minister Benoit Bouchard) insisted that the new system was not intended to close the door on genuine refugees... "We want a positive immigration program that permits the orderly entry of immigrants," he said. "But we cannot maintain such a program if we allow abuse of our refugee program to continue."
>
> –*Maclean's Magazine*, March 2, 1987, p. 12.

QUESTIONS

1. What problem did the Refugee Class of immigrants create for immigration officials?

2. What do you think Joyce Yedid meant when she charged the government with saying to would-be refugees "Die at home"?

The **Independent Class** included other relatives whose Canadian family members promised to help them get established or be responsible for them. Other potential immigrants in this class were entrepreneurs with the will and the means to set up businesses, people who would be self-employed, and people who could satisfy the point system.

In July, 1987, these refugees reached the coast of Nova Scotia after travelling by lifeboat under cover of fog and darkness. How had they come to be in a lifeboat off the coast of Nova Scotia? Why is refugee status so controversial?

The third category which the 1978 *Immigration Act* created was the **Refugee Class**, now official after many years of inconsistent application. Like the Loyalists of the eighteenth century or the Mennonites and Doukhobors of the nineteenth, these people feared or suffered persecution in their own country because of their race, religion, nationality, political ideas, or social identity. In the 1970's, such immigrants included "Boat People" from Vietnam, Asians expelled from Uganda, and political dissidents fleeing a military dictatorship in Chile. Because they were often in danger in their native land, these people were permitted to apply for immigrant status from within Canada.

It is important to keep in mind that even policies which are conscientiously intended to be free from bias may have biased results. For instance, the point system makes it difficult for many people from Third World countries to meet the requirements for education and skills. At the same time, it may help to drain those countries of their most highly qualified people. A trained doctor, nurse, or machinist represents an enormous investment of money, material, and time for any nation. A flow of professionals and skilled workers to Canada represents a form of foreign aid which few countries can afford to give.

Immigration remains a political issue in Canada; in a country where a quarter of the population is born elsewhere, any restrictive policy is bound to be controversial. Close to half of new immigrants since 1980 belong to visible minorities. Thus, Canada is undergoing the "fundamental alteration in the character of our population" which Prime Minister King promised to avoid just four decades ago. Many Canadians accept the change. Inevitably, there will be those who do not.

QUESTIONS

1. In the author's view, what are the two main questions that previously directed Canada's immigration policy?
2. Why were Hungarians accepted as refugees when they arrived in Canada in 1956?
3. How can an immigration policy be racist?
4. What are the four chief criteria assessed by the "point system"?
5. What are the three classes of immigrants outlined in the 1978 *Immigration Act*?

Citizenship—Joining Canada

Immigration is the first step in a new life for new Canadians. Admitted to Canada as permanent residents, they are known as **landed immigrants**. There is little difference in status between them and Canadian citizens. Most Canadian laws apply to everyone in Canada, whether citizen, landed immigrant, or visitor. Landed immigrants also benefit from medicare, unemployment insurance, and other programs, and pay the same taxes as citizens.

However, Canadian citizens have some privileges which landed immigrants do not. Only citizens can vote in any Canadian election, or run for public office. Many positions in the civil service are reserved for citizens. Assistance from a Canadian embassy or consulate in a foreign country can only be claimed by citizens. In addition, section 23 of the *Charter of Rights and Freedoms* grants only to citizens the right to choose between French and English as the language of education for their children. To obtain these benefits, and because they feel a sense of pride in their new land, most landed immigrants choose to become Canadian citizens.

Until 1947, Canadian citizenship did not even exist: Canadians were British subjects. Those who had not been born in Canada or who did not come from Britain were encouraged to become **naturalized** British subjects. The requirements for naturalization were three years' residence in Canada and an oath of allegiance to the Crown. The *Canadian Citizenship Act* automatically made all those who had been born in Canada or naturalized as British subjects Canadian citizens. Under the law, others could gain citizenship if they had been lawfully admitted and had resided in Canada for four of the previous six years, were of "good character", and had an adequate knowledge of English or French. If they could not meet the last requirement, they had to prove that they had lived in Canada continuously for 20 years.

In 1976, Canada got a new *Canadian Citizenship Act* which reflected some of the changes of the previous three decades. For example, it acknowledged that a person born in a Canadian aircraft could be a Canadian citizen; the earlier law had mentioned only ships. It recognized equality between men and women. Under the 1947 *Act*, a child born outside Canada of a Canadian mother and foreign father was not a Canadian, but a child born of a Canadian father and foreign mother was. The new *Act* removed these distinctions. It also reflected the influence of the *Official Languages Act*, and the practice which had grown up over the years of expecting new citizens to know something about their adopted country. Some of the criteria for citizenship are listed in the margin.

Applying for citizenship is a three-stage process. First, applicants fill out a form which indicates that the necessary qualifications have been met. Next, they appear before a Citizenship Court judge to prove their

Becoming a Canadian Citizen

To become a Canadian citizen, a person must

(a) be 18 years of age or over;
(b) be lawfully admitted to Canada for permanent residence, and have spent three of the previous four years preceding the application living in Canada;
(c) have an adequate knowledge of one of the two official languages of Canada;
(d) have an adequate knowledge of Canada and of the responsibilities and privileges of citizenship;
(e) not be under a deportation order, suspect as a security risk, or burdened with a serious criminal record.

An immigration official explains to a new applicant how to fill out the required forms.

qualifications. The process is not meant to be intimidating. Citizenship judges are normally chosen because of long political service, a fondness for humanity, and, often, because they too were once immigrants. The final stage of citizenship is a formal ceremony at which the new citizens swear or affirm allegiance to the Queen and her successors and obedience to the laws of Canada.

For all its advantages, taking Canadian citizenship can pose painful choices. It can mean the abandoning of a cherished national allegiance. It can bring a sense of awkwardness and the legal disabilities of a foreigner for those who return to their former homes. Furthermore, if they return to their homeland even for a visit, foreign-born Canadian citizens may find that they have not lost such duties to their land of birth as military service. Canadians should understand the reasons which may hold landed immigrants back from taking the final step of citizenship. They should also realize that becoming a citizen is one of the finest compliments a person can offer Canada.

QUESTIONS

1. It is not necessary for landed immigrants to become Canadian citizens. Why, then, do most immigrants choose to do so?
2. Do you think landed immigrants should be required to become Canadian citizens after a certain period? Explain your answer.
3. Why might taking citizenship in a new country pose "painful choices"?
4. Name a specific way in which the 1976 *Canadian Citizenship Act* recognized equality between men and women.

A Multicultural Nation

Despite Prime Minister King's promise, the nature of Canada's population has been fundamentally altered over the years. In the Laurier era, 95.4 percent of Canadians were of British or French descent. By the mid-1980's, the figure was down to just over 68 percent. No other ethnic group made up more than 5 percent of the population.

In the 1960's, the very title of the Royal Commission on Bilingualism and Biculturalism defined what many Canadians thought their nation was. Ironically, it was the commission itself which found, after years of research and hearings, that the definition would not fit. Its members said in their final report, "[Leaders of ethnic groups] want, without in any way undermining national unity, to maintain their own linguistic and cultural heritage." It is perhaps fitting that the compromise which Canadians now share as the official definition of their society was formulated in 1967, the centennial year. It was then that the government established as its policy "multiculturalism within a bilingual framework". Canada would have two official languages—but no official culture.

Critics—and some ethnic leaders—assumed that Ottawa would pour money into scores of individual cultural activities. That was not the government's intent. Multiculturalism meant respect for and sharing of all cultures, not the cultivation of difference. Pierre Trudeau believed strongly in the value of both individualism and multiculturalism, and the need for an interplay between the two.

The adoption of multiculturalism has brought a mixture of frustration and achievement. At times, it has been used for crassly political ends, with funds being spent with the next election in mind. Yet in the two decades since the definition of Canadian society was handed down by the Royal Commission on Bilingualism and Biculturalism, Canadians have come to recognize the need for multiculturalism. At the same time, understanding of the concept has become more sophisticated. There had been a shift from the vague notion of "culture" to the more precise one of "heritage", the collection of experiences and understanding which each ethnic community and each individual within it has brought to the daily life of Canada. In 1982, that newer understanding was entrenched as section 27 of the *Charter of Rights and Freedoms*: "This Charter shall be interpreted in a manner consistent with the preservation and enhancement of the multicultural heritage of Canadians."

The entrenching of multiculturalism in the Charter did not guarantee an end to discrimination. Disturbed by reports of racially-motivated incidents, in that same year the government was moved to found a race relations unit. Its aim was to discover the causes of racial tension in Canada and devise ways of reducing them. The government also began to give assistance to immigrant women from many cultural backgrounds, who as a group were often isolated at home with little chance to participate in society at large. In addition, it continued to fund writings about Canada's ethnic groups and other projects promoting multiculturalism.

What, then, is a Canadian? The answer is for each Canadian to decide, from a range of choices. Maurice Careless, one of Canada's greatest historians, described a reality of "limited identities". Canadians, he said, were people who could identify with an ethnic heritage, a region, a province, and a community, with economic interests, and with ideas and a religious faith, and still be good Canadians.

Can such a society work? By now, it may be too late for second thoughts. If Canada, with its wealth and space and its history of compromise, cannot succeed, what country can? In a rapidly shrinking world, showing that different groups can live together in harmony is one of the most important contributions which Canada can make to the survival of humankind.

CLOSE-UP

Black Like Me

Fil Fraser, a black Canadian born in Montréal whose parents immigrated to Canada from the Caribbean, grew up in the 1930's and 1940's in a "white man's country". In 1987, he wrote an article for the magazine *Saturday Night*, describing the changes he had seen since his childhood. *Saturday Night*'s editors introduced the article like this: "Black Like Me: In one man's lifetime Canada has evolved from a deeply (though subtly) racist society into a country that's multiracial, multicultural and so astonishingly diverse it ought to be the envy of the world." Below are some excerpts from the article:

> A boy in my class at Montréal High told me he couldn't get into McGill's medical school, even with first-class marks, because the quota for Jewish students had been filled that year... In the early years of World War II... marauding bands of English-Canadian soldiers roamed east-end Montréal, looking for Frenchies to beat up... Every so often an English-Canadian soldier was caught off base by a French gang. That was bad. But no one had it worse than the handful of French Canadians who enlisted voluntarily...
>
> When the war was over... Ukrainians were *out* in Edmonton. Germans were *out* in Winnipeg. Who was *in* never varied. To be of British descent was to have access to the corridors of power and prestige... Canada was a "white man's country"—as Mackenzie King put it... That meant a white Anglo-Saxon, Protestant, man's country. It never occurred to us, then, what that meant to women...
>
> And yet astonishingly, Canada today is unique in the world, embracing more diversity than any other country. We are officially, and by degrees, viscerally, a multicultural country... Multiculturalism is enshrined in the Canadian Charter of Rights and Freedoms, is reflected in our institutions, and is seeping, far more rapidly than we realize, into our collective psyche. Canada has become a country that says its citizens are equal, regardless of race, or religion, or origin, or age, or physical or mental status, or sex. The courts back up that idea, it seems, almost weekly...
>
> Most of the world's countries are either unicultural, uniracial, and religiously homogeneous, or else caught up in internal strife... Canadians have yet to discover the creativity of their social order. If we can solve the problems of making it possible for people of every kind to live together in reasonable harmony, we have a message for the world. The problems of this shrinking planet are problems we're solving in Canada.

QUESTIONS

1. In your opinion, what helped Canada become the multicultural country it is today?
2. Are there still groups in Canada who are "out"?

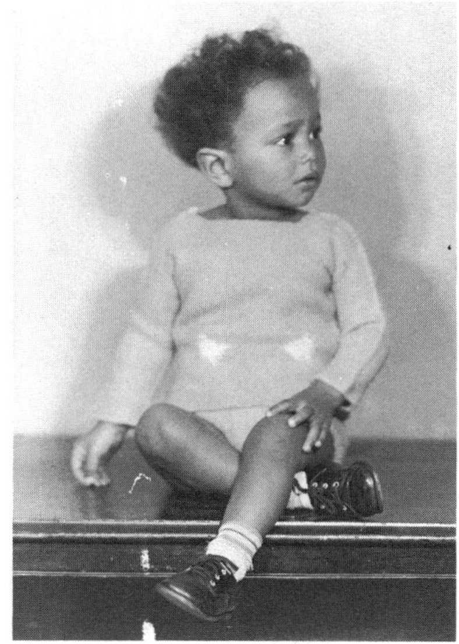

Fil Fraser as a small boy in a racially divided Montreal. Today he recognizes the changes evolving in a multicultural Canada.

QUESTIONS

1. How does multiculturalism contribute to national unity?
2. How do culture and heritage differ?
3. Why is the funding of writings about ethnic groups an effective way to promote multiculturalism?
4. Why did Canada establish its multiculturalism policy within a bilingual framework?

Into the Future

Except for Joe Clark's few months of power in 1979–1980, the Conservative government elected in 1984 was the first real change in 21 years. With backing at the polls, in the House of Commons, and from eight of ten provincial premiers, Brian Mulroney had fulfilled his first promise: uniting Canada.

Three years later, much of his support had vanished. His party was backed by fewer voters than the Liberals or the NDP. For a time in 1987, Ed Broadbent's NDP was the most popular party in Canada. By the end of 1987, Liberals had won power in four provinces, partly because the Mulroney government was unpopular.

The reasons for this unpopularity were not obvious. Though much of Canada suffered from bad economic times, inflation fell and employment rates increased. Canada's economy grew faster than those of other industrialized countries, such as Japan and Germany, which Canadians had envied in the 1970's. At Meech Lake, Québec, in May, 1987, Brian Mulroney got all the provincial premiers to help him keep his promise to get Québec to accept the Constitution. When the Finance Minister angered pensioners by trying to cut the growth rate of their pensions, the government quickly reversed itself. In power, the Conservatives tried to be moderate. They did not change such popular programs as unemployment insurance. As they promised, they allowed a debate on bringing back the death penalty, but Mulroney's own eloquent speech against capital punishment turned the tide. Meanwhile, the government could claim credit for cutting the deficit and creating new regional development agencies for Atlantic Canada and the West.

Why, then, did the government become unpopular so quickly? One reason was that the long years out of power made it hard for the Conservatives to get used to governing. It was hard to trust civil servants who, for years, had helped the Liberals. Inexperienced ministers made mistakes. So did the Prime Minister. During the campaign, he had claimed that social programs were "a sacred trust". Why, then, had he even thought of changing old-age pensions? He had also condemned John Turner for political patronage—granting jobs and favours to political friends. Most governments use patronage, and so did Brian Mulroney—but voters remembered the television broadcast in which he had attacked such actions.

Governments make enemies as well as friends because of their decisions. Many in the West were furious when the government favoured Montréal over Winnipeg in a contract to repair Canada's supersonic fighters. Montréalers, who always had assumed that their industries would get the business, were hardly grateful. Winnipeggers, who wanted more high-technology industry and who had offered a lower price, felt cheated by a government which most westerners had supported in 1984.

Most governments fall out of favour between elections, and many come back. When Canadians vote in their next general election, they will have to take into consideration the accomplishments of Mulroney's government. One of them, the biggest tax reform in many years, cut rates for many low-income earners. Another was the Meech Lake Accord. Critics might complain that the constitutional agreement gave too much power to the provinces and unique status to Québec, while ignoring the demands of women and Native people. Nevertheless, Brian Mulroney could answer that he had completed important business left undone by the Trudeau government.

The leading issue of the Mulroney years, however, had not even been promised in the 1984 campaign: free trade with the United States. In opposition, Mulroney had opposed the idea as too dangerous for

As Prime Minister Mulroney looks on, Premier David Peterson of Ontario (left) exchanges a symbolic handshake with Premier Robert Bourassa of Québec (right), after the signing of the Meech Lake Accord. The Accord was designed to heal the constitutional rift between Québec and the other provinces.

Canada, but he had also promised to rebuild the friendship between the two nations. "Good relations, super relations with the United States will be the cornerstone of our foreign policy," he had said in 1984. Almost at once the new Conservative government ended the National Energy Program and weakened the Foreign Investment Review Agency, two annoyances for American business. Canada also pleased the U.S. by promising to spend more money on defence, including rebuilding the North Warning System and sending more soldiers to Europe.

In March, 1985, when the Prime Minister and President Ronald Reagan met in Québec City, many problems seemed to be solved. Even though Reagan refused to believe that acid rain was destroying forests, he agreed to discussions by special envoys. He also agreed to back special talks to negotiate the wide-ranging free trade deal which Mulroney had once feared and condemned.

Why had Mulroney changed his mind? One reason was that powerful Canadian business leaders had urged him to do so. The report of a Royal Commission appointed by the Trudeau government echoed the plea. It warned that, without free trade, Canadian exports might be shut out of the United States. As Canadians waited through 18 months of bargaining, that fear came true for products ranging from British Columbia softwood lumber to Ontario steel. Yet many people also feared, as their Prime Minister once had, that any such deal with the United States would give Americans too much power in Canada. Would medicare or unemployment insurance join B.C.'s low stumpage fees as "unfair" competition for any American producer opposed to Canadian imports? Earlier Conservative Prime Ministers, such as John A. Macdonald and Robert Borden, had argued that free trade would undermine national sovereignty. The same arguments now came from Liberals and New Democracts, trade unions, and church leaders.

On October 3, 1987, after dramatic last-minute negotiations, Canadian representatives signed an agreement with their American counterparts. As critics had foreseen, American officials had given very little away. If the border was open, it could still be shut for any product which annoyed a U.S. competitor. At the same time, Canada, as the smaller country, was opened to American business. Critics were angry at the deal and warned that hundreds of thousands of Canadians could soon lose their jobs. Yet did a country which conducted 80 percent of its export business with a single customer, the United States, have much choice but to make the best deal it could before Washington added still more barriers? Would Canadians be forced to muster the energy and ingenuity to survive and compete in a single North American market? Were Canada's culture and social institutions so valuable that they deserved protection on the new "level playing field"?

An able American diplomat, George Ball, predicted in 1965 that the time would come when Canadians no longer wanted to pay the price for belonging to a separate country. Then, at last, Ball said, the "manifest destiny" of the United States to rule all of the northern part of the continent would be fulfilled. Had that moment come in 1988 with the ratification of the Canada-U.S. Trade Agreement?

History does not answer such questions. It leaves the choices to each generation. Nor does history repeat itself; too many circumstances change. We are not the same people as our ancestors, and our times are not theirs. All that history can give us is the wisdom of experience and the strength of hope. Canadians have good reason to believe in their future. They will handle it better if they remember their past.

QUESTIONS

1. On what basis could Brian Mulroney claim after the 1984 election that he had united Canada?
2. In what instance did Mulroney's statement that social programs were "a sacred trust" seem ironic?
3. When he was in opposition, did Mulroney oppose or support free trade with the United States?
4. What did some Canadians suggest might have happened to Canada if a free trade deal with the United States was not worked out?

Chapter Summary

The 1980's took Canada past historic milestones. Faced with the choice, Québec chose to remain within Confederation. In 1982, Queen Elizabeth signed a Constitution Act *which gave Canadians a* Charter of Rights and Freedoms *and full responsibility for changing their system of government. However, five more years passed before further major amendments satisfied Québec. The Meech Lake Accord's transfer of authority to Québec and to other provinces left critics wondering whether Canada would have strength enough to serve all its people equally and fairly.*

Among those unsatisfied by the constitutional settlements of 1982 and 1987 were Canada's Native people. Their claims to land and self-government went unanswered. Nor did constitutional debates settle the economic problems that seemed to deepen the gulf between rich and poor.

A proposed solution to these problems was free trade with the United States and a continental sharing of energy and other natural resources. By 1988, that century-old vision seemed on the verge of realization. But could such an arrangement with the United States allow the survival of Canadian industries, institutions, and social programs, or would they be flattened to create a "level playing field"? Did enough Canadians really care?

Canadians in the 1980's were busy redefining who they are. In a crowded, interdependent world, the old dominance of the so-called "founding nations" of English and French was challenged by an increasingly multicultural heritage. Canadians now have ties of family and culture with every part of the world. In turn, Canada is linked to the conflicts and suffering of the world by the obligation to find homes for refugees, fleeing not only from political oppression but also from hunger and economic constraints.

In the 1980's, Canada has been both more conservative and more individualistic than it was in earlier decades. Sometimes, on issues concerned with moral values, that trend has produced deep social conflict. At the same time, it has also reversed many Canadians' belief that governments have a central role in solving Canada's economic and social problems.

History is, of course, an unfinished story. Each generation writes its own chapter. Your time is about to begin.

IN REVIEW

1. The May 20, 1980 referendum asked *Québécois* whether they would "authorize the Québec government to negotiate the terms of sovereignty-association with Canada." Study the wording of the referendum question carefully. Is it neutral, or biased? Explain your answer.

2. An amending formula included in the Constitution was intended to allow changes to be made to it in the future. Why was it so difficult to design an acceptable formula?

3. In the 1984 election, Québec voters turned away from the Liberals after decades of supporting the party. What element of the negotiations about the patriation of the Constitution may have prompted this move?

4. How did the plans for the James Bay hydroelectric project result in the first significant recognition of Native land claims?

5. What two problems seem continually to make amendment of the *Indian Act* difficult?

6. Persons with a large amount of capital to invest in a business in Canada are often readily admitted within the Independent Class of immigrants. Some Canadians, however, consider this policy unsatisfactory. Suggest a basis on which such a policy might be supported, and one on which it might be opposed.

7. Why was there so much controversy about the immigration policy intended to keep out "bogus refugees"?

APPLYING YOUR KNOWLEDGE

1. Why did both Native and women's groups feel it was extremely important for their rights to be entrenched in the Constitution?
2. Provinces which have no, or few, treaties with Native groups seem to be the most eager to avoid the subject of Native claims. Why might this be so?
3. Why do provincial premiers want a precise definition of "aboriginal rights"?
4. What was Prime Minister King really saying when he announced that there would be no "fundamental alteration in the character of our population" as a result of immigration?
5. **(a)** What did the government have in mind when it used the word "biculturalism" in the name of the Royal Commission on Bilingualism and Biculturalism?
   (b) Was the view of Canada expressed in this name accurate? Explain.
6. How can the requirement that immigrants to Canada must meet a certain level of education and skills harm poorer countries?

FURTHER INVESTIGATION

1. Some Canadians have suggested that Canada should celebrate April 17, the date of the proclamation of the Constitution, as its national day, rather than July 1. Do you think this idea has merit? Why or why not?
2. Jeanette Lavell knew that, to an Indian, the community is more important than the individual. How would the majority of Canadians regard this attitude? How would you?
3. Name three qualities or characteristics that you think should be included in an assessment of an applicant's suitability to be admitted to Canada as an immigrant.
4. Why were some Canadians suspicious of the Mulroney government's promised policy of "super relations" with the United States?

GLOSSARY

dialectic A logical process of development which always progresses through certain defined stages.

enemy aliens Defined during World War I as anyone from an enemy country who had not sworn an oath of allegiance to the government of the country he or she lived in.

Family Class A classification of immigrants to Canada that includes spouses, unmarried children under 21, parents, or grandparents of people who are already citizens or permanent residents of Canada. (*Immigration Act, 1978*)

Independent Class A classification of immigrants to Canada that includes relatives (not included in Family Class) whose Canadian family members promise to help them get established or to be responsible for them. Also includes entrepreneurs, the self-employed, and those who satisfy the point system. (*Immigration Act, 1978*)

indexation A means of adjusting income tax to the rate of inflation.

landed immigrants Immigrants who are admitted to Canada as permanent residents. There is little difference in status between them and Canadian citizens. Landed immigrants do not have federal or provincial voting privileges.

manifesto A public declaration or statement of policy, opinions, intentions, or motives.

naturalise To grant full citizen rights to someone from a foreign nation.

non-status Indians Those native people who for some reason do not have full status as Indians.

primary sources The records, letters, diaries, interviews, and other material produced by people who saw or participated in historical events.

reciprocity A system by which special trading considerations are exchanged between nations.

Refugee Class Immigrants to Canada who fear or suffered persecution in their own country because of their race, religion, nationality, political ideas, or social identity. (*Immigration Act, 1978*)

secondary sources Books and articles written after an event.

status Indians Those native people who are registered as members of one of the 565 bands of 2274 reserves across Canada.

INDEX

Aberhart, William, 89, 96, 97
Aboriginal rights, 209, 210
Agricultural Rehabilitation and Development Act, 157
Aircraft, in World War I, 47
Air force, Canadian, 47, 114, 116, 119-121
Alaska Highway, 135
Alaska Panhandle dispute, 26
Alberta, 31, 87, 94, 96, 97, 131-132, 190; resources, 147, 191, 192, 205; schools, 17
Amiens, battle, 62
Anti-Inflation Board (AIB), 193
Anti-Semitism, 99, 101
Appeasement, 102
Arctic, 138, 198; Canadian claims, 135-136
"Arms race", 159
Army, Canadian: in World War I, 47-54, 58, 59-60; in World War II, 114, 121-127
Art, Canadian, 77-78, 151
Asians, immigration of, 17-19, 212
Atomic bomb. *See* Nuclear weapons
Atomic Energy Commission, 137
Automation, 191
Automobiles, 21, 47, 73, 75, 76, 82
Avro Arrow, 160, 161

"Baby boom", 150, 177; baby boomers grow up, 190, 191
Balfour Report (1926), 98
Ball, George, 224
Bank of Canada, 81, 95, 158
Battle of Britain, 109
Battle of the Atlantic, 117-119
Bennett, Richard B., 20-21, 80, 81; attitude to Empire, 98; fights Depression, 81, 84, 85, 87, 89; letters to, 93-94; "New Deal", 92
Bennett, W.A.C., 149, 157, 167, 175
Beveridge Commission (U.K.), 131
Bilingualism and biculturalism, 168, 169, 172, 174-176; Royal Commission, 174-175, 219
Bill 101 (Québec), 189, 203
Bill 22 (Québec), 189
Bill of Rights (1960), 157
***Blitzkrieg*,** 108, 117
Bloch, Ivan, 48
Boer War, 24-25
Borden, Robert, 30, 31, 33, 36, 39, 44-45, 71; changing attitudes to Empire, 60-61, 62, 65; committed to war effort, 55-57, 58, 61
Bourassa, Henri, 17, 31, 33, 38, 40, 174; opposed to involvement in wars, 26, 28, 41, 54, 56
Bourassa, Robert, 185, 189, 193-194, 203
Bracken, John, 130
Branch plants, 14, 75-76, 147
British Columbia, 76, 96, 157, 167, 190, 205; election in 1933, 91; Asian immigration to, 17-19
British Commonwealth, 137, 159
British Commonwealth Air Training Plan, 119-120
British Empire, 60, 61, 98, 135; Canada's role in, 24-27, 28-30
Broadbent, Ed, 195
Byng, Sir Julian (Lord Byng), 52; King-Byng controversy, 73

Cambrai, 52, 53
Canada Council, 151
Canada Development Corporation (CDC), 198
Canada Pension Plan (CPP), 171
Canadian Broadcasting Corporation (CBC), 95, 151
Canadian Citizenship Act, 217
Canadian Expeditionary Force (CEF), 47-54, 59-60
Canadian International Development Agency (CIDA), 196
Canadian Legion, 70
Canadian National Railway (CNR), 71
Canadian Northern Railway, 13, 20, 21, 71
Canadian Pacific Railway (CPR), 12, 13, 70-71
Canadian Patriotic Fund (CPF), 43
Canadian University Services Overseas (CUSO), 196
Canadian Wheat Board, 70
***Canadiens*,** 9, 17, 29, 40, 41, 78-79, 157; attitude to British Empire, 26; conscription issue, 54, 56, 57, 108, 114, 126, 127. *See also* Québec
CANDU reactor, 147
Caouette, Real, 162
Capital punishment, 222
Cardinal, Harold, 208, 211
Careless, Maurice, 220
Carr, Emily, 77-78
Centennial celebrations (1967), 180-181
Chamberlain, Neville, 102
Charter of Rights and Freedoms, 179, 206, 211, 217, 220
China, People's Republic of: Canada recognizes, 199; wheat sales to, 157, 167, 197
Chinese immigrants, 17
Chretien, Jean, 203
Churches, 24, 150-151; and "liberation", 179. *See also* Roman Catholic Church
Churchill, Winston, 109, 120, 122, 135
Cities, 14, 21, 23, 147, 150
Citizenship, 217-218
Clark, Clifford, 113
Clark, Joe, 194, 199, 222
Cold War, 139-143
Coldwell, M.J., 155
Communists, 84, 91, 132, 139-140
"Community of communities", 199
Company of Young Canadians (CYC), 177
Computers, 191
Confederation, 6, 7; Newfoundland joins, 147
Congo, peacekeeping in, 159
Conscription, World War I, 54-60; how it worked, 58-60; World War II, 103, 107, 108, 114-115, 126-127, 132
Conservatives, name change to "Progressive Conservatives", 130. *See also* Elections, federal; Progressive Conservatives
Constitution, Canadian, patriation of, 157, 168, 179, 203-204, 206; Meech Lake Accord, 222, 223
Constitution Act (1982), 204
"Continuous passage" rule, 18-19
Convention, meaning, 204
Co-operative Commonwealth Federation (CCF), 90-91, 130-131, 132, 149, 155, 156; New Democratic Party formed, 162; rivalry with Communists, 139, 140. *See also* New Democratic Party
Corvettes, 117-118
Coyne, James, 158
Creditistes, 162, 169. *See also* Social Credit
Cree Indians, 208-209
Crosbie, John, 194-195
Cross, James, 185, 186
Crown corporations, 148
Cuban missile crisis (1962), 163
Currie, Sir Arthur, 52-53, 60, 61, 62-63
Czechoslovakia, 102, 103

Dafoe, J.W., 98, 102
Dandurand, Sen. Raoul, 109
D-Day (June 6, 1944), 124-125
Defence, 27, 28-30, 72, 224; of North America, 138, 160-161, 163-164
De Gaulle, Charles, 180-181, 197
Depression, 1870s, 8, 9; 1913-1914, 33, 40; 1921, 70; Great Depression, 79-88, 98
Devaluation of the U.S. dollar, 191-192
Dialectic, 3
Diefenbaker, John, 152-153, 154; domestic policies, 156-158; external affairs, 158-161, 163-164, 167
Dieppe raid, 122
Dominion status, 61, 65, 98
Douglas, Tommy, 149, 162, 169; on War Measures Act, 186, 187-188
Drapeau, Jean, 114, 180
Drought, 80, 87
Duff, Lyman, 58
Dulles, John Foster, 145
Dunsmuir, Sir James, 17
Duplessis, Maurice, 96, 108, 143, 149, 152, 156, 163, 170; Padlock Law, 96, 97, 140
Dust storms, 87

Easter riots (1918), 59
Eden, Sir Anthony, 144, 146
Education, 76, 82; changes in 1960s, 177; French-language, 17, 170-171, 175-176, 188, 189
Eisenhower, Dwight, 159
Elections, federal: 1896, 10; 1911, 30, 32-33; 1917, 57; 1921, 72; 1925, 73; 1926, 74; 1930, 81; 1935, 94; 1940, 108; 1945, 132; 1957, 152-156; 1958, 156; 1962, 163; 1963, 164, 166; 1965, 167; 1968, 168-169; 1972, 192; 1979, 194, 199; 1980, 195; 1984, 205-206, 222
Elections, provincial: B.C., 1933, 91; Québec, 1936, 96; Québec, 1976, 188-189; Saskatchewan, 1934, 91
"Enemy aliens", 40
Energy projects, 147, 191
Entertainment, 76-77, 82, 88
Environmental activists, 177
Ethiopia, 101
European Economic Community (EEC), 197, 198-199
Expo '67, 180

Fact checking, 4-5
Family allowances, 131
Farmers, Diefenbaker aids, 157; farmers' movements, 72, 94; in Great Depression, 80, 81, 87-88; Wheat Board, 70; wheat pools, 76
Federal-provincial relations, 9, 31, 95-96, 157, 203; Meech Lake Accord, 222, 223
Flavelle, Joseph, 43, 44
Fleming, Donald, 158
Foreign Enlistment Act, 101
Foreign Investment Review Agency (FIRA), 198
Foreign policy, Canadian, opinions in 1930s, 98. *See also* British Commonwealth; British Empire; United Nations; United States; and subentries under Diefenbaker, John; King, William Lyon Mackenzie; Trudeau, Pierre Elliott
Forestry, 14, 15
Fourteen Points (Wilson), 64
Franco, Francisco, 101
Fraternal orders, 22
Freedom Riders, 181
Free trade with the U.S., 9, 32, 33, 139, 223, 224
French-Canadians. *See Canadiens*
***Front de Liberation du Québec* (FLQ),** 185-188
Frost, Leslie, 156
"Functional principle", 136, 137

George VI, 102-103
Gold, and world money supply, 11
Gold rush, Klondike, 10, 11, 14
"Good Neighbour" policy, 102
Gouzenko, Igor, 139-140
Government bonds, 44, 46, 129
Grand Trunk Railway, 12-13, 71
Grasshoppers, plague of, 87
Great Depression, 79-88, 98
Green, Howard, 161
Groulx, Abbe Lionel, 78-79
Group of Seven, 77-78

Haig, Sir Douglas, 52, 53
Halibut Treaty (1923), 73
Halifax, Lord, 134-135
Halifax explosion (1917), 42, 57
Hammarskjold, Dag, 146
Hepburn, Mitchell, 96-97, 108
History, how written, 1-2; study of, 2-3
Hitler, Adolf, 99, 101; attacks Treaty of Versailles, 99, 100; invades Poland, 103
Homestead Acts (U.S.), 9
Hospital insurance, 149
Houde, Camillien, 108
Howe, Clarence Decatur, 112-113, 148, 152, 160
Hughes, Colonel Sam, 38-39, 43, 54
Hungarian Revolution (1956), 213
Hydroelectricity, 10, 14, 147, 167; James Bay project, 170, 191, 194, 208-209
Hydrogen bomb, 159

Ilsley, J.L., 107, 112
Immigration, 12, 13, 14, 16, 17, 74, 212-216; 1920s law, 77; 1945-1957, 150; attitudes to immigrants, 16-18, 19, 22, 82; point system, 213, 215; to Québec, 175, 176; refugees, 100, 212, 213, 215, 216; from Third World, 196; three classes of immigrants, 214-215
Immigration Act, amended, 214, 216
Imperial Conferences, 1923, 98
Imperial Munitions Board, 43
Imperial War Cabinet (1917), 55, 61
Income War Tax, 47
Indexation, 192-193, 194, 205
India, 137
Indian Act, 179, 208, 209, 210-211
Indians, 208-209; status and non-status, 207, 210-211. *See also* Native people
Inflation, 22; 1917-1921, 47, 70; danger in World War II, 107, 129; 1970s, 191-194
Influenza epidemic (1918), 64
Intercolonial Railway, 8, 71
Interest rates, 205
International agreements, signed independently, 72
International Control Commission (1954), 143
Inuit, 207, 208-209
Isolationism, Canadian, 97-100
Israel, 143

James Bay hydroelectric development, 170, 191, 194, 208-209
Japan, 101, 196, 197; Pearl Harbour attack, 109
Japanese Canadians in World War II, 115-116
Johnson, Daniel, 168, 171, 173, 180, 181
Johnson, Lyndon B., 181
Judicial Committee of the Privy Council, 76

Kashmir, 143
Kennedy, John F., 161, 163, 181, 182
King, Martin Luther, 181, 182
King, William Lyon Mackenzie, 23, 29, 72-74, 95, 97; 1930 election, 80-81; caution over wartime involvement, 106-108, 112; conscription issue, 126; foreign policy, 72, 98, 101, 102, 103, 135, 136, 198; immigration, 212, 215; King-Byng controversy, 73; "new social order", 131, 132; opposes free trade with U.S., 139
King-Herzog principle, 98
Komagata Maru (ship), 19
Korean War, 141-143

Labour Party, 81
Landed immigrants, 217
Lapointe, Ernest, 102
Laporte, Pierre, 185, 186
Laurendeau, Andre, 114
Laurier, Sir Wilfrid, 6, 9, 17, 18, 38; 1911 election, 30-33; attitude to British connection, 26, 30; Boer War, 25, 26; close-up, 11; "Laurier boom", 10-15, 23; life in Laurier era, 19-24; master of compromise, 27, 29; opposes conscription, 56
Lavergne, Armand, 17

Leacock, Stephen, 20, 46
League of Nations, 65-66; Canada's role in, 101
Le Devoir, 33, 114
"Lend-lease", 113
Lesage, Jean, 163, 168, 170, 171
Levesque, Rene, 168, 170, 174, 175, 185, 204; *Parti Québecois*, 173, 189, 194, 203; vision of Québec, 172-173
Liberals, 153-154. *See also* Elections, federal
Liberation decade, 176-180
Ligue pour la defense du Canada, 114
Living conditions, early years of century, 20-24; flaws of 1920s, 74, 76, 79; Great Depression, 81-88, 93-94; home life in wartime, 127-128, 129; postwar boom, 147, 149, 152; 1960s, 167; 1970s, 190-191
Lloyd George, David, 43, 55, 61
Low, Solon, 155

Macdonald, Sir John A., 6, 7-8, 9, 14, 26; nation-building strategy, 8, 12
Mackenzie, Alexander, 8
Macmillan, Harold, 146
Macphail, Agnes, 98
"Maitres chez nous", 163, 170
Manhattan (ship), 198
"Manifest destiny" of U.S., 224
Manifesto, 185
Manion, Robert, 102, 108
Manitoba, 8, 71, 147. *See also* Prairies
Manning, Ernest, 132, 149, 174
Marchand, Jean, 168, 213-214
Maritimes, 73, 76, 190; freight rates, 71
Marx, Karl, 3
McCarthy, Sen. Joseph, 140
McNaughton, Gen. A.G.L., 84, 122, 126
Meech Lake Accord, 222, 223
Meighen, Arthur, 58, 70-71, 72, 73, 74, 114, 130
Mercier, Honore, 9
Metis, 8, 9, 209
Middle powers, Canada a leader of, 136
Military Service Act (1917), 55, 57, 58-60
Military Voters' Act, 56
Mining, 14-15
Mons, battle, 63-64
Montreal, 14, 150, 223
Movies, 77
Mulroney, Brian, 205, 206, 222-223; accomplishments of his government, 222-224
Multiculturalism, 15-16, 219-221
Munich conference (1938), 102
Mussolini, Benito, 99, 101

Nader, Ralph, 177
Nasser, Gamel Abdel, 144
National Energy Board, 157
National Energy Program (NEP), 198, 223-224
National Housing Act, 131, 149
Nationalism, Canadian, 61, 65, 77-79, 98, 198-199, 203-204
"National Policy", 8
National Resources Mobilization Act (1940), 108, 121
National Selective Service (NSS), 113
National War Labour Order, 131
Native people, 17, 179, 206-211; groups, 207; land claims, 208-209; self-government, 209-210
NATO (North Atlantic Treaty Organization), 141, 142; Canada cuts forces, 198, 199
Natural gas, 147; pipeline, 152
Naval Service Act (1910), 29, 33
Navy, Canadian, 27-28, 33, 72, 113-114, 116-119
Nehru, Jawaharlal, 137
New Deal, Bennett's, 93, 94; Roosevelt's, 92, 97
New Democratic Party (NDP), 162, 164, 222. *See also* Co-operative Commonwealth Federation
Newfoundland, 135, 157; joins Confederation, 147
Newly independent nations, 195-196
"New Social Order", 131, 132
Niagara Falls, 10, 14
Nishga tribe, 208
Nixon, Richard, 191, 197
NORAD (North American Air Defence Command), 160, 161, 163
Northwest Territories, 8, 147
Nuclear power, 147
Nuclear weapons, 159-161, 163-164; crusade against, 161; spy ring, 139-140

Official Languages Act (1969), 175
Ogdensburg agreement (1940), 109
Oil, Alberta, 147, 157, 205; prices increase, 192
Olympics, Montreal, 1976, 194
One Big Union (O.B.U.), 69
Ontario, 9, 14, 76, 96, 203
"On-to-Ottawa" trek, 84-85
Organization of Petroleum Exporting Countries (OPEC), 192
Ortona, 122-123

Padlock Law, 96, 97, 140
Parti Québecois, 173, 189, 194, 203
Passchendaele, 52-53
Patriotism, 41
Patronage, 223
Pattullo, T.D., 85, 86, 91, 96, 97
Pearl Harbour, 109
Pearson, Lester B., 98, 156, 158, 163, 164, 182; helps solve Suez Canal crisis, 145, 146; problems of his government, 167, 168, 174-176, 181
Pelletier, Gerard, 168; on the War Measures Act, 186-187
Petro-Canada, 198
Pioneering, 14
Plebiscite on conscription, 114
Poland, 103
Population increase, 149-150, 196
Prairie Farm Rehabilitation Act (1935), 88
Prairies, 12, 31, 46, 76, 205; in Great Depression, 80, 81, 87-88; homesteaders, 14; overcropping, 43, 44; politics, 71, 91, 94, 156
Price-fixing, 91, 92
Primary sources, 3
Progressive Conservatives, 130, 154. *See also* Elections, federal
Progressives, 72, 73, 81
Prohibition, 45, 73
Propaganda, 41, 49
Prosperity, of Laurier years, 10-15; of mid-1920s, 74-76; after World War II, 147-151; 1960s, 167; 1970s, 190-191
Protest marches of 1960s, 177
Provincial powers, 9, 76, 203
Purvis Commission, 95

Québec, attitude to Korean War, 142-143; Duplessis attains power, 96; immigrants to, 213-214; James Bay hydroelectric project, 170, 191, 194, 208-209; Quiet Revolution, 163, 168, 170-171; referendum on "sovereignty-association", 203; separatism, 168, 171-176, 189; "special status" for, 168, 171; two visions of, 172-173; unilingualism, 175-176, 188, 189
Québec Pension Plan (QPP), 171

Race issue in Canada, 17-19, 212-213, 220-221
Race riots in U.S., 182
Radio, 77, 88
Railways, 70-71, 74, 147; Canadian National, 71; Canadian Northern, 13, 20, 21, 71; Canadian Pacific, 12, 13, 70-71; Grand Trunk, 12-13, 71; Intercolonial, 8, 71; riding the rails, 82-83; transcontinental, 8, 44-45
Ralston, J.L., 113, 115, 122, 126
Rand formula, 149
Rationing, wartime, 127-128
Reagan, Ronald, 224
Rearmament, 102
Recessions, 1957, 158; 1982, 205
Reciprocity, 9, 32, 95. *See also* Free trade with the U.S.
Reconstruction Party, 92, 94
Referendum on sovereignty-association, 189, 203
Refugees, 100, 212, 213, 215, 216
Regina Manifesto (1933), 90-91
Regina riot (1935), 93
Regional inequalities, 76, 95, 147, 190
Relief, 82, 87, 88

Relief camps (1930s), 84, 85
Reparations, German, 99
Resources, control transferred to provinces, 76; development, 14, 148, 157, 192
Riddell, W.A., 101
Riel, Louis, 8, 9
Roman Catholic Church, in Québec, 163, 170-171
Roosevelt, Franklin Delano, 92, 109, 113, 135
Royal Commission on the Arts and Letters in Canada (Massey Commission), 151
Royal Commission on Bilingualism and Biculturalism, 174-175, 219
Royal Commission on Dominion-Provincial Relations (Rowell-Sirois Commission), 95-96
Royal Commission on Price Spreads (1934-1935), 91-92
Royal Commission on the Status of Women, 178

Saskatchewan, 17, 31, 87, 190; 1934 election, 91. *See also* Prairies
Secondary sources, 3
Separatism, Québec, 168, 171-176, 189, 203; Western provinces, 192
Service clubs, 76
Settlers, prairie, 8-9, 14
Shell Committee, 43
Sifton, Clifford, 12, 16-17
Skelton, O.D., 72, 98, 102
Smallwood, Joey, 157
Smythe, Conn, 125-126
Social Credit, 89, 94, 96, 97, 131-132, 149, 155, 156, 164; Creditistes, 162
Socialism, 90-91
Social programs, 46, 76, 129, 130, 131, 132, 167
Somme offensives, 52
South Africa, 159
Sovereignty-association for Québec, defeated, 203
Soviet Union, spy ring in Canada, 139-140; Stalin's dictatorship, 99. *See also* Cold War
So You Want a War Job!, 128-129
Spain, civil war in, 101
Sports, 77, 150, 190
St. Laurent, Louis, 137, 139, 143, 149, 153-154, 156; Suez Canal crisis, 145-146
St. Lawrence Seaway, 81, 147-148
Stalin, Josef, 99
Stanfield, Robert, 169
Statute of Westminster (1931), 98
Stevens, Harry, 91-92, 94
Stock market crash (1929), 80
Stratford Shakespearean Festival, 151
Strikes, 131, 139, 148-149, 168, 193-194
Submarines, German, 117, 118, 119
Suez Canal crisis, 144-146
***Survivance,* la,** 170, 203

Tanks, 52
Tariffs, 8, 10, 14, 31, 72, 75, 87, 88; U.S., 12, 80, 197
Taxes, 47, 129; reform, 223
Technology, 191
Television, 151, 182, 190
Thalidomide, 177
Third World, 195-196, 205
"Three Wise Men", 168
Toronto, 150
Trade with U.S., 74-75, 197; free trade, 9, 31-32, 33, 139, 223, 224; partial reciprocity, 94
Trans-Canada Airlines (now Air Canada), 95
Trans-Canada Highway, 148
Transportation. *See* Automobiles; Railways
Treaty of Versailles, 65; attacked by Hitler, 99, 100; harshness criticized, 102; terms, 99
Treaty of Washington (1871), 8
Trench warfare, 48-49, 50
Trudeau, Pierre Elliott, 116, 168-169, 182, 184, 192, 194; foreign policy decisions, 198-199; goals before leaving politics, 202-205; individualism, 178-179, 219; international efforts, 205; use of War Measures Act, 185-186, 188; vision of Québec, 172, 173, 174
Turner, John, 192-193, 205

U-boats, 117, 118, 119
Unemployment, 88, 191, 205; a national problem, 95; Great Depression, 80, 81, 82-86, 87, 88; low in 1965, 167
Unemployment insurance, 129, 130
Unilingualism in Québec, 175-176, 188, 189
Union government (1917), 57
Union Nationale, 96, 170, 171, 189
Unions, 17, 22-23, 55-56, 69, 70, 76, 158, 193; legal rights established, 131; Rand Formula, 149; strikes, 131, 139, 148-149, 168, 193-194
United Farmers, 72, 94
United Nations, 136, 142; Emergency Force (1956), 145-146; Security Council, 136; veto rights of great powers, 136-137
United Nations Relief and Rehabilitation Agency, 137
United States, anti-Communist "witch hunts", 140; Canada's economic ties with, 74-76, 102, 138-139, 147, 149, 197-198; and Canadian culture, 76-79, 151, 181-182; criticism of, 79, 181-182; declares war, 55, 109; Depression in, 80, 92, 97; devaluation of dollar, 191-192; free trade with, 9, 31-32, 33, 139, 223, 224; joint defence of North America, 138, 160; wartime attitude to Canada, 135-136

Vancouver, 14, 150
Veterans, of World War I, 70
Victoria, 150
Vietnam War, 182, 192, 197
Vimy battle, 52, 55

Wage and price controls, 193, 194
War Measures Act, 38, 45, 107, 185-188
Wartime Elections Act, 56-57
Wartime Prices and Trade Board (WPTB), 107, 127, 129
Wheat, new varieties, 12; production increases, 13; sales to China, 167, 197
Wheat pools, 76, 80
White, Sir Thomas, 44, 47
Wilgress, Dana, 140
Wilson, Woodrow, 64, 65-66
Winch, Harold, 84, 86
Winnipeg, 14, 223; general strike, 69-70
Winter works program, 158
Women, demand social programs, 76; in the Laurier era, 21, 22; liberation, 178; National Council of Canadian Women, 23-24; and prohibition, 45, 46; rights entrenched in Constitution, 206; rights of Indian women, 210-211; voting rights, 45, 46; working, 191; in World War II, 113
Woodsworth, J.S., 23, 24, 40, 81, 90, 98, 103, 130
World University Services of Canada (WUSC), 196
World War I, 37-66; Canadian participation, 38-42, 47-53; changes in Canada, 42-47; conscription crisis, 54-60; international background, 37-38; postwar world, 60-66; words from the front, 50-51
World War II, Air Training Plan, 107-108, 109, 119-120; Battle of Britain, 109; Battle of the Atlantic, 117-119; *blitzkrieg*, 108; bomber attack on Germany, 120-121; Canada declares war, 103; Canadian army, 114, 121-127; Howe's industrial programs, 112-113; Japanese Canadians, 114-115; King's initial reluctance, 106-108; life at home, 127-132; timetable, 110-111
Writing, Canadian, 78, 151
Wrong, Hume, 136

Ypres, 49